Strategy Making during Ambidext

D I S S E R T A T I O N
of the University of St. Gallen,
School of Management,
Economics, Law, Social Sciences
and International Affairs

to obtain the title of
Doctor Oeconomiae

submitted by

Marko Rillo

from

Estonia

Approved on the application of:

Prof. Steven W. Floyd, PhD

and

Prof. Claus D. Jacobs, PhD

Dissertation no. 4490

SeriousPlayPro, Tallinn 2016

The University of St. Gallen, School of Management, Economics, Law, Social Sciences and International Affairs hereby consents to the printing of the present dissertation, without hereby expressing any opinion on the views herein expressed.

St. Gallen, October 16, 2015

The President:

Prof. Dr. Thomas Bieger

Acknowledgements

Many thanks to my dissertation committee consisting of Professors Floyd and Jacobs. Steve - your continuous patient and friendly insights in response to any, no matter how silly, questions provide a true role model of an academic mentor. Claus - your encouragement and support have helped me get through tough times and I hope that our mutual passion for pathways off the beaten track will continue to provide interesting discussions. Thank you both for your support throughout the past years!

There are many to be grateful to at St. Gallen. Professors Christoph Lechner and Markus Kreutzer helped to get a quick start. Prof. Sebastian Raisch gave the inspiration for the dissertation topic and Prof. Winfried Ruigrok's feedback on early ideas was appreciated. Fellow academic community members elsewhere: Charles Baden-Fuller, Xavier Castaner, Walter Ferrier, Javier Gimeno, Anil K. Gupta, Tomi Laamanen, Saku Mantere, Joakim Netz, Milvi Tepp, Henk W. Volberda, Richard Whittington, Peter Zemsky and others.

My sincere thanks go to Dr. Christian Junnelius, Prof. Jaak Leimann and Dr. Franziska Breuning - your personal support and financial contributions from the SIAR Foundation, the CARPE Foundation and the Swiss Gebert RÜF Stiftung SBN made it possible to study at St. Gallen in the first place and participate in the doctoral schools and research conferences.

I would like to thank people working at both case organizations, whose sincere interviews and open workshops gave invaluable insights. Allowing an outsider to enter your companies for many years and providing limitless access to almost everything that I asked for was a risky leap of faith on your part. Without this, the dissertation could not have been possible.

In addition, the support of two fellows who took this research journey together with me has been invaluable: Egert Valmra, my co-researcher who shared some of the interview leg of this journey with whom I could bounce around the ideas for the draft. Madis Talmar, who also assisted in collecting data and untangling the data analysis.

And other friends: Thomas Schrettle - thank you for the fun we had during spring 2007 when we were the only two PhD students who started with classes during that semester, and many thanks for your assistance with the German language for this thesis summary. Florian Überbacher - for your thoughts on an earlier draft of this study. Thanks to Ergo Metsla, Rando Rannus, Mike Wahl, Mait Rungi and the SPUR team at the TUT. But also others from St.Gallen with whom we shared coursework as well as free time: Martin Rajes, Carola Wolf, Markus Kreutzer, Markus Menz, Alexander Zimmermann, Widar von Arx, Sven Kunisch, Stefan Grösser, Alexander Fust and Christian Welling (†) - just to name a few.

I would also like to thank my family: parents, in-laws and Grete Elise for being our sunshine. Krista - for dedicating so much of your free time to being with our little daughter.

Finally - Kersti! Thank you for your patience and push in reaching the milestone. I dedicate this work to you!

Tallinn, October 2015   Marko Rillo

Table of Contents

List of Figures

List of Tables

List of Abbreviations

ARPU	Average revenue per paying user
AXE	Automatic Cross-Connection Equipment - a contemporary technology for telephone exchange systems
CEO	Chief executive officer
CFO	Chief finance officer
CSO	Chief strategy officer
DAI	Digital Access Index (OECD)
DTMF	Dual-tone multi-frequency signaling - touch tone dialing system of phones which enables to interact with interactive voice response systems
EBITDA	Earnings before interest, taxes, depreciation and amortization
KPI	Key performance indicator
IaaS	Infrastructure as a Service
ICT	Information and communication technology
IDI	ICT Development Index
IPTV	Internet Protocol Television - protocol through which television is delivered via internet
ITU	The International Telecommunications Union - www.itu.int
IVR	Interactive Voice Response - technology which allows to interact with computerized customer service via voice and DTMF tones
MBT	Mobile base transceiver
Mgmt	Management
MM	Middle management
NPV	Net present value
OECD	Organization for Economic Co-operation and Development
OTT	Over The Top (services) - services delivered over an infrastructure that is not under the same control as the primary service provider (e.g. Skype connection running over traditional internet connection)
RQ	Research question
SaaS	Software as a Service
SO	Strategic orientation
Telco	Telecommunications (firm, industry)
TBE	Top Broadband Economy
TMT	Top management team

Glossary of Definitions

Ambidexterity, ambidextrous organization	Organizational ability to engage in practices that allow alignment and efficiency while simultaneously being adaptive to changes in the environment by effectively combining exploratory and exploitative activities. Term coined by Duncan (1976).
Ambidexterity cycle	See *cyclical ambidexterity*.
Contextual ambidexterity	Behavioral capacity to demonstrate simultaneously alignment and adaptability across an entire business unit that arises from the context of the organization (Gibson & Birkinshaw, 2004, p. 209).
Cyclical ambidexterity, ambidexterity cycle	A type of sequential (temporal) ambidexterity in which organizations engage in periods of exploitation interspersed with periods of exploration - Simsek et al. (2009, pp. 882-4). Cyclical ambidexterity is a subtype of sequential ambidexterity.
	This concept relies on the literature on *punctuated equilibrium* (Tushman & Romanelli, 1985; Gersick, 1991) according to which, cyclical ambidexterity involves a cyclical allocation of resources and attention to either exploitation or exploration.
	This phenomenon has several names, e.g. "punctuated equilibrium" (Burgelman, 2002; Tushman & Romanelli, 1985). "Sequential allocation of attention to divergent goals" or "temporal achievement of exploration and exploitation" (Gupta, Smith, & Shalley, 2006). "Relentlessly shifting organizations" (Brown & Eisenhardt, 1997). "Structural modulation", "modulating structure", "cycling structure" or "vacillation" (Nickerson & Zenger, 2002). "Sequencing" or "temporary decentralization with subsequent reintegration" (Siggelkow & Levinthal, 2003). "Switching strategy" (Reeves, Haanæs, Hollingsworth, & Pasini, 2013). "Regular creation and losing of business charters" (Galunic & Eisenhardt, 1996). "Sequential, cyclical and reciprocal ambidexterity" (Simsek, Heavey, Veiga, & Souder, 2009). "Organizational cycling" (Cummings, 1995), "Temporal division before centralizing" (Siggelkow & Levinthal, 2003).
	The terms *cyclical ambidexterity* and *ambidexterity cycles* have become the most popular during the recent years and hence used in this thesis, too.
Exploration	Entrepreneurial activities consisting of variation, risk taking, experimentation, play, flexibility, discovery and innovation in the domains of new products, technologies, markets, customers or geographical regions.
Exploitation	Expertise-building related activities consisting of refinement, choice, production, efficiency, selection, implementation and execution in the domains of existing products, technologies, markets, customers or geographical regions.
	There seems to be dissention concerning the use of the words *exploitive* or *exploitative*. There are sources that consider the two words synonymous (e.g. Merriam Webster online - http://www.merriam-webster.com/). Others define them differently (e.g. http://www.eudict.com).
	Exploitive - using somebody unfairly; take advantage of (for selfish reasons)
	Exploitative - utilizing for profit, pertaining to the exploitation of people or resources.
	For this reason, in the present thesis I have used the adjective *exploitative*
Organizational Actor	Any individual who has impact on strategy creation, formulation or implementation in that firm by either participating directly in strategy making or having influence on strategy indirectly.
Punctuated equilibrium	Long stable periods of exploitation sporadically interrupted by short radical bursts of exploration (Tushman & Romanelli, 1985; Romanelli & Tushman, 1994).
Reciprocal ambidexterity	A type of sequential ambidexterity in which organizations pursue exploitation and exploration sequentially across units via complementary streams of exploitation and exploration that occur across time and units - in which the outputs of exploitation from Unit A become the inputs for exploration by Unit B and the outputs of Unit B

cycle back to become the inputs of Unit A. Unlike cyclical ambidexterity, which involves managers simply passing the baton at some point in time, this type requires relationships characterized by ongoing information exchange, collaborative problem solving, joint decision making, and resource flows between the managers of the units - Simsek et al. (2009, pp. 886-7).

Sequential ambidexterity	Method for achieving ambidextrous balance between contrasting strategic orientations of exploration and exploitation through temporal division, where during certain periods the company's strategic orientation is exploration-directed and during other times exploitation-directed. Sequential ambidexterity may either be cyclical or reciprocal - Simsek et al. (2009, p. 868).
Strategic renewal	Strategic renewal includes the process, content, and outcome of refreshment or replacement of attributes of an organization that have the potential substantially affecting its long-term prospects (Agarwal & Helfat, 2009, p. 282). A process associated with promoting, accommodating and utilizing new knowledge and innovative behavior to change in an organization's core competencies or product market domain" (Floyd & Lane, 2000, p. 155)
Strategic orientation (SO)	Terms of what business the firm is in, how it competes and how it ensures its continuous superior performance. Strategic orientation sets the primary target and bearing of organization's activities. In the present study - exploratory or exploitative strategic orientation demonstrate opposite and contrasting goals whereby one is targeted towards exploration of new businesses and the other is targeted towards exploiting existing business. Strategic orientation may also be described and measured by an organization's "1) core beliefs and values regarding the organization, its employees and its environment; 2) products, markets, technology and competitive timing; 3) the distribution of power; 4) the organization's structure and 5) the nature, type and pervasiveness of control systems". (Tushman & Romanelli, 1985, pp. 174-178).
Strategy practices	Various routines, concepts and technologies through which strategy work is made possible, including strategy reviews and off-sites meetings, academic and consulting tools and material technologies and artifacts (PowerPoints, flip-charts etc.). (Jarzabkowski & Whittington, 2008, p. 101)
Strategizing	Behavior of strategy actors in creating strategy. In the present study, strategizing can be both structured, administrative activity as well as non-routine behavior with implications on strategy of the firm.
Strategy	A phenomenon or a process that sets out the core principles based on which a company operates, which drives long-term success of the organization, ultimately determining its success or failure. (Definition partially based on (Agarwal & Helfat, 2009)).
Strategy as practice	Research stream that focuses on arrays of situated and context-driven socially-accomplished activity of organizational actors that is strategically consequential and thereby knowingly or unintentionally shapes firm's strategy. The strategy as practice research focuses on three pillars. 1) Strategy practitioners - "strategy workers" - individuals within the firm or as external consultants, who have a key role in shaping strategy; 2) praxis - the flow of activity through which strategy is achieved and 3) practices - the social, symbolic and material tools through which strategy work is done (Whittington, 2006; Jarzabkowski, 2005; Jarzabkowski & Spee, 2009).
Strategy process	Consecutive patterns of deliberate and organized or emergent activities carried out to create or develop an organization's strategy. The strategy process research focuses on the factors that govern the formation and execution of strategies at different organizational and network levels (from Strategic Management Society website, description of the Strategy Process interest groups domain statement - strategicmanagement.net/ig/strategy_process.php).
Structural ambidexterity	In order to manage trade-offs between conflicting demands of the dual nature of exploration and exploitation, organizations put in place "dual structures" so that

	certain business units or groups within business units focus on alignment, while others focus on adaptation (Duncan, 1976).
Temporal ambidexterity	A subtype of ambidexterity, whereby an organization is in certain periods more oriented towards exploration and in other periods more towards exploitation

Abstract

Broader context. The research stream on organizational ambidexterity has identified possibilities of achieving contradictory goals of exploration and exploitation simultaneously (March, 1991; Raisch & Birkinshaw, 2008; Gibson & Birkinshaw, 2004). Some companies shift between these extremes. This phenomenon is termed *cyclical ambidexterity* where firms change their strategic orientation between the contrasting aims periodically ((Simsek et.al. (2009), Uotila et al. (2009) Boumgarden et al. (2012)).

Research focus. This study focuses on a particular aspect of cyclical ambidexterity. It focuses on strategy making in firms shifting between exploration and exploitation. The aim of the thesis is to analyze what happens within the organizations in the course of these shifts. To observe and explain the inner workings of this change process, the study takes the strategy as practice view (Johnson, Langley, Melin, & Whittington, 2007).

Method. Due to its exploratory nature, a focus on contemporary events and lack of control over behavior of actors, this study employs a longitudinal case study method with partial retrospective data collection elements (Yin, 2008). The case organizations were selected based on purposive theoretical sampling (Patton, 2001) and sample variation in crucial categories (Eisenhardt, 1989; George & McKeown, 1985) where one case organization was in a phase of changing its primary strategic orientation from exploration to exploitation, and the other in the opposite direction - from exploitation to exploration. To allow for a comparison of practices, the organizations were selected from a single industry and geographical location.

Contribution. This study results in a better understanding of the process of shift in strategic orientation. It therefore informs the ambidexterity literature and the strategy-as-practice literature streams about practices used during ambidexterity cycles. It shows that when engaging in cyclical ambidexterity, companies keep multiple capabilities for strategy-making in-house, activating the latent practices that are deemed suitable for the associated upcoming shift of strategic orientation and deactivating those active practices that have become redundant.

Keywords: Ambidexterity, Cyclical Ambidexterity, Shift in Strategic Orientation, Exploration, Exploitation, Strategy as Practice, Strategic Change, Strategy Process

Zusammenfassung

Hintergrund. Im Zentrum der Forschung zum Thema "Organisationale Ambidexterität (Organizational Ambidexterity)" steht die Frage, wie es Organisationen gelingt, die gegensätzlichen Ziele von Erkundung von neuem (Exploration) und Ausnutzung von bestehendem (Exploitation) miteinander in Einklang zu bringen. Manche Unternehmen sind hierbei in der Lage, zwischen diesen beiden Extremen zu wechseln, ein Phänomen das man als "Zyklische Ambidexterität (Cyclical Ambidexterity)" bezeichnet. Diese Unternehmen verändern ihre strategische Orientierung regelmäßig und wechseln entsprechend zwischen gegensätzlichen Zielen ((Simsek et.al. (2009), Uotila et.al. (2009) Boumgarden et.al. (2012)).

Forschungsschwerpunkte. Diese Dissertation fokussiert sich auf eine spezielle Facette dieser Zyklischen Ambidexterität. Während der Prozess der Strategieentwicklung in Unternehmen mit einer reinen Erkundung den oder einer rein ausnutzender Ausrichtung bereits ausführlich untersucht wurde, gibt es keine Studien die die Strategieentwicklung in Unternehmen untersuchen welche sich in einem Wechsel zwischen diesen beiden Modi befinden. Das Ziel dieser Arbeit ist es diese Lücke zu füllen. Es wird analysiert wie Strategien in Unternehmen entwickelt werden die zyklisch ambidexterität sind und einen Wechsel von Erkundung zu Ausnutzung durchlaufen oder umgekehrt. Grundlage der Beobachtung und Erklärung der zugrunde liegenden Prozesse bildet die Literatur des Strategischem Wandel und der Strategischen Erneuerung (Huff et al. 1992; Pettigrew et al. 2001; Agarwal & Helfat 2009). Um zu entsprechenden empirischen Erkenntnissen zu gelangen, liegt der Studie eine aktivitätsbasierte Strategie-als-Praxis ("*Strategy-as-Practice*") Perspektive zugrunde (Johnson, Langley, Melin, & Whittington, 2007; Jarzabkowski 2005).

Methodik. Aufgrund ihres erkundigenden Charakters liegt der Fokus der Studie auf der Beobachtung von Prozessen in Echtzeit, ohne Kontrolle über das Verhalten der Akteure. Sie ist als Längsschnitt Fallstudie angelegt, verwendet jedoch teilweise auch retrospektive Elemente (Yin, 2008). Die Fallgeber wurden anhand eines theoretischen Stichproben Prozesses ausgewählt (Patton, 2001) wobei die Fallgeber in entscheidenden Kategorien variieren (Eisenhardt, 1989; George & McKeown, 1995). Eine der Organisationen befand sich zum Zeitpunkt der Untersuchung in einem Veränderungsprozess ihrer Strategischen Orientierung, von einer erkundigenden explorativen hin zu einer ausnutzenden Ausrichtung, eine andere dagegen in umgekehrter Richtung - von der Ausnutzung zur Erkundigung. Um eine Vergleichbarkeit der Aktivitäten zu gewährleisten, wurden Organisationen aus derselben Branche gewählt, dem Telekommunikationssektor einer bestimmten geografischen Region in Estland.

Beitrag. Das daraus resultierende bessere Verständnis über "Zyklische Ambidexterität" bereichert sowohl die Ambidexteritäts- als auch die Literatur des Strategischen Wandels um das Verständnis strategischer Praktiken, die während einer Veränderung der strategischen Orientierung zur Anwendung gelangen.

Schlagwörter: Ambidexterität; Zyklische Ambidexterität; Erkundung; Ausnutzung; Strategie-als-Praxis; Strategieprozess

Strategy Making During Ambidexterity Cycles

1   Introduction

The research question of this dissertation is "Which practices are used by organizational actors involved in strategy making in the context of cyclical ambidexterity?" In order to illustrate what *cyclical ambidexterity* is, and how it is implemented in companies, I start with a story that is a simple metaphor for this research project.

> *Jack decides to start a corner shop. He mortgages his house to buy and renovate a suitable space. In the next six months, he will monitor his costs closely to save for an ice cream booth that he plans to set up early in the summer to attract the youngsters in his neighborhood to come by for a daily sweet bite.*

Jack demonstrates cyclical ambidexterity whereby he engages in periods of exploration (i.e. change - focusing on investments and expansion) and exploitation (i.e. relative stability - focusing on managing sales and costs). Due to resource constraints, he allocates his attention to either one or the other - to exploitation or exploration (Simsek et al. 2009, pp. 882-4). Sanchez and colleagues have discussed firms that shift between the two extremes (Sanchez, Heene, & Thomas, 1996). These firms plan the timing of their exploratory moves well ahead and they only invest in expansion during certain periods to make sure that they are later able to manage. Cyclical ambidexterity manifests itself in effectuation behavior - focusing attention via smart risk-taking on actions that are under management control (Sarasvathy, 2001).

While small companies instinctively take a cyclical approach to exploring and exploiting, larger multinationals are more deliberate in this process. Companies need to expand their business by introducing new products, new technologies or enter new markets, while at the same time maintaining their profitability. Hence, Duncan coined the term *organizational ambidexterity* to depict the duality and the paradoxical tensions between the two classical strategy tradeoffs (Duncan, 1976). As a rule, large multinationals seek *simultaneous ambidexterity*. They manage this conflict by pursuing exploration and exploitation simultaneously through a variety of means as explicated by Simsek et al. (2009, pp. 869, 881-2).

This dissertation positions itself in the field of cyclical ambidexterity. Some studies have demonstrated that cyclical ambidexterity, as a well-patterned vacillation strategy between exploration and exploitation, may yield higher performance gains than simultaneous ambidexterity (Nickerson & Zenger, 2002; Boumgarden, Nickerson, & Zenger, 2012). Ongoing discussions of research on cyclical ambidexterity have revealed some reasons why companies engage in the sequential behavior of exploration and exploitation. The choice can hinge on the inertia of organizational learning and unlearning (Sastry, 1997; March, 1991), attention allocation (Ocasio, 1997), cognitive limits (Simsek, Veiga, Lubatkin, & Dino, 2005), resource limits (Uotila, Maula, Keil, & Zahra, 2009), external technology cycles (Benner & Tushman, 2003) and the inherent dynamics of the firms (Nickerson & Zenger, 2002). In addition, previous studies have described how change behavior leads to organizational renewal through periods of stress and inertia, which form the building blocks of cyclical ambidexterity (Hannan & Freeman, 1984; Huff, Huff, & Thomas, 1992).

However, previous studies have not focused on how organizational strategies unfold in a cyclical ambidexterity context. Activities associated with exploring and exploiting are associated with incongruent organizational architecture and processes (Smith & Tushman, 2005; Smith & Lewis, 2011). Some argue that they are even mutually exclusive, as competencies need to be learned and unlearned during every change endeavor (March, 1991). However, the ambidexterity studies have not yet used the strategy-as-practice toolkit to understand what happens at the micro level during shifts.

The gap within the existing body of research got me interested in what happens during the times when companies take turns between exploration and exploitation. Do managers carefully plan the moves between the extremes? Do they abandon their companies' competencies or retain some of them? How do people in these organizations cope with the times when they need to carefully create new practices, and at other times abandon them? A related question also applies to strategy work: How do the firms that engage in cyclical ambidexterity manage strategy creation? Strategy making in exploitative organizations follows a primarily rational mode and in exploratory organizations mostly a symbolic or generative mode (Hart, 1992). Strategy work in ambidextrous firms relies on an adaptive mode (Andersen, 2000; 2004; Andersen & Nielsen, 2009). Do people vacillate between rational and generative modes or do they rely on a certain type of adaptive mode?

To answer these questions, the study, of necessity, draws from two streams of research:

1. The literature on organizational ambidexterity and the duality of exploration and exploitation (Raisch & Birkinshaw, 2008; Gupta, Smith, & Shalley, 2006; Simsek, Heavey, Veiga, & Souder, 2009). Ambidexterity research focuses on the contrasting aims of staying competitive via streamlining an organization's activities while simultaneously trying to adapt to changes in the environment. The exploration-exploitation literature defines three main subtypes of ambidexterity: a) structural (Duncan, 1976), b) contextual (Gibson & Birkinshaw, 2004) and c) temporal (Nickerson & Zenger, 2002). The present study focuses on the third subtype, where organizations choose to achieve the contrasting aims of exploration and exploitation via temporal cycling - during certain periods their strategic orientation is exploration-directed and during other times exploitation-directed. Simsek et al. (2009, pp. 882-4) were the ones who coined the term *cyclical ambidexterity* for this type of behavior.

2. The present study also relies on strategy-making concepts that are rooted in research on strategy-as-practice (Johnson, Melin, & Whittington, 2003), to understand the micro-level practices that constitute work on strategy (Whittington, 2006; Jarzabkowski, 2005; Jarzabkowski & Spee, 2009).

While the above-mentioned research streams have analyzed the phenomena in question, the studies to date have not focused on a combination of the two principles - the linkage of strategy-as-practice and cyclical ambidexterity. Therefore, the purpose of the present dissertation is to map the practices of strategy making as cyclical ambidexterity unfolds within an organization. The central research question of the thesis is:

> *Which practices are used by organizational actors involved in strategy making in the context of cyclical ambidexterity?*

The research question entails focusing at two levels. 1) *the macro level*: identifying the ways business units change their dominant strategic orientation during a shift of cyclical ambidexterity 2) *the micro level*: identifying the associated practices used by organizational actors who are involved in strategy-making.

Methodologically, the study employs two longitudinal case studies, analyzing firms where one is going through a shift from exploration to exploitation mode, and the other is moving in the opposite direction. At the macro level, it identifies the dominant strategic orientation and the shifts of cyclical ambidexterity by analyzing the strategic initiatives reported in company annual reports. At the micro level, the study utilizes a strategy-as-practice lens to review strategy documents, interview managers and observe the strategy meetings of the management teams.

The findings of this study lead to the central argument of the dissertation, which is:

> *When engaging in cyclical ambidexterity, companies keep multiple capabilities for strategy making in-house, activating the practices that are deemed appropriate to the associated upcoming shift of strategic orientation, and deactivating the practices that have become redundant.*

The structure of the dissertation is the following: After the current introductory chapter, I will lay out the research background, specifying its theoretical and conceptual scope, spelling out the current working definitions of key constructs, and clarifying the research focus. The third chapter is about method. I shall describe the logic of the research design, the data sources and the methodology that was followed. In the fourth chapter I will summarize the results of the study and present the conceptual model of how I will analyze the case study data. I thereafter demonstrate how the ambidexterity shift unfolded in the two case organizations. In the final chapter, I will discuss the contribution and implications of the present thesis.

The results of this study inform the ambidexterity literature. Previous studies have primarily engaged in analyzing *harmonic ambidexterity* or *contextual ambidexterity*, whereby firms attempt to keep high levels of exploration and exploitation going at all times (Birkinshaw & Gibson, 2004). This study demonstrates that there are firms who, instead, decide to fluctuate between relatively high levels of exploration and exploitation, alternating at different times. The findings of this study demonstrate that while the previous literature on ambidexterity cycles has described this phenomenon via the concept of *punctuated equilibrium*, whereby long periods of exploitation are interrupted by short periods of exploration (Tushman & Romanelli, 1985; Tushman & O'Reilly, 1996), this study demonstrates that the periods of exploration can be longer than previously reported.

It also informs the strategy-as-practice stream about micro-level practices that are used in reshaping strategic orientations in the ambidexterity continuum. Strategy-as-practice research has described the practices that people engage in during the periods of shaping and reshaping the practices. This study demonstrates that organizations that engage in cyclical ambidexterity keep their ability to explore and exploit ready to go at all times. During a shift towards exploration, they activate exploration practices and deactivate exploitation practices. During a shift towards exploitation, they likewise activate exploitation practices and deactivate exploration practices. The contribution of this study is to demonstrate the dynamics of alternating activation and deactivation practices of companies that engage in cyclical ambidexterity.

2 Background

To answer the research question: "Which practices are used by organizational actors involved in strategy making in the context of cyclical ambidexterity?", I need to focus upon two areas in my literature review:

- The primary literature stream focuses on organizational ambidexterity;
- The second literature stream focuses on strategy-as-practice, concentrating on the practices and organizational actors.

The term *organizational ambidexterity* renders 400 results for academic papers in the EBSCO Business Source database, and a citation count of more than 3,000 sources in Google Scholar[1]. An increasing number of studies on ambidextrous organizations have focused on performance antecedents, moderators, and outcomes (Raisch & Birkinshaw, 2008; Gupta, Smith, & Shalley, 2006; Simsek, Heavey, Veiga, & Souder, 2009; Cao, Gedajlovic, & Zhang, 2009). As Raisch and Birkinshaw (2008) noted in their review paper: "The discussion on the duality of exploration and exploitation on organizational adaptation has grown and today spans several sub-streams of organizational learning, technological innovation, strategic management and organizational design". I have therefore focused my literature review in this dissertation on papers published in the top 21 journals in the field of strategic management and strategy as practice, taking into consideration only the relevant research papers with the most rigorous publishing quality checks.[2] To identify the most relevant literature in the subfield of cyclical ambidexterity I searched the databases for the terms *ambidexterity, exploration, exploitation, cyclical, temporal and sequential.* The resulting literature analysis of the field of organizational ambidexterity, which defines the core constructs, the gaps in the literature and my planned contribution through this paper, is below.

Likewise, I have framed the literature review for strategy making in a similar manner. The strategy-as-practice literature stream is a growing field of study that focuses on strategy agendas in organizations. It focuses on who is involved in strategy work; what they do; how they do it; what tools they use and what organizational implications these elements have (Jarzabkowski & Spee, 2009, p. 69). The bibliography on the Strategy-As-Practice community website includes more than 800 entries, including books, journal articles, conference presentations and working papers. Given the breadth of the discussion, I have focused in the literature review in this dissertation on the papers

---

[1] The sites ebscohost.com and scholar.google.com accessed on February 26, 2015
[2] A-level journals, including four journals of The Academy of Management, three journals of The Strategic Management Society, and The Administrative Science Quarterly, The California Management Review, The European Management Review, Human Relations, The International Journal of Management Reviews, The Journal of Business Research, The Journal of Management, The Journal of Management Studies, Long Range Planning, Management Science, Organization Science, Organization Studies, The Sloan Management Review and Strategic Organization.

of the same top 21 journals mentioned above, plus 3 books.[3] The generic definition of practices tends to be broad - e.g. "practices are socially recognized forms of activity done on the basis of what members learn from others and are capable of doing well or badly, correctly or incorrectly" (Barnes, 2001, p. 16). Even the *strategy-as-practice* camp defines strategy practice broadly as "something that people do rather than something organizations have" (Johnson, Langley, Melin, & Whittington, 2007, p. loc.131). To identify the most relevant studies, I therefore searched the databases for the keywords *strategy-as-practice, strategy making and strategizing,* and thereafter the focus in the literature review was on the core constructs associated with my dissertation.

The following chapter will be a review of the literature on ambidexterity, and thereafter the focus will be on the combination of strategy making and ambidexterity.

2.1   Ambidexterity

The word *ambidexterity* is derived from the Latin *ambos* "both", and *dexter* "right" – and hence means the ability to effectively use both hands (Simsek, 2009, p. 599). The metaphorical term *organizational ambidexterity* was coined by Duncan (1976) to describe organizational ability to manage trade-offs between the conflicting demands of the dual nature of exploration and exploitation. Duncan presented those trade-offs as mutually exclusive. Since the seminal work of March (1991) the research discussion has evolved in scope and depth, following two important waves. The first was comprised of a number of works written by Michael Tushman and his colleagues (Romanelli & Tushman, 1994; Tushman & O'Reilly, 1996). Thereafter a second wave was set in motion a decade later when a special edition of The Academy of Management Journal opened a research forum on managing exploration and exploitation (Gupta, Smith, & Shalley, 2006).

Appropriate choices between exploratory innovation and exploitative operations significantly influence organizational performance (Jansen, Van den Bosch, & Volberda, 2006). As firms in volatile industries are trying to simultaneously take advantage of existing opportunities and also discover new ones, managers have become interested in the subject area. This provides consulting businesses with opportunities to advise the firms in this field[4].

2.1.1   Exploration and exploitation - theory and definitions.

Organizational learning theory was the first to explore ambidexterity as a combination of exploration and exploitation. James March defined exploration as "entrepreneurial learning-related activities that include search, variation, risk taking, experimentation, play, flexibility, discovery and innovation" (March, 1991, p. 71). He defined exploitation as "expertise learning-related activities

---

[3] Strategy as practice books: ● Golsorkhi, D., Rouleau, L., Seidl, D. & Vaara, E. (Eds.) (2010) *Cambridge Handbook of Strategy as Practice* ● Johnson, G., Langley, A., Melin, L. & Whittington, R. (2007) *Strategy as Practice Research Directions and Resources.* ● Schatzki, T.R., Knorr Cetina, K. & von Savigny, E. (Eds.) (2001) *The Practice Turn in Contemporary Theory.*
[4] Based on an unpublished PricewaterhouseCoopers report: *Strategy Frameworks Manual,* which lists a number of consulting tools that rely on enhancing exploration and exploitation capabilities. Among these are: value chain analysis, profit trees, cost structures, pricing tools, industry lifecycle models, which focus on exploitation, and value curves, customer segmentation tools, disruptive technology scanning, which focus on exploration.

consisting of refinement, choice, production, efficiency, selection, implementation and execution" (March, 1991). In his subsequent paper, he defined the duality between exploration and exploitation as inseparable different facets of learning, which occasionally drive actors into traps because of the myopia created by the bounded rationality that creates simplification and specialization (Levinthal & March, 1993). Floyd and Lane (2000, p. 156) specified two types of learning which roughly correspond to exploitation and exploration: *competence deployment* - a process to reinforce existing product market positions and *competence modification* - a process to encourage emergent adaptive change behavior. Sanchez et al. (1996) used the terms *competence leveraging* for exploitation and *competence building* for exploration. Tushman & Anderson (1996) weighed in with *competence destroying* for exploration and *competence enhancing* for exploitation. Birkinshaw and Gibson coined the terms *adaptability* and *alignment*. Adaptability signifies the ability to move toward new opportunities, to adjust to markets and avoid complacency by reconfiguring activities in the business unit to meet changes in the task environment. Alignment denotes the capability to streamline activities to exploit the value of proprietary assets and coherence among all the patterns of activities in the business unit - working together toward the same goals with a clear sense of value creation in the short term (Gibson & Birkinshaw, 2004, p. 209; Birkinshaw & Gibson, 2004, p. 47).

Dynamic capabilities theory provides a framework that relates closely to organizational ambidexterity. Dynamic capabilities are the tools of managers for adapting and reconfiguring organizational resources to match changing environments (Teece, Pisano, & Shuen, 1997; Eisenhardt & Martin, 2000). Likewise, managerial efforts drive the balancing of organizational tensions between exploration and exploitation, to ensure both present and future viability of the firm (March, 1991). Hence, a number of authors have suggested that the predominant underlying theory for organizational ambidexterity relies on the dynamic capabilities view (O'Reilly & Tushman, 2008; Taylor & Helfat, 2009; O'Reilly & Tushman, 2013). O'Reilly and Tushman suggest that "dynamic capabilities help an organization reallocate and reconfigure organizational skills and assets to permit the firm to both exploit existing competencies and develop new ones" (2013, p. 332).

Contingency theory opened the discussion about the dominant strategies of firms (Miles & Snow, 1978; Donaldson, 2001), which has evolved into prescriptive suggestions arising from *multiple contingency theory* or *configuration theory* (Burton & Obel, 2004). Exploration centers on the external strategic goals of an organization, focusing on steps taken to improve new product development, expand market share or intensify competition. Exploitation, on the other hand, focuses on the internal strategic goals of an organization: increasing productivity, efficiency and overall operational effectiveness. Miles and Snow (1978) established a typology of four dominant strategies for a firm. They used *prospector strategy,* characteristic of an organization actively expanding to new markets and product domains, and which resembles exploration strategy; and *defender strategy* to depict organizations keeping their stable market via efficiency-oriented activities, analogous to the exploitative strategy. *Analyzer strategy* captures the essence of ambidextrous organizations that are trying to do both at the same time. According to Miles and Snow, organizations should ideally respond to the environment in a relatively consistent manner. If the environment demands it, then the firms should revise their dominant strategy and change their strategic bearing to one of the new dominant strategies that are more appropriate in the new changed circumstances. Gupta et al. (2006, p. 698) also point to contingency theory as having merit if observing exploration and exploitation within a single domain indicates adaptation, depending on the context.

Social evolutionary theory's core conceptual framework of *variation, selection and retention* is a representation of the exploration and exploitation cycle. Exploration probes the environment and provides variation, whereas the retention process happens through exploitation (Chen & Katila, 2008, pp. 200-201). Evolutionary theorists started using the idea of *search* in generating variations of ideas, issues or products to select and retain (Nelson & Winter, 1982). The search notion was thereby originally synonymous with exploration. Katila and Ahuja took this notion further in their 2002 study. They distinguished levels of exploitation and argued that firms can differentiate themselves not only to the extent to which they explore new activities, but also to the extent to which they master the old ones. Thus, they drew attention to the importance of exploitation not just for fine-tuning and economizing the efficiency of an existing technology, but also for creating new knowledge. While exploratory search would have focused on new solutions, exploitative search had the role of combining existing solutions with generating new value-generating combinations (Katila & Ahuja, 2002). Nerkar and Roberts (2004) differentiated search domains and geography: defining proximal localized search activities as exploitation ("shifting through the haystack") and distal global search activities as exploration ("exploring uncharted territory").

According to the typology of Sidhu et al. (2007; 2004), local and non-local search divides into three categories: 1) demand- and 2) supply-side search and 3) geographic search, local and non-local. Gavetti and Levinthal describe both local and distant experimentation as subtypes of exploration (Gavetti & Levinthal, 2000). In a similar manner Rosenkopf and Nerkar describe four types of exploratory search in the CD-ROM industry: 1) *Local exploration* using a firm's existing patents to improve existing products incrementally; 2) *Internal boundary-spanning exploration,* integrating knowledge that already resides within the present firm, but is distant from the present products technologically; 3) *External boundary-spanning exploration,* relying on knowledge that is derived from other organizations, but which relates closely to the company's existing knowledge; 4) *Radical exploration,* which brings in radical technology from outside the firm (Rosenkopf & Nerkar, 2001). Sidhu et al. (2007; 2004) , however, maintain that "local exploration" as defined by Rosenkopf and Nerkar may be categorized as "exploitation".

Several recent conceptualizations of ambidexterity have focused on particular facets of a business and boundaries within a firm, for example *product ambidexterity* and *market ambidexterity* (Voss & Voss, 2013) and *technology sourcing ambidexterity* (Rothaermel & Alexandre, 2009). Rothaermel and Alexandre (2009) analyzed the ambidexterity of technology sourcing and determined the respective types of technologies (exploiting existing technology vs. exploring new), sourcing them either internally or externally. This can be presented on a 2x2 matrix, where a firm sources already-known technology from internal sources, engaging in *internal exploitation,* or alternatively from external sources - *external exploitation*. The third option is that the firm sources new technology from internal sources - internal exploration and finally from outside - external exploration.

Another relevant study for the present context is a work by Voss & Voss. They outlined ambidexterity across product and market domains and defined four subtypes: *Product exploration* - developing new products, and changing product subsystems, that is, underlying technologies and production capabilities; *Product exploitation* - increasing returns from existing product capabilities; *Market exploration* - marketing programs, which attract new customers by either broadening the market geographically or by a local non-targeted market segment; *Market exploitation* - focused marketing programs designed to retain and increase purchases from current customers. (Definitions adapted from Voss & Voss [2013]).

Organizational ambidexterity also relates to the theory of change - shifts in degrees of ambidexterity as a type of organizational change (Gilbert, 2006). *Paradox theory* refers to organizational ambidexterity as a set of organizational tensions on the learning and performing continuum: building capabilities for the future while maintaining the successes of the past (Smith & Lewis, 2011; Andriopoulus & Lewis, 2009). To ensure coherence with the practice literature, I use the following definition based on the above:

> **Ambidexterity** - *the organizational ability to engage in practices that allow alignment and efficiency while simultaneously being adaptive to changes in the environment by effectively combining exploratory and exploitative activities.*

The table below summarizes the main theoretical underpinnings of the duality of exploration and exploitation.

Table 1. Research on duality of exploration and exploitation

Theory stream	Concepts	Main authors
Organizational learning theory	Entrepreneurial learning vs. expert learning	(March, 1991)
	Competence destroying vs competence enhancing	(Tushman & Anderson, 1996)
	Competence modification vs. deployment	(Floyd & Lane, 2000)
	Competence building vs. aging	(Sanchez, Heene, & Thomas, 1996)
	Adaptation vs. alignment	(Gibson & Birkinshaw, 2004)
Dynamic capabilities theory	Exploration vs exploitation as a modality for managing organizational trade-offs to increase management capabilities	(O'Reilly & Tushman, 2008; Taylor & Helfat, 2009; O'Reilly & Tushman, 2013)
Contingency theory	Prospector vs. defender	(Miles & Snow, 1978)
Evolutionary theory	Exploratory search vs. exploitative search	(Katila & Ahuja, 2002)
	Proximal experience and localized search vs. distal experience and global search	(Nerkar & Roberts, 2004)
	Distant search vs. local search coupled with demand side- and supply-side search	Sidhu et al. (2007; 2004)
Functional view (depending on boundaries of the firm)	Internal exploitation, external exploitation, internal exploration, external exploration	(Rothaermel & Alexandre, 2009)

Market exploration - exploitation vs product exploration - exploitation	(Voss & Voss, 2013)

Based on the conceptualizations above, relying on the definitions of March (1991, p. 71), Sidhu et al. (2007) and Voss & Voss (2013), I define the terms in the context of the present thesis as:

Exploration: Entrepreneurial activity consisting of risk taking, experimentation, play, flexibility, discovery and innovation in the domains of new products, technologies, markets, customers or geographical regions. And

Exploitation: Expertise-building activity consisting of refinement, production and execution in the domains of existing products, technologies, markets, customers or geographical regions.

2.1.2   Exploration and exploitation duality.

The duality of exploration and exploitation is a construct that designates a firm's dominant strategic orientation in terms of "how the firm competes". The four configurations delineating the duality of exploratory and exploitative strategic orientations are: 1) discrete and mutually exclusive choices (Duncan, 1976); 2) orthogonal capabilities to be developed simultaneously (Gibson & Birkinshaw, 2004); 3) the endpoints of a continuum (Tushman & Romanelli, 1985), and 4) complementary - enabling and interdependent dimensions which are constantly reinforcing each other (Farjoun, 2010).

Early studies focused on the discrete approach towards exploration and exploitation, noting that as a single domain does not allow the achievement of conflicting demands simultaneously, the management should consider dividing them into different parts of the organization via structural division. One part of the organization should deal with exploratory activities whereas the other focuses on exploitative activities, thereby establishing a partition through structural ambidexterity within the organization (Duncan, 1976).

Birkinshaw and Gibson (2004) surveyed more than 4,000 individuals in 41 multinational business units and observed *contextual ambidexterity* where the individual employees of the organizations were multitasking and effectively dividing their time between alignment-focused and adaptability-focused activities. Markides called for ambidextrous professors at universities (2007). They point, in other words, to the ability of individuals to both explore and exploit.

Simsek et al. (2009) suggested categories of ambidexterity, which divide combinations of exploration and exploitation into a 2x2 matrix based on a temporal and a structural dimension. Temporal division determines whether exploration and exploitation are simultaneous or time separated. Structural division determines whether exploration and exploitation are in the same organizational unit or span across units.

Several authors have noted that despite the attempts of companies to strive for both exploration and exploitation simultaneously, it is difficult to achieve that in practice without structural adjustments. Therefore, companies would have to identify the optimal spot on the continuum that would allow the most favorable amount of exploitation and exploration (Gupta, Smith, & Shalley, 2006; Gomez, Raisch, & Rigall, 2007).

Zollo and Winter (2002) suggested a relevant typology for the continuum wherein exploitation primes exploration and vice versa. Instead of a trade-off between exploration and exploitation processes, there is a recursive and co-evolutionary relationship between them. Ultimately, the notion of the complementarity of exploration and exploitation via their reinforcing loop also suggests that cyclical ambidexterity is a layer of the other forms of ambidexterity and implies that the cyclical nature is a combination of the above forms[5].

Farjoun (2010) supports this argument. He argued that the reliability of stable systems increases through variability, that is, by introducing "moderate" exploitation that uses the tools of exploration as a means of keeping it going. Furthermore, exploration may be made more fruitful by experimenting more frequently, but with fewer painful failures – that is, by introducing "moderate" exploration, which uses tools of exploitation to keep experiments under control. He pointed to the mutually reinforcing roles of organizational stability and change, arguing that the reliability of exploitative systems increases through variability. Exploitation is also more fruitful when experimentation is more frequent, but with fewer painful failures (2010, pp. 208-9). Floyd and Lane argue that for a company to remain adaptive, it has to both exploit existing resources as well as explore new ones. Hence, the two facets of organizational learning are inseparable (Floyd & Lane, 2000, p. 155).

Based on the discussions above, the present dissertation will focus on a particular type of ambidexterity: cyclical ambidexterity. In the present dissertation, I use the definition:

> **Cyclical ambidexterity** - *a subtype of sequential (temporal) ambidexterity in which organizations engage in periods of exploitation interspersed with periods of exploration.*

2.1.3 Cyclical ambidexterity.

The cyclical ambidexterity concept relies on the literature of punctuated equilibrium (Tushman & Romanelli, 1985; Gersick, 1991), according to which cyclical ambidexterity involves a cyclical allocation of resources and attention to either exploitation or exploration. A variety of terms and theories describe this phenomenon, for example punctuated equilibrium (Burgelman, 2002; Tushman & Romanelli, 1985); "sequential allocation of attention to divergent goals", "temporal achievement of exploration and exploitation" (Gupta, Smith, & Shalley, 2006); "relentlessly shifting organizations" (Brown & Eisenhardt, 1997); *structural modulation, modulating structure, cycling structure* or *vacillation* (Nickerson & Zenger, 2002); *sequencing* or "temporary decentralization with subsequent reintegration" (Siggelkow & Levinthal, 2003); "switching strategy" (Reeves, Haanæs, Hollingsworth, & Pasini, 2013); "regular creation and losing of business charters" (Galunic & Eisenhardt, 1996); "sequential, cyclical and reciprocal ambidexterity" (Simsek, Heavey, Veiga, &

---

[5] Steven Floyd suggested *cyclical ambidexterity* as an overlay form, commenting on an earlier draft of this study.

Souder, 2009); "organizational cycling" (Cummings, 1995); and "temporal division before centralizing" (Siggelkow & Levinthal, 2003).

The terms *cyclical ambidexterity* and *ambidexterity cycles* have become the most popular and are therefore used in this thesis.

While studies have demonstrated that simultaneous ambidexterity is possible (Gibson & Birkinshaw, 2004), there are also some analyses that have demonstrated companies failing to achieve exploration and exploitation simultaneously and choosing cyclical ambidexterity instead. March explains this tension between exploration and exploitation via learning (1991, p. 72). Constant exploration of new alternatives increases competencies to work on exploratory activities and diminishes the exploitative ones. In addition, improvements in competence at existing procedures make experimentation with others less attractive (Levitt & March, 1988; Levinthal & March, 1993). Ultimately, the abilities of working in the other mode are reduced.

The second line of reasoning for the adoption of cyclical ambidexterity relates to the cognitive limits of individuals. The predominant brain function mode is subject to individual traits, whereby one function dominates over the other. Hence, exploratory and exploitative tasks are difficult to carry out simultaneously (Gazzaniga, Ivry, & Mangun, 1998). Cognitive limits may also be collective. A unified opinion about strategic orientation among the top management team also tends to carry with it a behavioral inertia in the leading group; that is, it becomes difficult to establish a strategic agenda for the organization that allows it to achieve multiple goals, in the direction of both exploration and exploitation (Simsek, Veiga, Lubatkin, & Dino, 2005). Organization may also be subject to becoming more uniform, either externally via the attraction-selection-attrition effect (Schneider, 1987) or internally via the homophily effect (Rillo, 2008). Hines has criticized this view for being overly simplistic, especially with regard to managerial cognition (1987). There is a related constraint – the attention-allocation capacity of the decision-makers (Ocasio, 1997). Organizational choices are limited via attention structures, procedural and communication channels as well as particular issues brought to the managers' attention. The firm's attention structures are a basis for valuation and legitimization of the issues and answers available to decision-makers (Ocasio, 1997, pp. 194; 196-199). Adler et al. describe another example of limited attention allocation in their study of model changeovers at the Toyota NUMMI plant, whereby a production plant that was highly exploitative revised its procedures during the introduction of new models to structurally facilitate attention allocation to exploration (1999).

In a situation where firms operate in industries requiring significant upfront investments or depend heavily on sunk costs, the resource constraints pose a limit. An organization that has dealt with exploratory activities and invested substantial amounts into entering new markets will likely not have enough resources to proceed with expansion, and has to exploit its investments and increase efficiency. Resource allocation largely determines the behavior of the firm on the exploration-exploitation scale (Bower, 1970; Noda & Bower, 1996).

Another reason stems from external technology cycles. In turbulent environments that are subject to disruptive technologies there are periods characterized by market uncertainty created by the adoption of new technology. These turbulent times are interspersed with relatively stable periods while the businesses harness this technology. These external forces make organizations adapt periodically to either exploratory or exploitative mode (Brown & Eisenhardt, 1997; Benner & Tushman, 2003).

The reason for balancing may relate to the inherent internal dynamics of the firms as the managers attempt to handle the conflicting demands of organizational inertia and performance and are actively attempting to facilitate a search for these types of efficiency gains (Tushman & Romanelli, 1985; Nickerson & Zenger, 2002; Cummings, 1995).

Furthermore, performance-orientation pressure may arise from stakeholders seeking specific innovation or cost-cutting initiatives as a clear message concerning the company's future. Those outside pressures may create an additional attention-seeking burden for the managers of the organization and thereby increase the likelihood that the management team will have to devote part of their attention span to handling the outside stakeholders, thereby having less time to deal with simultaneous exploration and exploitation.

Table 2. Tensions arising from simultaneous exploration and exploitation.

Key reasons why exploration and exploitation are difficult to achieve simultaneously	Main authors
Organizational learning inertia. While individuals work on one type of activity (exploration vs. exploitation), they learn it better, but at the same time lose skills in the other.	Levitt & March (1988), March (1991), Levinthal & March (1993)
Cognitive limits of employees and teams. Some individuals are more inclined to deal with exploration-type activities, others with exploitation-type activities. Furthermore, during a given period, it is difficult to divide one's attention equally between the two. If top management teams share demographic similarities, duration of their tenure and unified goals, they are more likely to choose one type of strategic orientation and subsequent activities over the other.	Gazzaniga, Ivry, & Mangun, (1998) Simsek, Veiga, Lubatkin, & Dino (2005)
Attention allocation. Where the behavior of the firm is the result of how its decision-makers channel and distribute their attention, during the limited amount of time when they focus their attention more on one type of activities, they do not have enough for the other.	Ocasio (1997), Adler, Goldoftas, & Levine (1999)
Resource limits. When an organization has invested heavily into exploratory activities it does not have enough resources to continue, so it is predestined by the legacy of past decisions to deal only with the exploitation of the existing resources.	Bower (1970), Noda & Bower (1996), Uotila et al. (2009)
External technology cycles. In a turbulent environment, there are periods characterized by market uncertainty and other periods characterized by relative stability, which force the companies periodically into exploratory or exploitative mode.	(Brown & Eisenhardt, 1997; Benner & Tushman, 2003)
Inherent dynamics of firms. Due to the reasons specified in institutional theory or population ecology, managers in firms may be attempting to handle the conflicting demands of organizational inertia and performance with a search for efficiency gains dominated by outside players.	(Tushman & Romanelli, 1985; Nickerson & Zenger, 2002; Cummings, 1995)
Requirements of the external stakeholders. Stakeholders may seek for messages from the TMT on the company future via an easily comprehensible strategic direction. It is easier to understand either innovation or cost-cutting initiatives separately rather than simultaneously.	Author

The argument above spells out the reasons why cyclical ambidexterity occurs. However, sometimes firms actively seek cyclical ambidexterity. Tushman and Romanelli first described the cycling behavior in more detail in 1985 as punctuated equilibrium, whereby long periods of exploitation were sporadically interrupted by short bursts of exploration. First, they established propositions summarizing the main reasons and contingencies that cause organizations to cycle periodically between exploratory and exploitative strategies, and in the latter paper they tested those empirically (Tushman & Romanelli, 1985; Romanelli & Tushman, 1994).

Pettigrew and Whipp argued that in a number of economic theory streams there are underlying concepts of cyclical behavior in observing organizational and economic change. They point to institutional theorists, Schumpeterian economists and new competition protagonists (Pettigrew & Whipp, 1993). Social evolutionary theory supports the exclusivity of the exploration and exploitation phenomenon (Nelson & Winter, 1982). The variation-selection-retention cycle mirrors the cycle of exploration and exploitation. Whereas exploration provides variation for new businesses, exploitation facilitates selection, retention and replication of dominant designs within an organization (Chen & Katila, 2008). Zajac and colleagues have argued that according to contingency theory, firms should try to identify possibilities for achieving a fit between environmental and organizational variables. The achievement of fit in constantly changing situations leads organizations into the constant flux of change, which forces them to cycle between exploration and exploitation while seeking for a balance between inertia and changes (Zajac, Kraatz, & Bresser, 2000).

Gupta et al. (2006, p. 697) argue in their review article that the sequential approach provides a combinatory mechanism to alleviate resource and administrative constraints; there exist two main reasons for this kind of sequential strategic behavior, which are both related to resource or attention limitations:

1. The scarcer the resources needed to pursue both exploration and exploitation, the greater the likelihood that the two will be mutually exclusive: high values for one will imply low values for the other.
2. Within a single domain or tightly-coupled domains (i.e. an individual or a subsystem), exploration and exploitation will generally be mutually exclusive.

Studies have demonstrated that cyclical ambidexterity is more prevalent in investment-intensive industries with less available capital resources, where firms have to invest substantially into a new technology and focus on making this technology profitable before any new exploratory investments are possible. The companies therefore periodically exploit existing resources and during other times explore new resources (Uotila, Maula, Keil, & Zahra, 2009). Cyclical ambidexterity predicts sales growth significantly in comparison with simultaneous ambidexterity in the software industry (Venkatraman, Lee, & Iyer, 2007). Cyclical ambidexterity is prevalent in narrowly-defined business domains (Gupta, Smith, & Shalley, 2006), subject to higher competitive rivalry (Jansen, Van den Bosch, & Volberda, 2005), or more intensive R&D (Uotila, Maula, Keil, & Zahra, 2009). Cyclical ambidexterity may also facilitate more efficient specialization of exploitative and exploratory activities and innovations within an organization (Simsek, Heavey, Veiga, & Souder, 2009). Cyclical ambidexterity facilitates meeting the conflicting demands of organizational inertia and performance (Sastry, 1997, p. 244). Cyclical ambidexterity may occur due to low competence periods resulting from a poorly-managed change process (Sastry, 1997, p. 266); a continuous search for efficiency gains (Nickerson & Zenger, 2002); the inherent internal dynamic within firms (Cummings, 1995); or an intra-organizational periodic requirement to manifest the results of the work of the alliance partners (Rothaermel & Deeds, 2004). Geerts and colleagues (2010) have suggested that service firms tend to prefer cyclical ambidexterity.

Furthermore, Khanaga et al. (2013) carried out a longitudinal study of a large telecommunications firm where they analyzed the firm's adoption of emerging technologies that were about to impact existing core technologies. The case analysis revealed the properties of cyclical ambidexterity whereby the case organization went through the cycle of exploitation - exploration - exploitation through a time-span of 3 years. The telecommunications firm first revised its resource allocation practices; thereafter it developed new incentive structures and experimental routines, and at the third stage it continued with exploratory initiatives via newly developed routines, and finally returned to the initial structures associated with the exploitative mode after having put in place the routines supporting further exploration (Khanaga, Volberda, Sidhu, & Oshri, 2013, pp. 58-62).

A number of authors have discussed the properties of cyclical ambidexterity. There are studies on timing and the extent of shifts and cycles. Tushman and Romanelli (1985) argue that organizations go through periods of convergence and reorientation. Convergence is a "process of incremental and interdependent change activities and decisions which work to achieve a greater consistency of internal activities with a strategic orientation, and which operate to impede radical or discontinuous change." Reorientation is a "simultaneous and discontinuous shift in strategy (products, markets and/or technology), the distribution of power, the firm's core structure, and the nature and pervasiveness of control systems". Whereas convergence periods last around 4-6 years, Romanelli and Tushman (1994, p. 1159) found that fundamental transformations were carried out mostly within a span of 2 years. However, Sastry took the textual variables of the original propositions of Tushman and Romanelli and modeled them in a turbulent environment and concluded that in addition to sharp periods of punctuated equilibria, two additional management routines come into play. Managers measure and assess organization-environment fit and keep a longer trial period following a change initiative to check on the validity of the change (Sastry, 1997). Sasson and Minoja confirm this by arguing that an organization needs to keep its change volatility at a relatively low level "to invest enough time to develop routines that would manage internal paradoxes of exploration and exploitation" (Sasson & Minoja, 2010). They suggest that if managers attempt to exploit short-term opportunities, it leads to constant changes. If routines and structures to align organizational resource allocation, remuneration, incentive systems, hiring, training and budgeting are constantly adapted, it hinders development of the ability to explore and exploit (Sasson & Minoja, 2010, pp. 247-8).

Nickerson and Zenger analyzed the past cycling behavior of Hewlett Packard and found periods of transformation that spanned between 2 to 7 years, fluctuating between extreme centralization and decentralization (Nickerson & Zenger, 2002, pp. 548-9). They further noticed that KPMG had been cycling between 5 structures during 7 years, while Ford had cycled between two extremes over 5 years. They also added that sometimes the cycling was not limited to internal structure, bringing examples of a medical supply firm that cycled its internal and external sourcing five times over the previous 20 years, and a gas firm that fluctuated between internal and external distributing (pp. 550, ibid.).

The frequency-of-cycling theme is expanded by Klarner & Raisch (2013). They focused on the rhythm of change and its implications for the performance of European insurance firms, and concluded that it is not so much change and stability per se, but the regularity of the shifts in question that contribute to the long-term success of the firms in question.

The literature review above has provided us with a detailed take on the studies of cyclical ambidexterity. Khanaga et al. (2013) focused on a single-case study where a telecommunications firm initiated and adopted cloud computing through a single cycle of exploitation-exploration-exploitation. However, based on my reading, no further studies to date have analyzed the internal dynamics of the practices of cyclical ambidexterity unfolding within organizations that engage in a more long-term implementation of cyclical ambidexterity. To address this gap, I intend to take practice-based view.

2.2   Strategy as Practice Research

In addition to looking at cyclical ambidexterity, this study focuses on strategy making. Two streams of research look into strategy making within organizations. One is the strategy process stream (Burgelman, 1991; Chakravarthy & Doz, 1992; Pettigrew, 1992; Lechner, 2006; Hutzschenreuter & Kleindienst, 2006), which observes strategy work resulting from patterned action (Huff & Reger, 1987), from budgetary process (Pfeffer & Salancik, 1974), resource allocation (Noda & Bower, 1996), an annual strategy creation cycle (Ansoff, 1965), decision-making (Mintzberg, Raisinghani, & Théoret, 1976), and agenda building (Dutton, Walton, & Abrahamson, 1989).

Another underlying theoretical pillar is the strategy-as-practice stream (Johnson, Melin, & Whittington, 2003; Johnson, Langley, Melin, & Whittington, 2007), which aims to understand the micro-level practices constituting strategy work (Whittington, 2006; Jarzabkowski, 2005; Jarzabkowski & Spee, 2009). The strategy-as-practice research stream relates closely to the strategy-process stream. Some claim that strategy as practice and strategy process are the same (Carter, Clegg, & Kornberger, 2008), while others claim strategy as practice to be a sub-field of strategy process (Langley, 2007). However, the largest group advocates for strategy as practice being a separate field of study because process research is not deep enough in detail, misses the view of agency or separates content from strategy work (Johnson, Melin, & Whittington, 2003).

A number of fields of strategy received interesting insights from a micro-level analysis of strategy practices. The studies using strategy as practice as a lens were looking at organizational capabilities and routines (Whittington & Vaara, 2012; Johnson, Langley, Melin, & Whittington, 2007). Ambrosini et al. (2007) used a practice view to approach a resource-based view. Regnér (2008) analyzed dynamic capabilities via a strategy-as-practice lens. Given that ambidexterity theorists have suggested several theoretical frameworks to explain organizational ambidexterity, O'Reilly and Tushman have suggested that the most appropriate lens is that of dynamic capabilities (2013, p. 332). Given the suggestion for the connection between the two research agendas, ambidexterity literature would gain additional insights from looking at how internal strategy work affects degree of exploration and exploitation in firms.

Strategy-as-practice study focuses on 1) practitioners who are involved in strategy creation and implementation; 2) their practices - ways of going about doing strategy, some of them routinized, the others adopted; and 3) the praxis of strategy work - daily strategy-related activities (Whittington

& Vaara, 2012). Hence, its primary focus is on what managers do when they engage in strategy work and thereby link "macro" and "micro" in strategy (Golsorkhi, Rouleau, Seidl, & Vaara, 2010). Furthermore, the strategy-as-practice perspective also presumes that an organization's strategy is never finished, but is perpetually "in the making" by strategy practitioners who engage in continuous discussions about adapting strategy (Whittington, 2003).

Strategy practitioners, practice and praxis. The research question of this dissertation looks at practices used by *organizational actors*. In resolving the research question and finding the answer as to which practices are used by organizational actors involved in strategy making in the process of cyclical ambidexterity, it becomes apparent that the underlying question is associated with agency. Agents of strategy making are central in strategy-as-practice literature (Jarzabkowski, 2005). Organizational actors - "who they are, how they act and what practices they draw upon" - (Jarzabkowski, Balogun, & Seidl, 2007) form the backbone of strategy-as-practice literature. Instead of attributing strategy work only to top management teams it suggests that strategy practitioners at different levels of an organization have influence over how the intended or emergent strategy of a firm takes shape. Focusing solely on top management (Alexiev, Jansen, Bosch, & Volberda, 2010) or even middle management (Wooldridge, Schmid, & Floyd, 2008) cannot tell the whole story about how strategies are created however, since strategy rests largely upon the participants in strategizing activities, those who establish themselves as strategy practitioners. They are "individuals who are trying to influence strategic issues" (Mantere, 2005, p. 157). In addition to conscious strategy-making activity, which leads to direct impact on strategy (i.e. by participation in strategy making) some organizational actors may also influence strategy indirectly (i.e. via activities that have strategic effect). Hence, the organizational actor may be a manager, a person working at any level in the organization or someone who wields impact through a boundary-spanning role, for example as a consultant, a major shareholder or an influential customer. In the context of the present study, I therefore put forth the following definition:

> *Organizational actor - an individual who has impact on strategy creation, formulation or implementation in a firm, either by participating directly in strategy making or having influence on strategy indirectly.*

Another core aspect is the notion of *strategy practice*. Strategy practice is a term related to *strategy making*, which is an overarching label for various activities assigned to the creation of organizational strategies. This entails any activities that lead to the emergence of organizational strategies: deliberate and emergent strategy formulation, organizing work during the implementation of strategies or any other activity that precedes strategizing (Whittington & Vaara, 2012, p. 287). There are a number of definitions of strategy practice, which rely on the concept of *activity*. Strategy activities can be defined as "all day-to-day stuff that managers do and what organizational actors engage in" (Johnson, Melin, & Whittington, 2003, p. 15). While this all-encompassing definition might be unobservable, it has been refined as "activities that are consequential and have strategic (i.e. important) outcomes" or "practices (i.e. situated activity) that are essential for the survival and competitive advantage of the firm" (Jarzabkowski, 2005, pp. both: 12-13). Strategy practice includes, therefore, a whole spectrum of tools and methods that enable strategy making in a firm. Here are more examples of **strategy practices**:

> *... routines, discourses, concepts and technologies through which strategy work is possible. Examples of this are: strategy reviews and off-sites; activities embedded in using academic and consulting tools (e.g. Porterian analysis, hypothesis testing, etc.); different organizational norms and procedures for strategy work (e.g. the annual strategy-making cycle); and in applying material technologies and artefacts (e.g. PowerPoint presentations, flip-charts, etc.) (Jarzabkowski & Whittington, 2008, p. 101).*

The final tip of the strategy-as-practice classic triangle is strategy praxis, a Latin term also frequently used in the English plural: *practices*. This is the actual "flow of activities in which strategy comes about" (Jarzabkowski & Spee, 2009, p. 70) or "the actual activity in which strategy making happens, e.g. in strategic planning meetings" (Whittington & Vaara, 2012, p. 290).

On this basis, I propose the following definition for the present thesis:

> **Strategy practices** - *activities of strategy actors in creating a firm's strategy or having indirect consequential implications for the strategy of the firm. The practices may be both structured and administrative activities, as well as non-routine behavior.*

Previous studies in the field of strategy as practice have established a number of findings about various practices associated with strategy making. For example, review papers have looked at formal vs informal practices, material vs analytical practices and practices associated with strategy meetings (Jarzabkowski & Spee, 2009; Whittington & Vaara, 2012). In the context of the present study, the strategy-as-practice lens provides the framework for analyzing exploration and exploitation practices and the practices of shifting between strategic orientations.

2.3   Strategy Making and Ambidexterity

2.3.1   Strategy making in purely exploratory or exploitative firms.

A literature review using a key-word combination of *strategy-as-practice* and *ambidexterity* provided a modest list of sources. An EBSCO search revealed just two results. This indicates a potential gap in the research. There are a limited number of studies focusing on combining strategy work and ambidexterity constructs. Jarzabkowski et al. (2013) wrote a conceptual paper about institutionalizing collective practices to study organizational complexities. Andriopoulus and Lewis (2009) wrote an analysis of case studies that dealt with how five firms handled the paradoxes of innovation using profit breakthroughs, customer orientation and personal drivers.

One of the related challenges is the unit of analysis. The Raisch and Birkinshaw review article about ambidexterity (Raisch & Birkinshaw, 2008, p. 396) noted that there are a few multi-level studies (Birkinshaw & Gibson, 2004). Ambidexterity has primarily been explicated on the corporate (He & Wong, 2004) and business unit (Tushman & O'Reilly, 1996) level of analysis, with only a few attempts to focus at the level of the individual (Junni, Sarala, Taras, & Tarba, 2013) such as

(Birkinshaw & Gibson, 2004; Mom, 2006; Mom, Bosch, & Volberda, 2007; Mom, Bosch, & Volberda, 2009). Mom's analysis primarily focused on the ambidexterity activities of managers, and connected some of the findings to strategy process studies by quantifying the managerial interactions, especially "the extent of horizontal knowledge flows during individual exploration and exploitation activities" (Mom, Bosch, & Volberda, 2007). Also (Miller, Zhao, & Calantone, 2006) modeled a way to add interpersonal learning to the original exploration-exploration paper of March (1991), although their study was just a simulation of the constructs. However, none of them takes the process view to see how ambidexterity links to strategy making at the practice level.

There are several studies carried out to describe and analyze strategy making in organizations that have chosen either the exploration or exploitation extreme. The authors have observed modes and patterns within those pure types (Mintzberg & Waters, 1985; Hart & Banbury, 1994; Regnér, 2003). Based on the typology of Hart (1992), generative and symbolic modes of strategizing are mostly used for exploration, whereas rational and command modes are used for exploitation. The transactive mode lies in-between, depending on the content of discussions of internal cross-functional communication groups. Similarly, based on the typology of Bourgeois and Broadwin (1984), the cultural and crescive models are more appropriate for exploratory action, while the commander and change models are best related to exploitation. Regnér (2003) suggests that strategy process at the corporate center of large multinational organizations emphasizes the refinement of current knowledge (exploitation of prevailing resources), while strategy process at the periphery relies on trying out, and adjusting to new knowledge creation (exploration of new resources).

In exploitative organizations, the corporate center carries out most of the exploitation-focused strategy activity and thereby controls the strategy process (Regnér, 2003, p. 71). Strategic decisions focus mostly on evolution in small incremental steps towards increased profits or reduced costs to defend the current position on the market. (Hart, 1992) Hence, established top-down annual activity dominates the classical strategy process. In most cases the budget process, with its associated resource allocation, is the key driving force of decision-making, and frequently companies organize their strategy making around the annual budgetary process, which consists of a number of stages, mostly focused on responding to the question: "How do we achieve better results in the given environment?".

Exploratory organizations do not frequently have structured strategy-making systems in place to differentiate between strategy formulation and strategy implementation. In addition, strategy work does not necessarily link with budgetary process. Instead, employees are encouraged to be entrepreneurial and resourceful with ideas. Frequently we find structured, funnel-like systems that may rely on the principles of guided evolution (Lovas & Ghoshal, 2000), where designated agents select and sustain the business ideas that will survive. Furthermore, there are companies that have established purely entrepreneurial means for strategy making (Dess, Lumpkin, & Covin, 1997). As cited above, based on a longitudinal case analysis involving four multinational companies, Regnér found that in large organizations the periphery primarily carries out exploratory tasks (Regnér, 2003,

p. 66). Bradach further confirmed, after looking at five US fast-food chains, that exploration happens mostly in the franchise offices, which are more likely to engage in innovative practices, and exploitation through fully company-owned units, which tend to copy internal best practices and strive for company-wide uniformity (Bradach, 1997, pp. 276-278).

2.3.2   Strategy making in an ambidextrous context.

There are authors who have brought out the performance implications of combining the two strategy making modes. Andersen (2000; 2004) has analyzed how a number of manufacturing organizations operating in diverse environments have used a combination of decentralized decision structures and centralized planning activities to gain higher performance in dynamic environments. In another study, Andersen and Nielsen (2009) analyzed how adaptation is possible in appropriate variations between emergent and intended strategy-making modes in a complementary manner. Their findings analyzing 185 manufacturing business entities show that the companies which have introduced complementary processes of systematic planning and strategic emergence, hence combining intended and emergent strategy modes (Mintzberg & Waters, 1985), are able to demonstrate higher performance gains.

Using structural equation modeling, Andersen and Nielsen argue that while "allowing emergence is an important precondition for higher performance, a more valuable result is achieved when emergence is further facilitated with effective planning processes" (Andersen & Nielsen, 2009, pp. 102-4).

Their study has limitations. First, their exploratory and exploitative strategic planning definitions were very broad. Exploration measurement relied on distributed decision authority and participation in strategy work. Exploitation relied on the degree of formalization of strategy making. Furthermore, the findings did not allow explicating causal linkages, as they did not verify how two different strategy-making modes manifested within organizational units. Despite these limitations, they demonstrate that a correlation exists and therefore it is still interesting to note that an "ambidextrous mode" of strategy making yields higher returns in certain contexts.

This evidence allows us to deduce (for the later argument) that the situation wherein the organizations are shifting their strategy making between exploitative and exploratory mode - while being in the flux of change - could potentially also yield higher returns despite the costs associated with the learning and unlearning of the practices associated with the new mode.

2.3.3   Strategy making during cyclical ambidexterity.

Ambidexterity cycles pose challenges for strategy making. The question of how strategizing during a shift from exploration to exploitation happens could be rather straightforward were it not related to several elements of strategy making which are different in exploration and exploitation modes. Based on the literature to date we do not have an example of an appropriate design for strategizing in an organization during an ambidexterity cycle.

The organization in the state of flux is likely to carry out multiple changes that span its capabilities, processes and even organizational structure, shifting on the centralization, formalization and complexity scales. We can presume that at the ends of both sides of the continuum, some elements of the strategy process may need to change. During the shift from exploitation to exploration, the organization may have to transform its primarily top-down, formalized, alignment-driven, centralized strategizing activity into more bottom-up, informal, adaptability-driven decentralized strategizing. Moving in the opposite direction from exploration to exploitation, the organization has to reintegrate its strategizing in the opposite way.

Although previous literature has discussed the duality of deliberate and emergent strategy making (Mintzberg & Waters, 1985; Hart, 1992) it is difficult to identify whether or not shifts in strategic orientation are conscious choices following a thorough, purposeful analysis, formalized as deliberate decisions and implemented with impeccable planning and follow-up. Such shifts may arise in the form of everyday activities or be induced by bottom-up activities of the organizational actors at lower levels (Burgelman, 1983).

Furthermore, the debate on organizational structure – for example, "does structure follow strategy?" - raises another question. The classical prescriptive notion of Chandler's "strategy follows structure" (1962) was supported by Hall and Saias (1980). Mintzberg argued that structure follows strategy reciprocally, "as the left foot follows the right" (1990). In their study Amburgey and Dacin (1994) found that, indeed, a mutual relationship between strategy and structure does exist; however, strategy has a stronger impact on structure than vice versa. Fredrickson (1986), on the other hand, suggested that a reciprocal relationship exists, but it depends on a number of variables. These factors include whether or not there exists a dominant structure within a firm; what the strategic impact of the structure is; what the proportions are of existing synoptic and incremental strategy-making processes within the firm; and what the characteristics of critical strategic decision processes are (Fredrickson, 1986).

Finally, it is also difficult to assess how large an impact the context surrounding the organization under observation has. As Miller and Friesen point out, there are several different change archetypes depending on a particular context (Miller & Friesen, 1980).

2.4   The Research Question

A number of different papers have looked at change processes - of managing the duality of inertia and adaptation (Huff, Huff, & Thomas, 1992; Mintzberg & Westley, 1992). In addition, studies have described and analyzed the strategy process in organizations that have chosen a purely exploration- or purely exploitation-based strategic orientation. Apart from Anderson and Nielsen (2009), the previous research has not looked at strategy making in the organizations that have combined exploration and exploitation. The literature has not analyzed strategy making during ambidexterity cycles. For this reason, I intend to address this gap. This study focuses on the reasons and mechanisms that trigger ambidexterity cycles, and what the *practices* are that the organizations go through during ambidexterity cycles. Based on the research positioning spelled out above, the research question is:

> *Which practices are used by organizational actors involved in strategy making in the context of cyclical ambidexterity?*

The research question calls for an in-depth exploratory study. It also calls for studying practices across multiple levels. The research question requires adequate measurement of the degree of exploration and exploitation in a firm. The next chapter will describe the method and analytical strategy used.

3   Method

This study seeks to understand action at the micro level when changes in strategy unfold within an organization. In order to capture the unfolding of strategy making as a process, and to verify a firm's strategic orientation and its bearing at any given moment as a series of snapshots, the tools used in process studies are required. Temporal snapshots would provide quantitative information about the variance of exploration and exploitation at discrete moments of time. In order to capture actions and their meanings at the micro level, the study has to employ a qualitative approach to analyze and understand the subjective reflections of the strategy practitioners. The chapter will therefore cover the following questions:

-   The first subchapter will describe the logic of the research design, and how I decided to approach the study with the comparative interpretative case-study approach. I will also explain the criteria for choosing the empirical context, demonstrating how the study progressed via piloting to its final sample of two case studies as the most appropriate design for the research question.
-   Second, I will explain the measurement protocol for analyzing ambidexterity at the macro level, based on what the previous literature has suggested for calculating relative degrees of exploration and exploitation and the direction of the shift of cyclical ambidexterity. I will also describe the measurement approach at the micro level: the interpretive stance taken for analyzing strategy practices.
-   I will describe data sources per case and provide a time-line for each case that highlights important data points in my data set, including the interviews as well as observations of strategy days.

Thereafter I will focus on detailed description of both case organizations.

-   One case organization - FixTel has a longer history, dating back to its predecessor firms via various mergers, reorganizations, changes of country borders and regimes for over a century. However, in the present study I will primarily focus on the company's recent history. The company privatization took place in 1993 and I will therefore focus on the period since then to map retrospectively the ambidexterity cycles.
-   The other case organization - MobiTel has a shorter history dating back to 1996 and I will analyze the whole life span of the firm in order to map its ambidexterity cycles.

I will sum up the chapter with the outline of the qualitative data analysis.

3.1 Research Design

3.1.1 The research question framed through interpretive case study design.
Given the research question about strategy practices used by organizational actors during cyclical ambidexterity, the thesis applies the longitudinal, exploratory and interpretive case study format (Yin, 2008).

According to Yin (2008), the case study design is an "empirical inquiry that investigates a contemporary phenomenon within its real-life context, especially when boundaries between phenomenon and context are not clearly evident". Yin outlines the phenomena that are appropriate to research using the case-study format: 1) those which manifest as a series of contemporary events within their naturally occurring environment, 2) where direct control over the behavior of the actors is not required and 3) situations where an active exploration of the subject is necessary. Eisenhardt has further proposed that the case study is especially suitable when one needs to understand phenomena in complex settings (Eisenhardt, 1989).

The core focus of the research was to develop the existing theory of ambidexterity by studying cyclical ambidexterity in real-life situations where the organizations cycle between exploration and exploitation. Hence, the approach was to choose two case organizations, which were in the midst of the flux of cyclical ambidexterity.

The observation of case organizations happened via first-person involvement - by participating and observing strategy meetings. According to Joseph McGrath, this provides the highest realism for observational context, but less generalizability over populations and limited precision of variable control (1981, pp. 182-186).

In addition, interviews with the representatives of the case organizations provided the chance to reflect, to analyze and to synthesize the case data. The interpretive approach to the case studies reflects the subjective interpretations, reflections and understanding of the real life context by the people who experience them (Gioia & Chittipedi, 1991; Corley & Gioia, 2004). Interpretation in the present study happened at two levels. Interviews guide the informants - the members of the case organizations - to describe and reflect their personal interpretations of the situation. Thereafter it is the role of the researcher to interpret those subjective phenomena both during interactions with the members of the organization and during the later data analysis (Daft & Weick, 1984).

During interpretive analysis of the case organizations, I also became a part of the change process. We as a team of two researchers initiated the research project in which both the client (research subject) and we ourselves were highly involved. While we did not possess the content knowledge about strategy creation for those firms, we participated as process advisers who assisted the case organizations in uncovering the roots of the problems, point those issues out to organizational actors and suggest practices to address them. We initially mapped the strategy practices of the case organizations and participated actively in discussions with the management teams of the firms about the potential improvement initiatives.

During the second phase of the research intervention, the top managers of the case firms became more interested in our involvement and became themselves more active in shaping the role of their firms. Our role in content discussions and process support thereby diminished. Designated responsible managers within the case organizations took up process leadership and we assumed the role of facilitators of strategy discussions.

In the final phase of our research, our role became even more passive as we set out to primarily observe the discussions and regularly reflect upon our findings.

Hence, while we carried out a number of interviews and participated in strategy discussions, they bore distinctly different objectives during the different phases of the research initiative. At the outset, they were set up to serve a dual diagnostic role, for both the firm and us to understand what the strategy practices were and how this affected organizational performance. In the second phase, data collection served as a process support role - to assist the case organizations in their change practices and to provide them with feedback on their progress. In the final phase, the collected data provided information solely for our research purposes.

3.1.2   Context of the research.

3.1.2.1   Pilot phase.
At the outset of the present research initiative, early in 2008, I piloted an inductive multiple case study analysis of strategy practices. I carried out preliminary interviews in 14 organizations. In all of them, I interviewed top managers to discuss their strategy-making practices and to identify cyclical ambidexterity on the exploration-exploitation scale.

During the pilot phase, I took a cross-industry approach. I carried out 3 interviews in the construction sector as the industry had just gone through a rapid restructuring due to the collapse of the Estonian real-estate market; 1 interview in the furniture production sector; 4 in the IT and telecommunications sector; 3 among public service providers; 2 in the media and publishing industries; and 1 in the financial sector. The aim of these interviews was to:

- check whether the cyclical ambidexterity phenomenon actually exists widely in organizational practice, or whether it is rare in this sample and
- verify whether cyclical ambidexterity can be analyzed using interviews and strategy discussion observation.

Based on these interviews I managed to pinpoint that it was easier to find case companies in the process of changing their strategic orientation from exploration mode to exploitation mode, because the ongoing economic downturn forced the managers to focus their attention primarily towards efficiency. In order to provide a longitudinal view and control for industry variables, I interviewed managers of five case organizations again at the end of 2009 to verify the changes in their strategy-making practices and strategic orientation.

This dissertation does not present the data collected from the pilot study. However, piloting informed me about the existence of the phenomenon and guided my attention towards one particular industry for closer attention: namely the telecommunications industry.

3.1.2.2   Sampling a suitable industry – telecommunications.

Cyclical ambidexterity occurs in a number of industries, such as internet sales, banks, aviation, telecommunications (Markides C. C., 2013, pp. 315-6). My goal was to identify and sample information-rich cases that dynamically manifest the phenomenon under study (Patton, 2001). The telecommunications industry fulfils the criteria suggested by earlier theory on cyclical ambidexterity. Previous research showed that the probability of identifying cyclical ambidexterity is higher in sectors where:

- the subject domain is tight or narrow (Gupta, Smith, & Shalley, 2006);
- the industry is subject to an intense competitive rivalry (Jansen et al. 2005);
- the R&D intensity is higher (Uotila et al. 2009); and
- there is high propensity for product innovations that originate core technologies or dominant designs in those industries (Simsek, Heavey, Veiga, & Souder, 2009).

To fulfill the requirements vis-à-vis sample selection and to increase across-case comparability, the study hence focused on a single industry. Given the previous studies carried out on cyclical ambidexterity in the telecommunications industry (Khanaga, Volberda, Sidhu, & Oshri, 2013), I concluded that this industry fulfills the above criteria for theoretical sampling in the best possible manner.

It is an industry with a small number of strategic players. This traditionally oligopolistic industry witnesses frequent changes in its environment. It has relatively high market entry and market exit barriers. At the same time, regulatory pressure and constant rapid technology development have forced the players in the industry to be highly competitive. During the past decades the telecommunications industry has witnessed a number of product, service and process innovations stemming from research and development activities. Major innovations have forced the telecom firms to regularly invest in costly technologies (3G, 4G, 5G, ADSL, broadband, etc.). This in turn forces them to change their strategic orientation periodically. Hence, the telecommunications industry appeared adequately suited to observe shifts between exploration and exploitation.

3.1.2.3   Sampling individual case studies.

I selected case organizations based on purposive sampling (Lincoln & Guba, 1985; Patton, 2001) and sample variation in crucial categories (Eisenhardt, 1989; George & McKeown, 1985). I consulted theory, which implied different practices for companies changing their strategic orientation in opposite directions (Miller & Friesen, 1980; Weick & Quinn, 1999) and hence, I selected one case organization that was in a phase of changing its primary strategic orientation from exploration to exploitation and another from exploitation to exploration.

In order to fulfill the requirements spelled out in the research design protocol, the sample of the study includes two case organizations, which operate in the same market. When I started my research endeavor, I was open about the case study selection with the top managers of both the companies and asked if they would agree to participate in the analysis with the other company. They responded that they did not mind, because they do not consider each other direct competitors. One of them is operating in a fixed line market – the other in a mobile market. However, given the small size of the Estonian telecommunications market, the managers confirmed that they observe each other's actions.

- One case organization is FixTel[6] (primarily a fixed line provider telecom firm with 1,500 employees), which during this research endeavor was in the process of changing its primary strategic orientation from exploration to exploitation.
- The other case organization is MobiTel (a mobile operator firm with 390 employees), which was in the process of moving its primary strategic orientation from exploitation to exploration.

The selection of cases from a single industry and geographical location allows better comparison of practices across cases.

3.2   Description of data

3.2.1   Telecommunications industry.

3.2.1.1   *Telecommunications industry global trends.*
Telecommunications is an interesting industry to observe. It is subject to simultaneous technological innovation, deregulation and globalization, but it is at the same time both local and old-fashioned. It is the industry where highly capital-intensive infrastructure companies with relatively low "industry clock-speed"[7] meet rapid product clock-speed and technological advancements in the areas of mobile handset, internet and web-TV. For fixed telecommunications service providers, technological advances from two-century-old copper wires to contemporary optical connections have introduced merely gradual change since the early 1980s. While the advent of internet and the introduction of satellite technologies have radically increased the traffic across the channels, the changes in transmission technology have nevertheless been minor. Hence, there are several companies

---

[6] The company names are pseudonyms to preserve the anonymity of respondents.
[7] Industry clock-speed is the rate of industry change, which consists of three factors: product clock-speed (how fast do new products replace the old ones), process clock-speed (how fast the process technologies are changing) and organizational clock-speed (what is the rate of change of strategic actions and organizational structures) - (Fine, 1999).

operating today with more than a century of history because they have been able to easily adapt and partially even dictate the technological advances in this field.

As the cable networks became interlinked, the industry players ultimately established a globally-connected web both via landlines and over satellites. Due to economies of scale, this in turn has opened the doors to horizontal integration and the subsequent rise of large international conglomerates, such as AT&T, Vodafone, Verizon, Telefónica and Deutsche Telekom, which have put their foot in several countries globally.

At the same time, it is an industry where recent deregulation and privatization have started to open the doors for newcomers. Despite the efforts of policy-makers to reduce switching costs, the evidence shows that, at least in the European telecom market, in most countries competitive rivalry is not strong. It is possible to differentiate between higher rivalry countries, such as the UK, Sweden or Germany and low-rivalry countries such as France and Spain (Fuentelsaz, Maicas, & Polo, 2012, pp. 103-5).

The amount of investment to build infrastructure that the new entrants would have to deliver increases exit barriers, which in turn increases inter-firm rivalry. However, as the telecommunications business is very susceptible to economies of scale brought about by the network effects, it remains relatively oligopolistic, where the former monopolies hold the bulk of the market share and the remaining market is distributed between two or three competitors.

In addition to conventional business models, technological advances have opened the doors to allowing the entrance of numerous disruptive challengers such as "Over-The-Top" (OTT) voice, video or messaging services: Skype, Google Talk, Nimbuzz, Fring, Viber or WhatsApp (Arthur D. Little, 2011). Hence, there are companies in this industry that appear or disappear with the advent or demise of their recently invented products and services. While Skype was established in just 2003, since 2009 it has become the largest carrier of international calls with a 13% market share (Teleography.com, 2009). However, it still has not started to disrupt fully the conventional international calls market, which, even though at a slower rate, demonstrated an annual growth of approximately 5% in 2011[8].

While the global telecommunications network exists, facilitated by cables or satellite connections, most of the customer base of telecommunications firms is geographically local. The customer base connects to its source of delivery via physical cables or location profiles of mobile subscription, which makes the business model relatively old-fashioned, similar to a regular utility firm.

In order to broaden its customer base and provide the communications access to all the potential users, the telecommunication industry has grown considerably in the recent decade. Penetration of communications has reached into many countries, to the level where customers carry more than one phone. However, there are significant differences in the sources of growth and penetration rates of

---

[8] telegeography.com/press/press-releases/2012/01/09/international-call-traffic-growth-slows-as-skypes-volumes-soar [accessed on 13.01.2013]

mobile and fixed operators. For example, while in 1998 the average mobile penetration in European countries was approximately 30%, it reached 100% already by the end of 2005. By passing that goalpost the industry entered a mature phase (Fuentelsaz, Maicas, & Polo, 2012, p. 96). Broadband and fixed line penetration has been slower. The most recent OECD average was listed at 25.6%[9]. Mobile penetration is higher for several reasons. While broadband subscriptions are usually per household, mobile subscription is normally personalized - everybody owns a handset. In addition, network effects in the mobile industry are stronger because of a lower cost of purchase for a single connection while building and connecting of fiber cables remains more expensive.

At the same time, fixed operators have entered into an interesting phase of development because of technological advances that have enabled them to start bundling information goods - communication, media and IT services. The same fiber cable-based delivery channel can be used for the delivery of multiple OTT content - internet, voice, television, radio, video rental, gaming or other services. Hence the fixed line providers, while witnessing traditional voice communications moving to mobile handsets, have started using their existing user base to deliver innovative OTT media services (Rautio, Anttila, & Tuominen, 2006; Seo, 2007; Chan-Olmsted & Guo, 2011).

Additionally, the advent of reliable and user-friendly cloud computing solutions has widened the business scope for fixed telecommunications firms, giving birth to Infrastructure-as-a-Service (IaaS) and Software-as-a-Service (SaaS) solutions, which allow users and companies to handle their data and applications in a more convenient manner. This in turn has increased the IT-relatedness of the telecommunications firms, which have subsequently started to acquire more IT firms. According to a McKinsey report, while the overall mergers and acquisitions dynamics in the telecommunications industry have demonstrated a remarkable trend downwards - from over 201 billion USD in 2006 to slightly above 45 billion USD in 2010 - the acquisitions from the adjacent ICT sector have doubled: from 4.8 to 11.2 billion USD during the same period (Lebraud & Karlströmer, 2011).

In terms of the outlook, the industry is bound to keep changing. Some industry analysts predict that by the year 2017 households with two teenagers will have 25 internet-connected devices and already by 2022 more than 50 devices (OECD, 2013). This in turn raises the issues about additional data warehousing and connectivity to which there are no available solutions yet. The coming years will also create enough innovation-driven challenges for the telecommunications companies.

3.2.1.2   *Telecommunications industry in Estonia.*
After the collapse of the Soviet Union at the end of 1980s, Estonia was substantially a laggard amongst world countries in the fields of telecommunications and IT. In terms of generic development, access and quality of service, it ranked in the third quartile globally. Before privatization of the phone business, the telecommunications service was handled by a single, highly ineffective state monopoly.

---

[9] http://www.oecd.org/internet/broadbandandtelecom/oecdbroadbandportal.htm [accessed on 13.01.2013]

In 1991, the ratio of landline phones per inhabitant was less than 20%, and more than 10% of the country's population was on the waiting list, having requested a phone connection but not receiving it. Lacking investment capabilities and subject to Soviet-era bureaucratic rules, the state monopoly was having difficulties providing basic services and frequently it took 3-4 years from posting a subscription request to receiving a phone connection.

Over the following years, from 1991 to 2001, the telecommunications market in Estonia made significant progress. The Digital Access Index (DAI), published in 2003, had just ranked Estonia's connectivity the highest in Eastern Europe and in 28th position globally, ahead of Spain and Malaysia[10].

Since then it has constantly climbed the ranks published by the International Telecommunications Union (ITU). In the ICT World Report in 2012, Estonia ranked 23rd overall in the ICT Development Index (IDI)[11] and 19th in the ranking of Top Broadband Economy (TBE) - even ahead of countries like Austria, Australia, Italy, New Zealand and Singapore. In the detailed web of the index components, the country especially stands out in the number of mobile subscriptions - see the chart below.[12]

Figure 1. ICT Development Index - (ITU, 2012, p. 29)

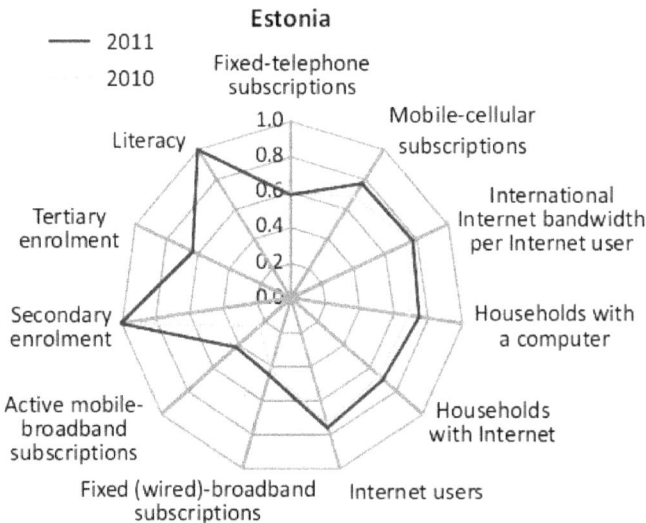

---

[10] http://www.itu.int/ITU-D/ict/dai/ [accessed on 13.01.2013]
[11] http://www.itu.int/pub/D-IND-ICTOI-2012 [accessed on 13.01.2013]
[12] http://www.itu.int/ITU-D/ict/facts/2011/index.html [accessed on 13.01.2013]

In order to achieve the above-mentioned rankings in such a short timeframe, investments in the IT and telecommunications infrastructure have been considerable. Partly financed by governmental support measures, telecom firms have also invested a significant percentage of their own revenues, partly from the companies themselves, but ultimately paid for by the consumers. While in most developed countries revenues from the telecommunications industry correspond to approximately 3.5% of the total GDP, Estonia is an exception with nearly 5%. This indicates the significantly high ICT uptake, particularly in mobile services. However, the telecommunication firms in Estonia have also been quick to adapt IPTV solutions[13], which adds broadcasting revenues to the figures and therefore covers a broader scope than data reported by most other countries[14].

Revenues from telecommunications services in Estonia have remained more or less constant during the years of the study, which indicate a stable, saturated market. The revenues have been stagnant and in some cases have even decreased from one year to another. One of the primary reasons for a shrinking market was the sharp decline in GDP growth during the years in question. While the country enjoyed a steady growth of GDP, between 6-10 % per annum for each year from 2000 to 2007, in 2008-09 the country faced a serious economic contraction, which was reflected also in the revenues of telecommunications firms:

Figure 2. Telecommunications revenue in Estonia (ITU, 2012, pp. 136-7)

	2007	**2008**	**2009**	**2010**
Revenues from all telecommunication services in Estonia	740,544	716,386	715,938	711,656
Real GDP Growth in Estonia in thousands EUR [15]	7.7%	-4.0%	-14.1%	2.6%

The overall trend in the telecommunications market has seen a constant reduction in fixed line phone usage, by approximately 5-6% per annum. It is predicted that by the year 2020, the fixed line phone will become an insignificant business segment. This has steadily reduced the stable income of fixed-line operators and has forced them to actively explore new business opportunities that would enable them to replace fixed-line products and services with viable long-term alternatives. One of the key markets for fixed-line providers has become digital television and internet-based value-added services.

In addition, it could be observed that this cyclical nature of business was affecting the overall behavior of companies in the telecommunications market. Recent market trends have shown that in 2008 the telecommunications sector in Estonia entered a downturn because of an overall slump in

---

[13] Household penetration of internet-based television as of 2011 in Estonia was 53% (3rd highest in the world after South Korea and Japan): TeleGeography's GlobalComms Pay-TV Research -
telegeography.com/research-services/globalcomms-pay-tv and telecoms.com/19015/estonia-little-country-that-coulddare-to-love-iptv/ [accessed on 13.01.2013]
[14] The ITU has pointed out comparison errors and has established an expert group to harmonize the indicators.
[15] The economic figures are taken from the EU eStat database: http://www.stat.ee/29958

the economy. During the interviews at both of the case organizations, the Finance Managers of the firms confirmed the following: they said that according to their observations, telecommunications has been one of the first sectors hit by any fluctuations in the business climate. When business overall is improving in a country then the telecommunications industry will be among the first to recover and when business is starting to suffer then telecommunications costs will be the first to be cut, both by private users and by businesses. The recent epic economic downturn in Estonia occurred in the last months of 2008 and the first part of 2009. By the end of 2009, the signs showed some stability and private customers especially started to make more purchases (Elion Ettevõtted AS, 2009).

Whereas earlier all mobile operators had their allocated number ranges, the Estonian Government introduced a regulation in January 2005 that allowed free movement of phone numbers between operators – known as *number porting* or *number transfer*. Transfer of a number to a new operator is a simple operation, which only requires a short application submitted either in person at a mobile company office or electronically with a digital signature. The transfer is effective within 6 days. As the transfer is free and the only switching cost relates to preparing the application, it has made phone contracts very fluid and has added pressure to lower costs via increasing rivalry between mobile service providers. The table below summarizes the dynamics of switching during the years, demonstrating the increasing trend. Given that the overall number of mobile subscriptions in the country is above one million, the annual switching accounts for between 5-10%.

Table 3. Number porting statistics (source: Estonian Technical Surveillance Authority)[16]

	2008	2009	2010	2011	2012
Mobile number transfers	45,526	48,799	69,363	73,616	102,595
Fixed number transfers	12,425	27,389	14,511	10,400	17,766

The main reason for the telecommunications downturn was the increasing competition over prices. Because of the overall downturn of the economy, the customers started to actively shop around for cheaper products, services and service providers. The active use of call services declined and many added-value services were reduced by a significant amount as well. A similar collapse was observed in the business client segment, which faced even more drastic cuts. Turnover from business clients declined from 2007 to 2008 by more than 15% for the total telecommunications market in Estonia. The biggest reduction was in calls made to international networks. Part of the reason was that during the time of the crisis many businesses started using Skype or other free providers to reduce their telecommunications expenses.

While the downturn in 2007-8 was rather sharp, already by the last quarter of 2009 and the first quarter of 2010 the downturn slowed and some services - such as internet-based television - even started demonstrating some growth. During 2010, the overall size of the telecommunications market

---

[16] http://www.tja.ee/numbriliikuvuse-statistika

turnover remained stable – decreasing only by approximately 1%. The continuous downturn was reduced further by the increasing use of mobile internet services (Elion Ettevõtted AS, 2010).

As the telecommunications industry is an oligopolistic market, in addition to the two case organizations selected hereafter, there are four more organizations that are identified as their competitors, which need to be describe adequately to give a picture of the status and dynamics of the industry:

- **SeriousMobile** – a telecom firm that solely provides mobile services. It has positioned itself strategically as a high-cost, high-quality universal service provider. The company was the first mobile telecom provider on the market in Estonia and was therefore ensured the largest subscription base to date. Even though the price of its services is roughly 10% higher than that of its competitors, it has remained the market leader in terms of their turnover in the field of mobile services primarily due to their focus on customer service.

- **LoveMobile** – a telecom firm that provides universal services: mobile, fixed line and internet services. Its traditional strength is in the field of business customers. It has strategically positioned itself as a personalized service provider and throughout the past has used personal and emotional marketing messages to gain a foothold among private consumers. It was the second mobile company that entered the market in the early 1990s, but after the first 4-5 successful years it had become 'stuck in the middle'. The company was trying to compete both as a universal high-quality provider and as a cheap solution simultaneously. Therefore, during 2000-2008 it lost a significant portion of its market share and eventually also began competing on price, starting from 2009 onwards.

- **MoonFix** – a telecom firm that provides fixed line, internet and television services. It has positioned itself as targeted towards private individuals, and low-cost options. It is famous for its popular, somewhat contradictory and humorous marketing schemes. However, in recent years it has faced difficulties because the business model was partially based on over-the-air technology, which has started lagging behind in quality to the optical fixed-service providers. While there have been a number of takeover attempts of the firm, it has continued to function as a standalone company.

- **RegionalCable** - a fixed-line operator that started primarily as a cable-TV provider and thereafter expanded to internet and fixed phone services. The company has geographically positioned itself mostly in urban centers and has only recently started to expand to smaller localities.

In addition to those mentioned above, there are 13 active telecommunications companies in the Estonian market. These mostly provide services either on a regional basis or to a narrow niche of clients and don't represent a significant interest in the overall telecommunications market. Their total revenues represent roughly 10 % of the overall market volume (in 2010 the overall telecommunication market volume in Estonia was 711,656 thousand EUR).

Table 4. Key players in the Estonian telecommunication market (2010)

Company	Service Lines	Key Figures	Networks	2010 turnover (thousand EUR)
Case 1 - FixTel	Fixed	1,550 employees	Subsidiary of a Pan-European Corporation	187,102
Case 2 - MobiTel	Mobile	390 employees	Subsidiary of a Pan-European Firm	95,752
SeriousMobile	Mobile	470 employees	Part of Pan-European Corp, roaming partnership with a global network	173,890
LoveMobile	Fixed and Mobile	450 employees	Subsidiary of Nordic Firm, roaming partnership with global network	89,882
IntlMobile	Mobile	65 employees	Local firm with international subsidiaries	50,326
MoonFix	Fixed	217 employees	Local firm with international partner contracts	25,445
RegionalCable	Fixed	214 employees	Local firm that provides fixed line, internet and TV	14,552
			Other providers (13 companies):	74,707
			Total market size:	**711,656**

In order to fulfill the requirements spelled out in the research design protocol above, the sample for the study includes two case organizations, which are two telecommunications companies operating in Estonian market:

- **Fixtel** - a fixed line telecom provider with a long industry background covering more than a century. During the past few years, the company has been actively engaged in dynamic business development; hence, in the exploration-exploitation continuum they are mostly at the exploration end. For this particular study, its exploitation-enhancing initiatives were also observed in detail as the company was in the process of shifting from exploration to exploitation during 2008-2010.
- **Mobitel** - a mobile telecom provider that has historically expanded through a number of acquisitions, but during recent years has positioned itself mostly at the exploitation end of the continuum due to its marketing efforts to prove itself as a low-cost efficient provider with a highly-streamlined low-cost supply chain. However, for the present study MobiTel's activities in exploration mode during 2007-2009 were observed.

Figure 3. Summary of the two case studies

FixTel	MobiTel
• Observed shift: exploration → exploitation • 1,550 employees (as of 2012) • Incumbent fixed-line provider, more than 100 years of history, privatized in 1993 • Market leader in product and service excellence • Part of MNC, headquartered in Scandinavia	• Observed shift: exploitation → exploration • 227 or 390 employees (as of 2012 - without or with subsidiaries) • Mobile telecom operator, established in 1996, • Market leader in operational excellence • Part of MNC, headquartered in Scandinavia

While the telecommunications market in Estonia is an oligopolistic market where the sales margins have throughout the years been between 15-30%, the rivalry between the players still exists and is occasionally aggressive.

While in larger markets the market leaders tend to expand their business aggressively through mergers and acquisitions, the Estonian market has been small enough and with little saturation, which has required the market players to develop their businesses primarily through organic growth. This in turn has forced them into more intense cyclical behavior between exploration and exploitation, because larger businesses tend to carry out their exploratory moves through purchases of exploratory start-ups and retain their presence in the one mode of strategic orientation.

During 2007-2010 LoveMobile, MoonFix and MobiTel sued the incumbent companies FixTel and SeriousMobile numerous times due to their inability to agree upon interconnection fees and rental prices for using the infrastructure: digital optical cables, cable piping systems and antenna masts. FixTel and SeriousMobile responded with counter-claims. Individually most of these claims have been from 0.6 million EUR up to 1.8 million EUR, which – while it would be circa 1 % of the overall turnover of FixTel - would represent approximately 6-7 % of the turnover for the smaller companies. This demonstrates that the rivalry, which has legal implications for the companies, is significant and affects their daily business.

3.2.2   Case 1 - FixTel: Shifting from Exploration to Exploitation[17]

3.2.2.1   *Background of the Case Study.*

FixTel is a telecom firm with 1,500 employees. The company is primarily a provider of fixed-line telecom, internet, digital media content- and IP-based television services. The history of FixTel dates to 1886 when the first phone network, together with a phone central exchange was built in the

---

[17] Source of this chapter: company annual reports of 1993-2012.

Estonian capital city of Tallinn. In 1889, the exchange became operational in the second largest town, Tartu[18]. The company that started this endeavor is the predecessor of FixTel. They subsequently carried out central phone network construction in order to cover all the cities of the country, which they finished by 1900[19]. During the following years, the company solidified its position as a state-owned company that built the fixed telephone lines all across the country and expanded lines gradually to smaller locations. Throughout Estonia's annexation by Soviet forces, the company continued its local operations, but all its international connections were rerouted through Moscow, Russia. After the collapse of the Soviet Union, the company was quickly privatized and reorganized.

When Estonia regained its freedom in 1991, the Soviet Ministry of Communications was abolished. Previously the Soviet ministry had dealt with both regulative functions. While there had been a state-owned enterprise that dealt with the operations of the communication network as a predecessor to FixTel, the handling of the phone communications networks was still under direct Moscow control. The newly established Estonian Ministry of Transport and Communications took up regulative functions. For network operations, the previous state-owned enterprise was restructured and the international phone connection through Moscow was severed and supplanted with new phone cables through neighboring countries - Finland, Sweden and Latvia.

While FixTel proudly presents the history of its predecessors on its webpage, the present case organization was legally established in 1993 through privatization. During privatization, a minority stake of 49% in FixTel was sold to a Nordic telecom operator with monopoly concession rights for 8 years, with the concurrent obligation for the company to invest a predetermined amount to provide full fiber-optic cable connections and a contemporary local network. 51% of the company ownership remained with the Estonian Government, which exercised its rights via a separate parent company that also kept shares of an incumbent mobile firm, an IT company, a paging service company, and that bought minority ownership in a company that provided internet services. During this time, FixTel had more than 4,800 employees and the company handled six different regional phone networks.

As we can see from the tables below, the company has been continuously profitable throughout the period 1994 through 2012. At the same time, the level of net infrastructure investments indicates that the company has simultaneously expanded extensively. In part, the monopolistic concession rights that the company had gave it a head start in a growing market, and has facilitated keeping its leading role.

Table 5. Indicators of FixTel - 1993-2012 (source: company annual reports)

	1993	1994	1995	1996	1997	1998	1999	2000	2001	2002
Revenue (mEUR)	28.0	39.3	53.7	75.2	99.2	138.4	157.0	160.2	170.0	163.9
Net profit (mEUR)	-3.6	3.1	8.4	12.5	11.4	16.8	8.9	26.7	3.1	18.3

---

[18] Kaasik-Aaslav, V. and Maripuu, H. 1999. *Tallinna Telefonivõrk 110 aastat 1886-1996*. Tallinn.
[19] History of phone networks in Estonia: http://vanatelefon.onepagefree.com/?id=18227

Investments (mEUR)	14.9	34.3	25.5	33.4	42.6	42.4	45.6	55.2	32.3	21.3
No of employees	4,774	4,373	4,380	3,784	3,590	3,305	2,772	2,535	1,798	1,420
	2003	**2004**	**2005**	**2006**	**2007**	**2008**	**2009**	**2010**	**2011**	**2012**
Revenue (mEUR)	164.8	146.1	144.6	155.5	164.0	187.2	190.2	187.1	207.4	200.7
Net profit (mEUR)	20.3	22.2	24.4	28.1	34.3	31.8	21.3	32.4	26.4	19.1
Investments (mEUR)	14.3	14.8	52.7	30.3	32.4	27.0	20.8	22.8	29.4	31.8
No of employees	1,354	1,281	1,279	1,237	1,332	1,292	1,346	1,334	1,569	1,550

Constant automation of the products and services has allowed the company to reduce its headcount threefold while revenues have grown eightfold. I will elaborate below on the individual periods of the company's history in order to describe the exploratory and exploitative periods in more detail.

In terms of its management and organizational systems, FixTel has had a functional organizational structure, the hierarchy of which divides its managerial levels according to five classes:

- Top management
- Managers of managers (i.e. middle managers)
- Leaders of a function or a large unit (with ca 100 subordinates)
- Leaders of specialist units (with ca 5-20 subordinates)
- Key personnel and functional personnel.

Despite the hierarchy and a functional approach, FixTel exhibited a participative management culture. It has created several cross-functional working groups, which meet on a regular basis to discuss new product development, the quality of products and services, the efficiency of operations and new trends and ideas.

3.2.2.2   History of FixTel

Figure 4. Exploratory and exploitative initiatives at FixTel

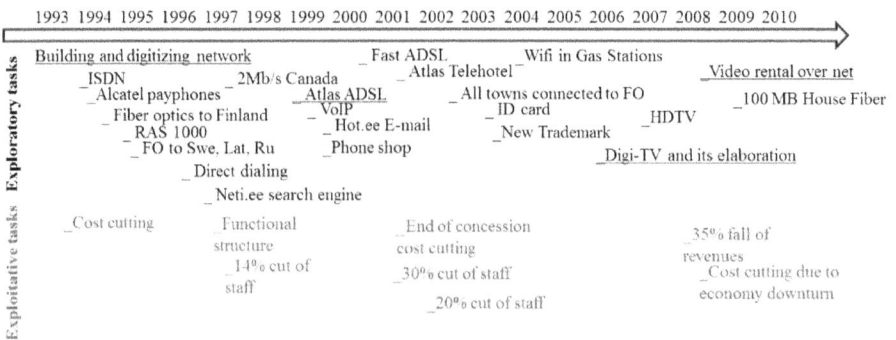

1993 - 1994 - Privatization and Exploitation Period.
During the early years, FixTel started its operations at the end of the exploration phase due to extensive investments carried out for building new infrastructure and soft systems. In terms of operations, this period was patterned by two contradictory goals. First, redesigning the Soviet-style management culture and ineffective management systems. There were many efficiency cuts by reducing the workforce from 4,774 employees to 3,784 in 1996 - a cut of ¼. The other goal was to break with the habit of not treating customers as the source of revenue for the company, but as 'consumers', who could be serviced when employees saw fit. Both initiatives required modifications in the competence profiles and a primary focus on efficiency gains.

In 1994, the company started to focus primarily on building new fixed networks. As described in the previous sub-chapter, FixTel inherited a Soviet-era infrastructure that needed a complete overhaul. The company started to work on replacing older copper wires with optical lines and installing digital call-exchange centers. They constructed optical lines between Estonia and neighboring Finland, Sweden, Latvia and Russia, which paved the way for a new communication transit service. FixTel also established new service centers in order to improve customer service, and this quickly led to a longer exploration cycle.

1995 - 1999 - Exploration Cycle
While building optical networks continued well into the following decade, during 1996-99 the company focused its primary investments in internet-based solutions to allow for new services. In 1996 they developed an internet search engine in-house, which included both the elements of a catalogue (like AltaVista and early Yahoo) and a web crawler (like WebCrawler and Google), and its freeware e-mail service (similar to Hotmail.com), which both immediately became the most popular internet websites in the country and are still among the Top 20 today.

To improve the capabilities for delivering new solutions, the company revised its organizational structure in 1997 and changed its regional divisional structure into one with a functional design. This allowed a part of the company to deal with maintaining the existing production and service-delivery functions – hence being more exploitative – and another part of the company to deal with future-oriented business development. While earlier exploratory activities concentrated on investments in physical infrastructure, this change also allowed exploration in business services.

In 1999, FixTel began expanding its services for fixed-mobile connection services for both business and private customers based on ADSL solutions. While the USA introduced ADSL the year before, FixTel was one of the first companies in Europe to start offering such a solution. ADSL technology allowed for the use of conventional phone lines to deliver high-speed internet to customers. This technology generated a possibility for earning revenues from a new line of service, which quickly gained momentum as a higher-speed and more reliable alternative to dial-up internet solutions.

2000 - 2003 - Exploitation Cycle

In 2001, Estonia was the first country in Central and Eastern Europe to deregulate the telecommunications market. This resulted in a change of the business model for FixTel as an incumbent operator. They were required to open their network to other service providers. As a result, during that year FixTel lost 9% of its monopolistic market share in the fixed telecommunications market (Heil, 2009, p. 63). The most significant drop was in the market segment with the largest margins - in international calls, where the company generated nearly 50% less revenue compared to the previous year.

The competition intensified for FixTel from multiple sources. The revenues from fixed calls started declining at a steady rate of 10% per year. Even though in 2001 they made up roughly ¾ of the overall revenues, the company was forced to start looking around for alternative income sources. In 2001, the company had two consecutive months of losses - the only time in history when FixTel had experienced loss since it was established in 1993.

At the same time, the company managed a second significant cut in workforce numbers. From 1999 to 2003, the headcount was reduced by more than 50%: from 3,305 to 1,354. This was partly achieved by selling the network service business. Another factor was a complete outsourcing of the IT function. This decision was made partially as a result of the months of revenue loss. The main reason however was lost illusions after the dot-com boom. As we found out later during interviews with managers however, both decisions were regretted afterwards.

Despite the difficult times, the company managers realized that another market segment had started gaining momentum - revenues from data communications increased more than two-fold during 2002-03 and a further increasing demand for high-speed internet promised to open up new business lines, which led to a new exploration cycle.

2003 - 2007 - Exploration Cycle

In 2003, FixTel changed its trademark. It replaced all the previous product and service trademarks of the different product portfolios with one, to represent them all . The primary reason for the trademark change was to respond to its declining share in the fixed phone segment and the company deleted the word "phone" from its name. While previously the company defined itself as a technology firm, the revised trademark positioned the company as a communications service firm. Together with unification of its trademarks, it also reorganized its service functions, combining phone service, internet service, data connection, IT and technology services under a single umbrella functionally led by communication services delivery.

During the following 4 years, the increased number of its optical fixed connections grew by more than 30% every year, which also led to a roughly equivalent increase of revenue from the segment.

In 2004, the company started to expand its sales network. It expanded its sales points and in addition to the previously-delivered phone service, it also started selling electronic equipment - computers, TV-sets and other electronic solutions. This segment tripled its revenues during the first 2 years.

Whereas previously FixTel had primarily focused its attention on private customers, during this same year the company expanded its business consumer value proposition considerably. FixTel started to expand long-term computer rental and computer maintenance services for large institutional customers and renting and hosting their server parks.

In 2005, FixTel increased its revenues from data connection solutions by 40%. FixTel was one of the first companies in Europe to deliver passive optical network solutions to private customers and with that they used their digital services investment to launch IPTV-based Digital Television over optical cable, being the second company in Europe to introduce this technology. In 2006, FixTel expanded IPTV Digital Television services considerably by adding a large number of television channels. It also started developing a video-on-demand rental solution via optical cable, launched early in 2007. In addition, FixTel further focused on the improvement of its service quality. While as recently as 1995-6 the company had serious service quality problems, by 2006 it received the highest ranking in the country for both personal service and phone service among its national competitors.

In 2007 the company expanded its service offering to business clients by providing the companies with VoIP phone service unified with website and e-mail hosting services. FixTel also collaborated with one of the mobile phone providers to start providing communications solutions where mobile internet connection backed up or combined fixed connections.

During 2007, the private clients received a number of new services – an online digital music sales service, online digital book sales service and an online digital photo album feature. All these solutions were interchangeably usable between the two platforms so the customers could view their online music and photos over the internet both on their computers as well as over their TV sets.

While the Digi-TV market was earlier shared between three large players and a number of smaller players, FixTel managed, within a year, to capture half of the overall cable TV market. As a result of this successful market penetration, Frost & Sullivan presented them in 2008 with its best practice award *The Best Market Penetrator of the Year in 2007* as well as an Estonian innovation award for 2007.

The company also entered into the personal and business lease market in collaboration with the largest local electronics sales chain where FixTel provided the necessary funding. .

2008 - 2010 - Exploitation Cycle.
In 2008, Estonia faced a significant economic downturn. During this year FixTel observed a reduction in its net profits, while the reduction of net revenues followed in 2009. As a result, the company started cutting its exploratory activities. During 2008, the primary developments focused on making Digi-TV multilingual and adding gaming solutions to TV sets. The volume of the financing market grew significantly during the following years. Due to the economic downturn, a number of customers decided to purchase services or goods on a lease. The company also established

an internet shop for second-hand computers and TV sets to address the needs of cost-conscious customers.

In 2009, the primary innovation was the preparation and delivery of high-speed 100 Mbit/s fiber-optic internet connections. In 2010, FixTel started offering High-Definition Television solutions to those customers who had received the 100 Mbit/s internet connection access. At the end of 2010, FixTel consolidated and merged with an IT firm that had earlier been a full subsidiary.

However, apart from these two initiatives, the company had largely abandoned all exploratory activity and was actively cost-cutting. This included reduction of staff and divestiture and outsourcing of its large-scale technology service division. FixTel simplified its primary sales channels and data packages into two main solutions for private customers and four solutions for business customers. It also closed down a number of services that demonstrated lower profitability.

3.2.3   Case 2 - MobiTel: Shifting from Exploitation to Exploration[20]

3.2.3.1   Background of the Case Study

Part of a Pan-European telecom group, the MobiTel Group has its headquarters in a Northern European country. The case focuses on its local arm, which has 390 staff members (without the subsidiary: 227 employees). The company was first established as a separate corporation as a start-up in 1996-97, with an aggressive trademark and employing a price challenger strategy.

The company started with exploratory activities and managed to increase its market share in a market with two strong incumbents (SeriousMobile and LoveMobile), who before the entry of MobiTel shared 97% of the market in Estonia. However, MobiTel was the first company on the market to offer subsidized handsets with long-term subscriptions. It also entered the market with a very aggressive marketing campaign, differentiating itself strongly from the two existing market players and primarily focusing on a more cost-conscious buyer, who until that moment had not contemplated owning mobile handsets at all.

By keeping its operating costs considerably lower, by renting the network equipment from the two incumbent companies instead of investing into a separate network, it managed to keep its costs lower and within the short timeframe of two years increased its market share to 25%, becoming the second largest mobile company in the country[21].

---

[20] Source of this chapter: company Annual Reports between 2001-2012.
[21] The 2nd largest incumbent LoveMobile kept three business lines dealing with mobile networks, fixed phone networks and handset sales separate until 2007, which meant that between 1999-2006 MobiTel exceeded the non-consolidated financial figures of LoveMobile 10-fold. However, since consolidation in 2007 the revenues of the two companies have been more or less equal.

Table 6. Indicators of MobiTel (from company annual reports)

	1997	1998	1999	2000	2001	2002	2003	2004	2005	2006
Revenue (mEUR)	4.5	11.5	12.3	16.9	34.5	52.5	71.0	76.8	90.2	108.3
Net profit (mEUR)	-4.1	-2.3	-3.7	-3.2	4.8	12.0	24.7	21.7	23.1	30.7
Assets (mEUR)	19.4	23.3	21.7	26.0	33.3	38.6	52.2	72.6	96.0	128.8
No of employees	N/A	N/A	N/A	N/A	148	169	156	144	126	135
	2007	2008	2009	2010	2011	2012				
Revenue (mEUR)	121.4	112.1	100.3	95.8	96.0	91.8				
Net profit (mEUR)	33.6	34.2	31.5	15.9	18.4	9.0				
Assets (mEUR)	171.3	202.9	230.8	71.2	90.7	99.4				
No of employees	153	209	235	234	217	227				

In terms of its management and organizational systems, MobiTel was run as a matrix structure across the boundaries of local firms; several local managers reported either through a secondary structure or in some cases even through a primary structure to supervisors in their corporate headquarters. In a similar manner, their daughter company reported directly via the matrix to its respective MobiTel managers.

From the hierarchical point of view, MobiTel was set up in a relatively flat manner, its sales division being the largest arm with four management levels, but most other divisions only had either two or three management levels. However, despite the flat structure, the managers had relatively little autonomy due to bureaucratization and a committee-based setup of management decisions throughout the MobiTel Corporation in Europe.

3.2.3.2   History of the Company.
Figure 5. Exploratory and exploitative initiatives at MobiTel

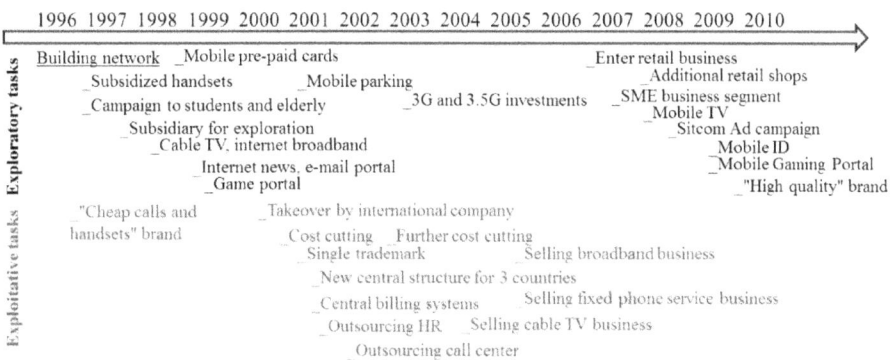

1996 - 1998 - Foundation of MobiTel
MobiTel was established on May 8, 1996 and spent its first year of startup investments focusing primarily on larger cities of the country. It officially launched its GSM mobile network on April 28, 1997 and was the third mobile network company in the Estonian market.

MobiTel differentiated its offers from two incumbent companies. It was the first dealer to start offering handsets at subsidized prices (with a fixed 2-year contract) to private customers. While the incumbents were primarily focusing on business customers and thereby both positioning themselves as "elite" providers, MobiTel focused on cost-conscious buyers - students, blue-collar workers and elderly people - people who had not even contemplated buying a mobile phone up to that moment. For this reason, MobiTel was able to substantially expand the existing market and identify large groups of completely uncovered segments.

The company also became a target for jokes that were emanating from the customers of the other two firms - they labeled the newcomer as "Cheapo". Due to MobiTel's lagging number of mobile network transmitter antennae in the country because of a later entry into the market, the incumbent firms' salespeople mocked them, saying that due to limited network coverage MobiTel should provide "a free shuttle bus to locations close to their antennae where people can use their phones".

However, as two existing firms had already built their antennae network MobiTel started negotiations with them and instead of building a full infrastructure it agreed to rent some antennae masts and network equipment, and managed to increase its coverage quickly up to par with the incumbents.

1998 - 2001 - Exploration Cycle

In 1998, MobiTel was the first mobile telephone company on the market that started providing pre-paid phone cards without a subscription contract. By the end of the year, the company became profitable and in terms of its profit ratio, it surpassed the second incumbent LoveMobile.

In 1999, the company established a subsidiary to start dealing with additional exploratory activities in order to enter the internet, cable TV, software development, and internet dial-up and broadband services. During this year, the company established its own wide-purpose internet portal, which included free e-mail, a news portal, a game portal, a search engine and a central information service directory with phonebooks and other extra functionality (similar to Yahoo!).

By the end of that year, MobiTel managed to increase its market share in the mobile communications business by 25%, becoming the second-largest mobile company in the country, by number of subscriptions.

While all the other network providers had used the strategy whereby calling inside their own network was substantially cheaper than calling other networks, in 2000 MobiTel was the first company to provide the possibility for calling all the networks at the same price. Combined with an aggressive marketing campaign the company managed to increase its market share. By the end of the year, the company managed to increase its network coverage to include 98% of the population.

2001 - 2006 - Exploitation Cycle

Until 2001, MobiTel had operated as an independent company with a number of major shareholders. In 2001, a Scandinavian-based multinational mobile phone company took it over and launched exploitative initiatives. It combined its different trademarks under a single global trademark, united the different companies and various subsidiaries in all three Baltic countries - Estonia, Latvia and Lithuania - under a unified management structure and combined the services into a single centralized framework.

In 2001, the company also established a centralized customer web portal and started offering the possibility of paying for the services directly online via bank links, or direct debit arrangements through the customers' banks. During this period, there was a substantial cut in their workforce (from 169 employees in 2002 to 126 in 2006):

- Their primary image and strategy in all the countries that they were operating in focused on a low-cost model. They had decided to keep the in-house personnel in all the countries where they operated to a bare minimum. During certain periods they achieved this partially by locally outsourcing a number of their functions – for example, another firm operated their customer support and call center in Estonia.
- Some product and service development functions were centralized to the parent company situated in Sweden. The function of product development at MobiTel Estonia was minimal - it consisted of only four service developers, one strategist, and three people who were dealing with product development on the technology side. Hence, MobiTel developers in Estonia primarily focused on applications of the services and products that were developed and handed over to them from Sweden.
- Likewise, a number of other core and support functions were centralized - procurement, global marketing, global roaming and connections, for example. This allowed the company in Estonia to achieve financially equal results with larger competitors but with a much smaller headcount. The other aspect of the centralization was related to stronger bargaining power - by centralizing the technology purchases across its 11 home markets MobiTel's parent company was able to bargain better with the technology providers than its competitors who were managing their purchases from a single country.

With respect to exploratory initiatives, the company joined the mobile parking network, giving its customers the possibility to pay for car parking using their mobile subscription. It also developed additional gaming possibilities for text message-based games, which did not gain popularity.

In 2002, the company streamlined its efficiency by combining billing systems for all business lines. It also restructured its systems for managing prepaid mobile services and thereby cut its costs on managing their services. It also increased its efficiency by starting to close its support functions and outsourcing some of its activities (e.g. customer support).

In 2003, the company managed to gain 1/3 of the market share in terms of subscription numbers. In order to achieve this for the second year running the company continued to cut prices for all services, and thereby its core services - mobile phone, text message and internet services - were circa 10-15% cheaper compared to the competitors. In order to achieve this the company continued its strategy, which was primarily focused on high efficiency and exploitation by simplifying the service packages delivered to its customers. It also centralized its procurement function for all of the Baltic countries, which allowed purchasing the infrastructure as well as handsets for a lower price than its two main competitors had to pay.

Regarding exploratory initiatives, in 2003 the company invested 4 million EUR into purchasing the license to build a 3G / UMTS network in the country.

In 2004, MobiTel had achieved, for the third year in a row, the top position in the Estonian Top 100 ranking (similar to the Fortune 500 ranking), which ranks the companies on the basis of the combination of their profit and turnover growth for the previous year. MobiTel occupied a unique spot. Neither before nor after this, not a single company has been able to grow both its profitability and turnover for 3 years in a row.

The company continued with its exploitative initiatives. It sold its cable TV business to MoonFix. It also further reduced its prices for a number of services. In addition, it was the first mobile phone company in the country that started providing a free mobile voicemail service. It also focused on aggressive expansion in some segments by providing dumping prices for the public-sector clients and for elderly clients. In order to increase the efficiency of its services the company started to actively promote the use of internet-based self-service and close down some of its physical service locations. Of exploratory initiatives, the company improved the provision of call services by building and installing 140 new stations for call network transmission in 2004.

In 2005, MobiTel further intensified its exploitative initiatives. It decided to close down and sell its fixed phone service. As the first mobile phone service provider to do so, it offered the possibility for small business customers to make phone calls within their firms for substantially lower prices, which further increased their market share within the business sector. Of exploratory initiatives, the company started building the aforementioned 3G network.

By 2006, the mobile service market in Estonia had become saturated. The number of mobile phones in use overtook the population number, which meant that this year the three companies started waging an active price war. As MobiTel had successfully implemented a low-cost strategy since the beginning of their operations, this helped them to gain even greater market share. Hence, MobiTel further intensified its exploitative initiatives starting to provide several service packages without a monthly fee. It also further reduced the prices of all its services. As a result, by the end of 2006, the company had managed to garner 36% of the market.

On the exploratory initiatives side, MobiTel opened its 3G network and started building the first 3.5G network stations. This allowed the company to enter the mobile internet business. As with other services, the company clearly differentiated itself from its competitors by providing the cheapest mobile internet service, supported by its bulk purchase of 3G technology transmitters to all three Baltic countries.

2007 - 2010 - Exploration Cycle.

In 2007, the company decided to revise its strategy and it initiated a number of exploratory schemes. It started expanding its sales network again and established both private-customer-focused and business-customer-oriented sales points in a number of commercial shopping centers and malls to be closer to the retail clients. The retail sales points also started selling related products such as laptop computers. The laptops were pre-configured to use the MobiTel mobile internet service for fast access. It also expanded its 3G network coverage extensively and started to provide and market internet services at 3.6 Mbit/s speed to an area covering more than 50% of the population. Additionally, it started offering mobile internet for the same price as the fixed internet subscription of its key competitors and thereby challenged the fixed internet service providers directly.

With regard to exploitative initiatives, the company further lowered its prices and was the first company that started providing a service by which a new type of cheap prepaid card - the *Friend Card* - was issued, whereby the users of the Friend Cards could make free phone calls to other owners of Friend Cards. Furthermore, price competition spread to the international calls market and roaming charges. MobiTel was the first to give its customers the opportunity to receive phone calls between Baltic countries without roaming charges.

In 2008, a gradual economic downturn started affecting the mobile business. However, MobiTel managers decided to strengthen their position with further exploratory initiatives.

The company established a 3.5G network in all urban centers and made further investments to increase the data connection speed to 7.6 Mbit/s all across its network.

To expand the retail business, it established a number of new retail outlets and started selling a number of different laptop computers that introduced pre-installed mobile internet packages. It also started renting mobile internet modems.

As the company had retained some of its original image of being a "cheap" provider, the potential large institutional customers did not consider their offers seriously. For this reason, MobiTel carried out a number of large investments to increase product and service quality, established a separate business line for business customers and commissioned impartial measurements across the country, which demonstrated that their network coverage and quality were on a par with its two competitors. It also initiated marketing campaigns to support opera, theatre and tennis events to attract the attention of decision-makers of large businesses. Finally, it created a number of specialized services for large-business customers.

It created additional services for its private customers by establishing an online music shop and developed an innovative service that allowed watching the 2008 Olympic Games in Beijing via mobile phones. This was developed further into a Mobile TV portal that included a number of local and international TV channels streaming via mobile phone.

During the same year the company launched an innovative marketing campaign, *MobiTel Sitcom*, which was set up as a unique series of amusing short soap opera episodes that were shown during commercial breaks. For a short period, the company acquired sole rights to show commercials on some TV channels. As a result, the marketing campaign became so popular that some polled viewers claimed to be more interested in watching the *MobiTel Sitcom* rather than their regular TV program.

In 2009, while the business climate became more difficult due to the continued downturn, with its strong impact on the telecommunications sector, MobiTel continued its exploratory activities.

Due to its active efforts to win over business clients, it managed to achieve a 34% market share among business customers (the market share was just 20% the year before). In order to gain in business market share, it also established add-in services that were primarily targeted towards business clients. Bearing the business customers in mind, MobiTel developed a Mobile-ID solution that allowed the use of special certified mobile SIM cards in combination with a password to use the mobile phone as a personal identity document. The Mobile-ID solution provided a comprehensive tool for secure user identification for logging into company portals using the phone, to confirm transactions, and to encrypt and sign documents[22]. With its subsequent infrastructure investments, MobiTel managed to cover 70% of the country with its 3.5G internet network.

For its private customers, MobiTel opened a Mobile Gaming portal, which featured both internationally- and locally-developed mobile apps. The marketing campaigns that it had launched the previous year were considered to be highly successful. They signed a highly visible contract to continue the support of tennis competitions. The CMO of the company was chosen Marketing Director of the Year by the leading marketing association of the country, and the continuing *MobileTel Sitcom* was awarded the prize for the Most Innovative Marketing Campaign of the Year.

On the side of exploitative initiatives, MobiTel further lowered call prices for a limited number of segments, targeting retired people and schoolchildren. It also started offering free phone calls between family members who were sharing their subscription.

In 2010, MobiTel witnessed a breakthrough year for the usage of mobile internet in terms of both usage statistics as well as business success. MobiTel was the first mobile provider to initiate a mobile internet package that did not have an upper-usage limit and its cost was on a par with the high-speed fixed internet packages available. As a result, the sales of the internet package grew exponentially. Every third mobile phone that MobiTel sold in 2010 was a smartphone and the company gained a third of the market for mobile internet.

The company also decided to revamp its brand for two reasons. First, MobiTel's investments in customer service had led to a situation where its customer service quality received the highest ranking in the customer-satisfaction segment. Second, the investments in network quality had paid off and independent measurements showed that in a number of locations MobiTel had reached the highest quality of network service among the three main mobile phone providers in the country. Due to these two quality assessments, MobiTel revised its brand to reposition itself no longer as "the

---

[22] Further information for Mobile ID at: http://mobiil.id.ee/mis-on-mobiil-id/

cheapest" provider, but as the "highest quality" service provider. This marked a significant change in both its outside image as well as in the handling of its internal processes.

3.3   Data Sampling and Data Collection at Case Firms

3.3.1   Units of analysis.

Pettigrew suggested that the theory surrounding the phenomenon requires gathering data at several complimentary levels of analysis. Case studies can employ an embedded design of multiple levels of analysis within a single study (Yin, 2008). To answer to the research question: *Which practices are used by organizational actors involved in strategy making in the context of cyclical ambidexterity?* I had to measure two types of constructs. 1) I first had to assess ambidexterity cycles at the macro level to witness shifts in strategic orientation between exploration and exploitation. 2) To understand the practices employed by organizational actors during cyclical ambidexterity I had to focus on micro-level strategic activity within the organization. Hence, the study analyses the span across two units of analysis as depicted in the table below.

Table 7. Data collection techniques used in the study

	Macro Level	Micro Level
Research issues	How does cyclical ambidexterity manifest itself at the organizational level?	What practices trigger a shift in strategic orientation at the micro level? What practices are used during cyclical ambidexterity? How do individuals perceive cyclical ambidexterity?
Data collection techniques	Analysis of relative ambidexterity based on annual reports and strategy documents. Interviews about the processes, routines and systems, confirmatory interviews	Observation, review of discussions of strategy workshops, reflections on participation in strategy workshops and interviews, documentary evidence

I collected data on individual practices from: 1) reviewing various company strategy documents, financial data and annual reports, 2) semi-structured one-on-one interviews and 3) facilitation or observation at strategy discussions.

3.3.2   Approach to data collection

In the first phase, I relied on secondary retrospective data - company annual reports, publicly available information on the company website, on news as well as comprehensive content analysis of several internal documents provided to me by the company representatives (historic business plans, internal presentations on particular business ideas, internal industry analysis documents and memos). Based on this primary data I drew up the macro-level measurement of degrees of exploration and exploitation throughout the case history. This gave me the opportunity to understand conceptually when the cyclical ambidexterity had appeared in the company history.

In the second phase, I carried out a number of interviews and thereafter participated in strategy sessions in both case companies to see how change was unfolding. This phase took place over a period of 2 years.

At the beginning of our research task we primarily carried out semi-structured interviews that lasted 60-110 minutes. These involved questions about the company, about the strategy practices, about the past, present and future degree of exploration and exploitation and perceptions about the upcoming shift in strategic orientation. As we proceeded with our research endeavor and the change was already unfolding, our interviews became shorter and they primarily focused on the particularities of the practices of shift. We conducted altogether 87 interviews with 39 respondents in the case organizations.

We recorded the interviews and participant observations with two modalities: with audio recordings and with supplementary rough transcripts that we created during our interviews using a laptop, typing up the respondents' replies as well as the key messages exchanged during strategy discussions. After each interview, I used NVivo qualitative data analysis software to create precise transcripts of all the interviews and discussions that I participated in or conducted.

Following the interviews, I used the principles of in-vivo coding (Strauss & Corbin, 1998) and I subsequently divided the categories into first order fragments, based on the actual language that the informants used in the interviews and strategy sessions, and second order constructs as theories to explain the findings (Van Maanen, 1979). I coded my data based on the example of the identity study by Corley and Gioia (Corley & Gioia, 2004). I appended the case data with the analysis of company strategic domains in order to provide a better comparison for in-company analysis and comparison across cases.

There were two of us who carried out the initial interviews at the top management level, where we targeted the people who were able to provide the most informed responses to the research questions. We asked the CEOs of the case organizations to identify the initial list of people whom we should target next. In addition, we finished each of our interviews with a question about who else the interviewee thought would be the most appropriate individuals to answer these questions (making use of what is known as the snowballing technique) and serve as our next interviewee.

We set off with slightly different research agendas. I was primarily focusing on the practices of cyclical ambidexterity, while the other researcher focused on strategic issue management. We therefore tried to establish our interview questionnaires in such a manner that they would first provide a holistic picture of strategy making in the given case organization and thereafter focus on our respective research topics.

As the two of us interviewers collected the data, we ensured the validity and reliability of the data collection by separate coding approaches, and later comparing our interview notes and generalizations. In the instances where one of us had interpreted the first order data in a different manner we discussed the underlying reasons and then jointly confirmed our understanding.

3.3.3 Data collection at FixTel.

Collection of in-depth strategy process and strategy practices data at FixTel AS (the telecom firm) began in July 2008 and finished in mid-2010. I conducted 66 face-to-face semi-structured interviews with 26 respondents throughout the organization. Sampling of the interviewees followed the purposeful sampling strategy (Lincoln & Guba, 1985; Patton, 2001).

During every interview we identified the status of the organization via a series of questions that mapped the actual elements of the strategy-making mode based on the models of Hart (1992), Burgelman (1983) and the conceptual framework spelled out above. In the interviews, I shift between *I* and *we* depending on whether a particular interview or a subsequent coding was performed by one researcher or two. The seeming presentational inconsistency is therefore intentional.

Table 8. List of informants at FixTel

#	Informant	Interv. Jul-Sep 2008	2 strat days Oct 2008	Interv. Nov-Oct 2008	2 strat days Apr 2009	Interv. Apr-Jun 2010	4 strat days Apr-Jun 2010	Interv Aug 2010
F1[23]	Top marketing manager	2	2	3	2	7	4	1
F2	Top finance manager	1	2	1	1		1	
F3	Top regulatory manager	1	1					
F4	Top service manager	1	2	1	2	1		
F5	Top technology manager	1	2	1	2	1		
F6	Top IT manager	1	2					
F7	Top sales manager	1	2		2	1		
F8	Top operations manager	3	2	2	2	1	1	1
F9	Middle operations manager	1	2					
F10	Middle technology manager	1				1		
F11	Development manager	1	1	1				
F12	Middle technology manager	1						
F13	Line marketing manager	1		2	2	4	4	2
F14	Specialist in operations	1		1	1			
F15	Line service manager	1						
F16	Specialist in operations	1						
F17	Middle retail manager	1						
F18	Middle strategy manager	1	2		2			
F19	Middle service manager	1	2	1		1		1
F20	Top HR manager			1	1			
F21	Top solutions manager					1	4	
F22	Middle service manager					1	4	
F23	Line manager in service					1	4	1
F24	Middle manager in sales					1	4	1
F25	Development manager					1	4	
F26	Middle manager in sales					1	4	
	Encounters with informants:	22	22	14	17	22	34	7

The interviews included top and middle managers as well as members of the operating core. All individuals had either direct or indirect influence on strategy making in their firm. With some respondents (e.g. F1, F13 and F19), we carried out a number of confirmatory meetings about some

---

[23] In this thesis, I have coded the informants to preserve the respondents' anonymity. Informant designations starting with *F* are representatives of FixTel and the ones with *M* are MobiTel managers. The excerpts from their interviews appearing later in the paper have been translated from Estonian to English

of our findings. At FixTel we also attended eight strategy days. At the outset of our collaboration with FixTel, we started our work as a team of two researchers to map the strategy practices of the firm and assist the company managers in their strategy discussions. In early 2010, our role was somewhat different because the managers again invited us - this time to join their team to facilitate strategy discussions that were ongoing relating to their efficiency agenda and to assist them in the acquisition of an IT firm. Finally, in August 2010 we carried out some confirmatory interviews just to map the progress of the firm and clarify as researchers the practices that had started to emerge during the final phase of cyclical ambidexterity.

3.3.4   Data collection at MobiTel.

Compared to FixTel, the other case company, MobiTel, was a smaller firm. The number of MobiTel employees made it roughly four times smaller in terms of headcount. Due to smaller scale and a much thinner middle-management level, the number of informants at MobiTel was also half that at FixTel. Subsequently the analysis was also based on a smaller amount of data than was that of FixTel.

Table 9. List of informants at MobiTel

#	Informant	Interv. Oct-Nov 2007	Interv. Mar-Apr 2008	4 strat days Apr-Jun 2008	Interv. Jun 2008	Interv. Dec 2009	Interv. Aug 2010
M1	Top operations manager	1	1	4	1	1	1
M2	Top development manager		1	4	1	1	
M3	Top HR manager		1	4			
M4	Middle sales manager		1	4			
M5	Top finance manager		1	4			
M6	Top sales manager		1	4			
M7	Top marketing manager		1	4		1	
M8	Top IT manager		1	4			
M9	Top technology manager		1	4			
M10	Middle technology manager					1	
M11	Middle technology manager					1	
M12	Top operations manager						1
M13	Middle marketing manager					1	1
	Encounters with informants:	1	9	36	2	6	3

I collected data in the framework of interviews concerning in-depth strategy process and strategy practices data during October 2007, thereafter during March - June 2008, and follow-up interviews in late 2009 and 2010 to review the data. The data collection included 21 face-to-face semi-structured interviews with 13 respondents. At MobiTel we also attended four strategy days over the period of three months between April until June 2008.

When we started our interviews, the company had for a long time operated in exploitative mode. MobiTel managers invited our team of two to help in developing new product ideas and revising their strategy. Hence, we have to clarify our dual roles. At the beginning of the encounters with MobiTel - from the end of 2007 until mid-2008, our role was to be a team of two in-house facilitators to help the management team brainstorm new business ideas. Then, in late 2009, I entered the firm as an impartial researcher with follow-up interviews with the aim of studying the way the shift had unfolded.

4   Results and Findings

4.1   Measuring ambidexterity at macro level.

While the study covers two cases as an unfolding process, through both the longitudinal approach as well as partial retrospective data collection elements, it also has the task of assessing temporal snapshots. This is necessary to determine levels of exploration and exploitation at a given point in time. It also informs the researcher about the variance in exploration and exploitation - how shifts unfold during cyclical ambidexterity.

Authors have compiled different means for measuring relative exploration and exploitation, but no universally-accepted measurement exists. Most studies to date have used survey techniques to assess the exploratory and exploitative focus of managers or firms (McGrath R. G., 2001; He & Wong, 2004; Gibson & Birkinshaw, 2004; Lubatkin, Simsek, Ling, & Veiga, 2006; Jansen, Van den Bosch, & Volberda, 2005; Jansen, Van den Bosch, & Volberda, 2006; Mom, 2006). Some of them have used their survey data to analyze linkages via structural equation modeling (Auh & Menguc, 2005; Rosenkopf & Nerkar, 2001). Two studies have relied on patent data (Rosenkopf & Nerkar, 2001; Katila & Ahuja, 2002). One study has used textual analysis of annual reports and company-related financial news to determine the relative exploration and exploitation in firms (Uotila, Maula, Keil, & Zahra, 2009). Some studies have conceptually discussed the constructs (March, 1991; Floyd & Lane, 2000).

In *Annex 2 - Summary of Studies Measuring Exploration and Exploitation* below, I have summarized studies that outline measurement protocols used for exploration and exploitation. However, given the multiplicity of previous research in this field, I have used my own protocol, which I shall describe in detail now.

To measure the degree of exploration and exploitation at the macro level, I have categorized the company initiatives reported in the annual reports of the case organizations.

- Variables that measured the extent of usage of entrepreneurial learning-related initiatives determined the *degree of exploration*, and included the initiatives that referred to search, variation, risk taking, experimentation, play, flexibility, discovery and innovation (March, 1991). Those initiatives unfolded in the demand side (discovery of new market structures and segments, product use, customer preferences), or the supply side (technological and organizational domains) or in the geographical sphere (spatial search in different regions).
- Variables that measured the *degree of exploitation* of initiatives referred to refinement, choice, production, efficiency, selection, implementation and execution (March, 1991) in the demand side, supply side and geographical sphere.

For measuring the degree of exploration and exploitation at discrete points in time, I used the following protocol:

- 1st stage - identification of strategic initiatives during 1993-2010 for one case organization and during 1996-2010 for the other case organization;
- 2nd stage - classification of strategic initiatives as "exploratory" or "exploitative";
- 3rd stage - allocating relative degrees of organizational importance to particular initiatives on the basis of 1) size of investment, 2) duration of the initiative and 3) extent of organizational attention allocated to the initiative;
- 4th stage - confirming the coding results with the managers of the case organizations.

4.1.1   First stage - identification of strategic initiatives.

First I reviewed the case organizations' annual reports and past strategy documents to identify exploratory and exploitative initiatives. I placed the initiatives into a quarterly timeline. In some historic accounts, where it was not possible to trace the precise start and end dates of the particular initiative, I indexed them for a full year. In some cases, where initiatives lasted for a longer period, such as for several years, I noted it accordingly. The example of the initiative coding is below in the table.

Table 10. Example of retrospective coding of timing of strategic initiatives

Timing	Initiative in Annual Report or Strategy Document	Year and Quarter
Dec. 16, 1992	Privatization of 49% of the company and signature of concession agreement for 8 years (until 29 Dec. 2000) providing monopolistic rights, but requiring the provision of a number of investments	I quarter of 1993
Jan. 1, 1993	Legal establishment of the firm according to the new legal framework	I quarter of 1993
During 1993	Restructuring of the firm - establishment of new internal structure and the revision of service procedures	During 1993
During 1993-97	Coin-based payphones replaced with card-based payphones	1993, 1994, 1995, 1996, 1997
During 1994-96	Reducing workforce from 4,380 (beginning of 1994) to 3,784 (beginning of 1996)	1994, 1995
Spring-summer 1996	Introduction of direct-dialing technology	II-IV quarter of 1996
During the 2nd half of 1996	Total digitalization of 3 mid-size towns (including building network, central AXE-type exchange)	III-IV quarter of 1996
During the 2nd half of 1996	Induction of IN-card	III-IV quarter of 1996
During the 2nd half of 1996	Installation of base network optical cable circuit in western Estonia	III-IV quarter of 1996
Winter of 1997	First Asynchronous Transfer Mode connection (precursor to ADSL)	I quarter of 1997
March 1997	First TV programs transferred via optical fiber	I quarter of 1997
During 1997	Construction of new service centers	1997
During 1997	Phone connections built to all small populated islands	1997
Summer 1997	Opening 2Mb/s data connection with Canada	III quarter of 1997

4.1.2   Second stage - coding strategic initiatives.

In the second phase, I coded the individual initiatives as "exploratory" or "exploitative". Some initiatives counted clearly as exploratory or exploitative. Some were neutral and some were ambidextrous. Combining the number of initiatives at hand at any given moment together with their degree helped to determine the actual extent of exploration- and exploitation-related activities that were present in the case organization in that particular moment of time. Thereby it assisted in deciding whether the managers in the organization during that period focused their attention on either one or the other facet of strategic orientation.

4.1.3   Third stage - relative degree of importance of an initiative.

The third stage concentrated on ascertaining the relative degree of managerial importance assigned to individual initiatives. Previous research has assessed the relative importance of initiatives with varying approaches. The strategic issue research stream has used a number of criteria to assess the importance of issues. For example, Dutton et al. (1989) suggested that the managers "separate the wheat from the chaff" by considering four dimensions. These are: 1) the analytical aspects of issues (complexity, impact, locus, threat, opportunity, visibility, time pressure); 2) the issue content (geography, type, competitive aspect); 3) the action aspect (likelihood and amount of payoff from action, controllability of issue and its resolution feasibility); and 4) the issue source (internal/external, strategic location, personal attachment to the manager).

In this thesis, the measurement of the relative degree of exploration or exploitation builds on the classification of Dutton et al. (1989) and creates a composite measure relying on three sub-variables.

Table 11. Criteria for measuring the relative degree of exploration and exploitation

Criteria for Measuring	Application of relative weight
Monetary importance, measuring the **financial aspect** of the particular initiative in question - whether the exploratory or exploitative initiative brings financial gains or savings to the firm.	Monetary importance, measured by the amount of investment in an initiative – up to 50 per cent ($x=0.5$) of the composite measure, where all investments above 1 million EUR were allocated a full 50% weighting and smaller investments respectively with the percentage ratio of the investment.
Organizational importance in terms of **timing** of the initiative. The duration of the initiative measures both the attention span of the managers and the overall organizational importance.	Organizational importance measured by the duration of initiative – up to 20 per cent ($y=0.2$) of the composite measure. The initiatives that spanned longer than 1 year were allocated a full 20% weighting, initiatives of 6 month received half of that and shorter initiatives another half less.
Organizational importance in terms of **scale** of the initiative. If the initiative involves multiple levels of organization or is even pan-organizational then it is of a relatively high importance. If only a limited number of employees or units handle it, then it is of a low importance.	Organizational importance measured by the scale of the initiative and multilevel nature, whereby the initiatives that spanned the entire organization received full 30% weighting ($z=0.3$). The initiatives that were isolated to a single functional unit received 5% and the initiatives that covered in-between were allocated 10% and 20% respectively, weighting depending on the scale of the initiatives

According to these variables, the following formula determines the extent of exploratory initiatives and exploitative initiatives at any given point in time (t). The extreme value of exploration is +1 and the extreme value of exploitation -1. Hence, the functions take into account the overall maximum extent of the exploratory and exploitative initiatives (max_t Expt and max_t Expr) during all times. They have values between +1 and -1. Resulting intermediate values of exploration at different time frames were plotted between 0 … +1 and values of exploitation were plotted between 0 … -1.

Function for exploratory plotting: $f(Expl_t) =$

$$[(P_t \times x)(T_t \times y)(L_t \times z)] \Big/ \max_t[(P_t \times x)(T_t \times y)(L_t \times z)]$$

Function for exploitative plotting: $f(Expt_t) =$

$$- \left\{ [(P_t \times x)(T_t \times y)(L_t \times z)] \Big/ \max_t [(P_t \times x)(T_t \times y)(L_t \times z)] \right\}$$

Where:

$Expl_t$ - relative exploration of initiative at given time (1 fully exploratory ... 0 no exploration);

$Expt_t$ - relative exploitation of initiative at given time (-1 fully exploitative ... 0 no exploitation);

$(P_t \times x)$ - relative investment allocated to initiative at a given time (P_t - investment, x - relative weight of the investment variable);

$(T_t \times y)$ - relative duration of initiative (T_t - duration, y - relative weight of the duration variable);

$(L_t \times z)$ - relative multi-level nature of initiative (L-number of organizational levels involved, z - relative weight of the multi-level variable).

Below are examples of measurements of exploratory and exploitative initiatives together with a graphical representation of the data.

Table 12. Measuring temporal snapshots - relative exploration and exploitation values

Initiatives in Annual Report or Strategy Document	Timing	Investment Size	Scale of Rating	Exploratory / Exploitative
- Introduction of direct-dialing technology; - Total digitalization of 3 mid-size towns (including building network, central AXE-type exchange); - Induction of IN-card - Installation of base network optical cable circuit in western Estonia	II-IV quarter of 1996	34 m EUR	In 1995: 0.7 In 1996: 0.7-0.8	Supply-side exploratory Demand-side exploratory Geographic exploratory
- First Asynchronous Transfer Mode connection (precursor to ADSL); - First TV programs transferred via optical fiber - Construction of new service centers - Coin-based payphones replaced with card-based payphones - Phone connections built to all small populated islands of the country - Opening 2Mb/s data connection with Canada	I-IV quarter of 1997	35 m EUR	In 1997: 1.0	Supply-side exploratory Demand-side exploratory Geographic exploratory
- Introduction of new billing system - Opening the monitoring center for network control	II-IV quarter of 1997	8 m EUR	In 1996: 0.2 In 1997: 0.2	Exploitative
- Cutting workforce from 4,380 in 1995 to 3,784 in 1996 to 3,590 in 1997 and to 3,305 by the beginning of 1998	Throughout 1995-97	N/A	In 1995: 0.5 In 1996: 0.1 In 1997: 0.3	Exploitative

Figure 6. Temporal representation of relative exploration and exploitation values

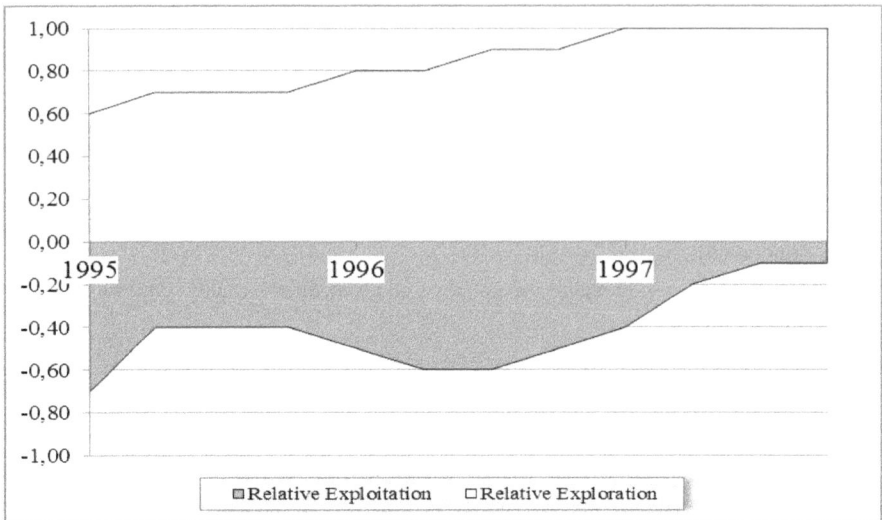

4.1.4   Fourth Stage - confirming coding with the case firm representatives.

To increase the precision of control related to the phenomena of interest and verify construct validity (McGrath J. E., 1981, p. 184; Scandura & Williams, 2000), I triangulated measurement with informants. Two managers of the case organizations who were well aware of their company history reviewed my data to comment about the accuracy of the judgments. To reduce their partiality, they saw the data without information about the aim of the present study (Huber & Power, 1985).

During this process, the FixTel representative suggested two corrections. Turnover data for the period 2008-2009 identified amounts mistakenly coded as exploratory gains, which should have been under "other income" in the profit-and-loss statement. Instead, both were one-off payments to FixTel by a competing firm who lost a court dispute. MobiTel representatives did not suggest any corrections.

4.2   Measuring ambidexterity at micro level

This subchapter will dig into the details of the micro practices of handling inertia and the (de)activation of latent practices associated with cyclical ambidexterity. To do so, I will first provide a summary of the qualitative data from the interviews and strategy sessions, which exemplifies the practices related to inertia and the (de)activation of practices associated with cyclical ambidexterity.

Thereafter I will describe the components of the data outlined in the findings categories, one by one. While I separated the tables summarizing the practices of the two case organizations, the following in-depth description of the findings attempts to combine the findings concerning the two case organizations into a consistent story, whereby the inert, activation and deactivation practices of exploratory and exploitative cycles are described by categories. This will feed into the following final chapter, where I will generalize those findings into a holistic model.

4.2.1 Case 1 - FixTel: shifting from exploration to exploitation

FixTel had been in primarily exploratory periods in 1994-2000 and 2003-2007 and it pursued primarily exploitative strategies in 2001-2002 and since 2008 to the present.

Figure 7. Relative degree of exploration and exploitation at FixTel

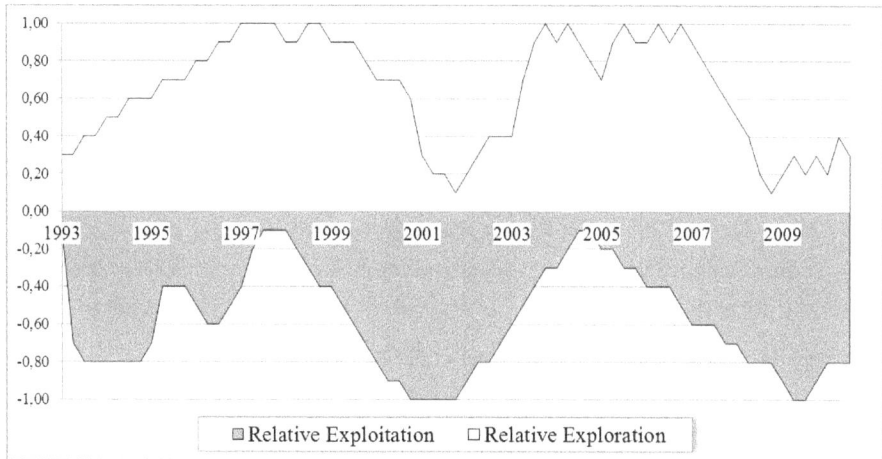

The detailed unfolding of ambidexterity cycles at FixTel with the following stages:

- **Exploitation**. In 1993, the company focused originally on an exploitation strategy by cutting costs and reducing their workforce, which was primarily of the old Soviet economy mindset, to enable a transition into a more effective market economy-focused organization.

- **Exploration and minor exploitation**. Immediately thereafter - starting from 1994 - the company began implementing extensive exploratory investments by building physical infrastructure and investing in new technologies and internet business solutions. The company also invested in customer relations exploration. Until 1996, there were still further cuts in workforce – mostly due to structural issues necessitating the cutting down of excessively large old Soviet-style regional departments.

- **Exploitation**. The company made a shift back to exploitation in 2001. The shift was made in order to cut costs in a changing post-concession business situation whereby FixTel lost nearly 50% of its most profitable international calls business. Subsequently, the company decided to cut 44% of its staff during 2 years and completely revise its business model from that of a technology firm to a service-delivery company, redesigned its brand and focused heavily on marketing.

- **Exploration**. The company simultaneously started a parallel shift to further exploration in 2003-05 by expanding its internet business and entering into the business of Digital Television. During this period, the company also elaborated a number of new technologies.
- **Exploitation**. After the extensive expansion of ADSL solutions and successful introduction of a number of solutions for Digi-TV the company reintroduced a shift to exploitation due to the need to cut costs in early 2008, in response to a request by the shareholders to keep up profitability in the post-economic-downturn situation. Exploitation activities intensified during 2009-10 due to the continuing poor economic situation, but also due to the preparation and execution of a major merger with an IT firm, which helped to consolidate business lines as superimposed by the parent company of the firm.

My study focused directly on the period 2008-10 and thereby observed the latest shift to exploitation.

4.2.1.1   Data on cyclical ambidexterity practices at FixTel

To be transparent about the findings, I have first summarized the representative quotes from the interviews. I have categorized the quotes according to summary themes in the table below. It contains supporting evidence to allow the reader to discover and consider the findings in more detail.

Table 13. Data on cyclical ambidexterity practices at FixTel

Themes	Representative quotes from interviews
Inert strategic orientation and triggering practices	
A) Positive reinforcement of active practices	**FixTel - practices demonstrating an unstructured strategy process with a high degree of autonomy, single basis for decision-making (innovation funnel based on EBITDA) and competition between TMT members, external competition unimportant.**
	FixTel.A1) "I don't think that during {last period} we had proper strategic priorities spelled out. We were focusing on new products and we could have said that anything that promised profits was an acceptable way of spending our time". (F15 - a middle manager in service area)
	FixTel.A2) "Our strategy was not very systematic. The only system that we had was our investment budget and we also refreshed our overall aims from time to time, but this has not been a very regular activity - just happens when one of us remembers it and thinks that we haven't discussed those issues for a long time. Perhaps just once or twice a year." (F8 - a top manager in Operations)
	FixTel.A3) "We are not observing our competitors in detail to report on their activity. We only observe global figures - e.g. if the market is growing or falling" (F2 - A top Finance manager)
	FixTel.A4) "We should not focus on competitors. Our primary focus should be on our existing customers. We have developed a rather elaborate CRM, which helps to identify patterns in the customers' behavior a few months before they give up on our service. Hence, our key priority in our direct sales is those potential departing clients and making attractive offers before they decide to leave us." (F14 - a representative of operating core)
	FixTel.A5) "It was easy. During [referring to exploratory inertia period], the Board was mostly hands off. They were only interested in our EBITDA figure. When we demonstrated good enough earnings - that was it!" (F2 - top Finance manager)

FixTel.A6) "I think that our management team still has to learn how to work as a unified team that is after the same thing. There are still lots of discussions at our meetings that focuses on "you vs. me" instead of 'us'". (F8 - a top Operations manager)

FixTel.A7) "I guess that our top management is just 'boys playing men'. At meetings, they go 'uh-uh-uh-uh' [gesturing and imitating a large gorilla]. They stand up and speak about their achievements instead of really discussing what matters". (F20 - a top HR manager)

FixTel.A8) "Of course, we have a system to measure the quality of business ideas. Just based on NPV calculations. The product developers are tech geeks. We don't know about finances. We know which is a cool product but for the [top management] selection committee we would have to accompany it with such a business plan that NPV would look promising. We started our meetings with [business analysts in finance department] to help us with that." (F11 - a middle manager in Development)

FixTel.A9) "I guess that the best way to describe our priorities is twofold. We have an EBITDA goal from our company Board and this we have to achieve no matter what. We revise our EBITDA goal at the Board twice a year. We have to find interesting services that would help them achieve this." (F2 - top Finance manager)

FixTel.A10) "We have introduced a system whereby four times a year we sit down with our development team [referring to a group of 20 middle managers from product development, marketing, IT and networks] and we do a long list of business ideas which we have baked somewhere in our departments. I remember that last time we had about 120 of them spelled out. We just did their screening and chose 15-20 that looked the most promising. Those are elaborated further to present to the management team for immediate financing. It is mostly up to product managers to make their ideas look good and work with analysts from the finance department to make sure that also their business projections would look good." (F11 - a middle manager in Development).

B) Handling of latent practices	**FixTel - practices rationalizing earlier ambidexterity shifts, pressure to become ambidextrous and referring to individual examples of isolated practices.**

FixTel.B1) "A few years ago, one top manager thought that it would be a good idea to start introducing metrics based on the Balanced Scorecard methodology. It was when BSC was a hot topic, but they agreed upon metrics only for our sales team. The others were left out of this initiative." (F14 - a representative of operating core)

FixTel.B2) "[During the exploitation period] we had a better system [for management], but at that time we did not have much content. Now it is exactly the opposite. We have many good ideas, but we have forgotten the system of how to get them properly done!" (F14 - A representative of operating core)

FixTel.B3) "It was 'management by hope' - most people were at random units, some outsourced. It was our mistake [during the previous exploitative period] when we decided to sack our entire IT." (F6 - top manager in IT)

C) Practices of reflection and triggering	**FixTel - triggering practices referring to revenue fall, reflection of internal myopia about the competitive situation and sorting out messy business.**

FixTel.C1) "We were observing already for some time that the market for fixed calls had been shrinking. We realized that it was not so simple any more to simply push something to the market and then start milking the opportunity with yet another aggressive marketing campaign. We had to revise our approach." (F1 - top manager in Marketing)

FixTel.C2) "Our product development people thought primarily about the toys we wanted to see in our own houses. [Referring to a recently developed product] required the client to read a 20-page manual or have our helpdesk guidance. At the same time, Apple sells gadgets that only have a single button and come without a manual." (F4 - top manager in Service)

FixTel.C3) "Our mobile competitors started offering cheaper internet service. Their quality was not so good, but it was good enough for many clients to start eating into our market." (F9 - A middle manager in Operations)

FixTel.C4) "During the past few years, we have always had a 'hit of the year'. When the downturn kicked in, it was obvious that we would not be having a hit with something new - the board required us to cut the costs." (F2 - a top Finance manager).

FixTel.C5) "(We had) inefficiencies with confusing processes and a colorful mix of disconnected competences. When the board gave us the signal that we should do something, we immediately started discussing the possibility of how to 'take out the garbage'". (F19 - a middle manager in Service).

Activation of latent and deactivation of active practices

D) Proactivity vs reactivity	**FixTel - activating practices to scan the environment.** *FixTel.D1) "In the new situation, we had to start thinking about how to manage in a competitive environment. How to constantly count money, how to constantly observe the competitor's positions, how to be competitive as a flexible service provider." (F3 - a top manager in the regulatory area)*
E) Creativity vs efficiency	**FixTel - activating practices to focus on strategic priorities and introducing efficiency-based objective-setting and tracking systems to resort to cost-cutting** *FixTel.E1) "If our board gives us a 20% profitability goal and the market is falling then the only way of making sure what we need to do is to discuss where we should cut and how much." (F1 - a top manager in Marketing).* *FixTel.E2) "We set up a couple of working groups at different levels that were discussing efficiency initiative. At our regular Friday meetings with our management board, we spent hours discussing the possibilities for cutting costs and seeking best practices from other companies on how to achieve some immediate results. Second - we created two working groups on efficiency. One in technology and another in the service division, who also met on a weekly basis to discuss the possibilities for cutting costs." (F2 - a top Finance manager).* *FixTel.E3) "In a training, we heard about the Japanese management model, whereby organizations discuss their difficulties openly with employees. For instance, it leads to decisions whereby people decide to reduce their salaries voluntarily to retain their long-term employment. We decided to do it, too." (F7 - a top manager in Sales).* *FixTel.E4) "The telecommunications business requires large-scale investments and most decisions have a time lag of 2-5 years. Larger investments are earned back in 5-10 years. Even for small services it takes between 1-2 years to get the service operational. If we were spending too much then during the following period we would have to cut double to meet our targets." (F15 - a line manager in Service).*
F) Single vision vs multiple agendas at the top	**FixTel - activating practices to harmonize shared vision held by the top management team and thereby systemizing the company strategy process with more analytical and deadline-driven approaches** *FixTel.F1) "Due to saturation of our market, we reprioritized our indicators. Hence, instead of overall growth EBITDA figures, we focused on ARPU, which reflects our present possibilities much better." (F8 - a top manager in Operations)* *FixTel.F2) "This year we started discussing 'cleaning house'. In essence, this means introducing the traditional centralized BSC-style metrics system, which is not exactly using BSC terminology, but what is important is that it has started to work." (F8 - a top manager in Operations).*
G) Efficiency silos vs collaboration at mid-level	**FixTel - activating practices to make efficiency-oriented improvement working groups actively operational and focusing management style to short-term goals** *FixTel.G1) "Before we had an approach based on 'key people' - every project idea, every new initiative had somebody identified as a key person who was responsible for it. If this person had a vision which matched the top management's, then he had all the resources in hand to just go ahead and do it. In the new situation all those projects were frozen, hence most people who were taking responsibility and acting responsibly simply stopped doing anything at all." (F11 - A middle manager in Development)* *FixTel.G2) "Before we were playing basketball - if you got the ball then all you had to do was to get close to the basket and then take a shot. If you were successful then you got your points. Now we are into bridge. You have to carefully plan and think with whom you are playing in pairs and contemplate what the other's hand might be." (an informant during a strategy workshop).* *FixTel.G3) "Before primarily the technology department ran our innovations. Then we were really dealing with innovation. However now the marketing department leads and I would say that what they are doing is just 'improvements'" (F12 - a middle manager in Technology).*

H) Coordination vs autonomy	**FixTel - activating the practices to respond to stricter governance style of the Board and create rules for handling and tracking cost cutting success**

FixTel.H1) "I remember that when we discussed the monthly results there was a recurring theme. Routinely, either one of the department leads or somebody else from among the participants at the meeting asked me at a certain point in the discussion the crucial question: 'Is what we are doing now good enough?' or 'Are we pleasing the supervisory board already?' or 'How much further do we still have to go?' At first, it was a difficult question. After a while, it became funny. Finally, I started preparing my presentations in such a way that I anticipated this question and tried to get to this upfront." (F14 - a representative of operating core).

FixTel.H2) "The newly revised NPV methodology has also had adverse effects. Have you heard about the advertisement with the theme how good ideas become reality? In our case - when we are so stuck in the financial analysis then ultimately the good ideas only turn into snails!"[24] (F6 -a top manager in IT)

FixTel.H3) "We might have worked on a business idea for 6 months, and ultimately at the end of the 6-month period we face the IT resource committee, and then we are simply told that: 'Your project is not a priority, forget it - we first have to finalize programming the other 4 large things here!'" (F11 - middle manager in Development)

4.2.2   Case 2 - MobiTel: shifting from exploitation to exploration

Figure 8. Relative degree of exploration and exploitation at MobiTel

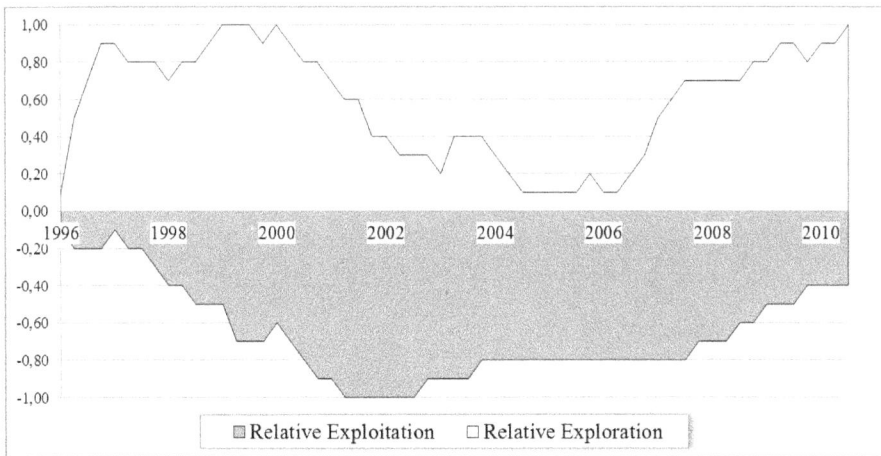

MobiTel used an exploratory strategy in 1997-98, a dual strategy of high exploration and exploitation in 1998-2001, a highly-exploitative strategy in 2002-06 and since 2007 in conjunction with mobile market saturation, the company has followed an exploratory strategy.

The ambidexterity cycles in FixTel unfolded in the following stages:

- **Exploration**. The company began in 1996 as an aggressive competitor in the market against two incumbent firms and to achieve its goal in the best possible way it focused

---

[24] Word play in Estonian language: "Hea mõte saab teoks" means both "Good idea becomes reality" and "Good idea turns into a snail".

during the first two years primarily on product and service exploration – on extensive building of infrastructure and selling the handsets for subsidized prices.

- **Both Exploitation and Exploration.** In 1998-2001, the company carried out a dual strategy with intensive investments, but compared with the incumbents it also focused intensively on efficiency to be able to capture a large portion of the market via lowered prices, and to increase profitability.
- **Exploitation.** Since the purchase of MobiTel shares by an international mobile operator the company repositioned and rebranded itself to consistently provide "the cheapest mobile service" in the country. Subsequently the company outsourced a number of its business areas, constantly lowered the prices to remain the cheapest alternative of the three major mobile companies and hence during 2002-2006 the company strategy was exploitative.
- **Exploration.** Starting from the saturation of the mobile market in 2007, and realizing that it is simply no longer possible to increase its market share by providing the cheapest service, MobiTel started focusing on service excellence, technology excellence and it introduced a number of new services primarily aimed at increasing its business segment market share, which led to an exploratory shift.

The focus of this in-depth study was on the latest shift to exploration and covered the period between 2008-10.

4.2.2.1   Data on cyclical ambidexterity practices at MobiTel.

I have also summarized the representative quotes from the interviews carried out at MobiTel. I have categorized the quotes according to summary themes in the table below. It contains supporting evidence to allow the reader to discover and consider the findings in more detail.

Table 14. Data on cyclical ambidexterity practices at MobiTel

Themes	Representative quotes from interviews
Inert strategic orientation and triggering practices	
A) Positive reinforcement of active practices	MobiTel - practices demonstrating a reactive strategy process with limited autonomy, patterned with an *efficiency mantra*, thorough competitor scanning procedures and reactive decisions to competitors' actions.
	MobiTel.A1) "Our ideas do not move fast enough in the list of priorities of our owners. For example, [our competitor] could create a solution for watching TV over a mobile connection. If we would like to do the same we would need some resources, but in our case, we cannot convince our owners and the committees. As Estonia is the most innovative in the region then our local competitors are constantly running ahead of us because we are unable to persuade the committees to make those investments." (M4 - a middle manager in Sales).
	MobiTel.A2) "There have been some examples where we managed to convince our bosses in Sweden. Like it would be a good idea to start with investments in 3G technology. We bought the license in 2003 and started building the network in 2005, which was much earlier than many other countries in the region. While today [in April 2008] the revenues from 3G services are rather small, however, if we would not have been able to invest at the same time with the others, today we would be 2-3 years behind

our competitors, who could easily use this as a marketing argument. "   (M4 - a middle manager in Sales).

MobiTel.A3) "I have 20 direct subordinates, but they all have direct sales responsibilities and daily tasks. Hence, when I am struggling with something out of the ordinary that needs to be done, I really cannot act as a Dilbert manager and just delegate it. I need to do it myself. When I am in doubt about something, then I usually just have a chat with some of my colleagues, go ahead, and then sort it out. " (M4 - a middle manager in Sales).

MobiTel.A4) "It does not matter what our source of efficiency is. What matters is that in order to retain our strategy as a price leader and our flexibility to be ready to lower the prices at any point, our cost base must be at all times 20% below the competitors. We cannot cut on sales nor on marketing, because these will have an immediate effect on our growth. The only things that remain are stronger bargaining with our suppliers, keeping our personnel costs down or delaying our investments. " (M7 - a top Marketing manager).

MobiTel.A5) "For market scanning, we employ two full-time people who review the marketing offers of the competitors and organize regular blind purchases of the competitors' products and services. Additionally, 20 people as business sales managers, also gather the offers of the competitors. Subsequently we make our advertising counter-moves on a weekly basis and the pricing counter moves every month. " (M1 - a top manager in Operations).

MobiTel.A6) "A number of important topics for our strategy process are delivered by our headquarters. They go through their annual process of defining the business at the beginning of the year and they deliver to us the core statements in February, explaining what business we are in and why we are doing this. They also deliver some core priorities, which act as a framework for our national strategy for the upcoming three years. Our work as a management team at MobiTel Estonia is to translate this framework via our own needs and possibilities into a strategy that would be implementable. "

MobiTel.A7) "Four times a year we have meeting with MobiTel consortium's top managers, which take place in February, May, August and December. At those meetings, we present our summary investment plans. We present our ideas about different investment projects, which vary in scope and scale. For example - when we plan to set up an MBT in the center of Tallinn then it earns back the investment within a month and nobody asks questions about it. However, we had conversations about investing in 3G technology for more than a year, because it is likely that the full investment will only become profitable in a decade. " (M9 - a top Technology manager).

B) Handling of latent practices

MobiTel - practices demonstrating isolated exploratory moves in exploitative situation.

MobiTel.B1) "In early phase of MobiTel in 2001, when it still was an independent company, a group of enthusiasts working at the IT department of MobiTel programmed its own billing system that was based on the architecture of Cerillion. The system was built on a modular basis partially using freeware software, which allowed the system to be set up within a short timeframe and with minimal resources. Based on MobiTel Estonia's billing system success story, which coincided with MobiTel Headquarters' failure, the group IT bosses concluded that the billing system built in Estonia was 'a strategic platform for MobiTel', which would be introduced in all countries. " (M8 - a top manager in IT).

C) Practices of reflection and triggering

MobiTel - practices demonstrating saturation of exploitation strategy and need to revise strategy making into less bureaucratic and more customer-focused.

MobiTel.C1) "It was a standard practice that we had to get at least a 20% discount on every partnership agreement. We negotiated with a number of advertisers for an all-in-one Christmas Cards service to our business and VIP customers. We only realized two weeks before Christmas that due to our negotiations the company was only able to deliver these cards shortly before Easter. After this we decided that we had gone too far with our approach and instead started talking about "smart efficiency" - that we will have to be efficient, but not cheap. " (M12 - a top manager in Operations)

MobiTel.C2) "[our competitors] registered trademarks that were similar to our name and claimed that 'SeriousMobile and LoveMobile are high-quality service providers, but MobiTel, MobyTel and Cheap Deal are cheap and lower-quality service providers. ' It was a wicked, but very effective campaign. In a way, they downgraded their own prepaid products, but by doing this, they strengthened the image of their core products. They also conveyed the message to price-sensitive customers that there are alternatives for our service. As they had now provided the alternatives, they could take a piece of the cake that was until that time only ours. " (M2 - a top Development manager).

Activation of latent and deactivation of active practices	
D) Proactivity vs reactivity	**MobiTel - activating practices to reduce reactivity to competitors and insourcing customer service to increase proactivity** *MobiTel.D1) "It bothers me that we are sometimes almost twitching to act. When SeriousMobile does something on Monday then we have to respond by Wednesday. I don't know if this is the best approach - we might earn some extra money with the fast response, but I am sure that we are also losing a lot because of our overly reactive approach. Perhaps we should be focusing more on our own way of doing certain things." (M4 - a middle manager in Sales).* *MobiTel.D2) "We discussed this amongst ourselves for a long time. While it does not matter to small household customers who answers their questions about their latest phone bill, we cannot use the same approach with our larger business customers. There are two problems. First, our outsourced partner can never be as flexible as our customers would need. Second, we look unreliable in the eyes of our customers when they realize that the service to them is not provided in-house." (M4 - a middle manager in Sales).* *MobiTel.D3) "It might be interesting that despite all those dramatic changes that have been carried out during the lat two years, the most dramatic change is that it has become more peaceful. Two years ago we were only firefighting, but now we have got much more time for discussing between ourselves and for thinking ahead. In part it is because we have much more agreement concerning our priorities." (M9 - a top Technology manager).*
E) Creativity vs efficiency	**MobiTel - activating practices to establish idea generation mechanisms and creative problem-solving tools** *MobiTel.E1) "Given that our IT development team in Estonia created the billing system for the entire Corporation, we have created a strong reputation among the group companies and we could build on this reputation to move ahead with innovation projects." (M8 - a top manager in IT).* *MobiTel.E2) "Now the number of product development projects has grown substantially. While before we managed 3-4 projects concurrently, at this moment there are 31 development projects in the pipeline, which is an exponential growth compared to two years ago. Some of them are related to improvements of existing products, the others are completely new services that we are about to bring to the market." (M2 - a top Development manager).*
F) Single vision vs multiple agendas at the top	**MobiTel - activating practices to handle multiple new businesses by bringing in new talent and facilitating solutions to serve more customer groups** *MobiTel.F1) "I guess that at a certain moment we realized that too much was going on to make sure that the three of us [referring to the head of business development, head of finance and head of operations] would be able to oversee it all. We realized that the only way to achieve our goals would be to involve as many people as possible from our company to be able to tap into the opportunities and test out the ideas that we were unable to absorb." (M1 - a top manager of Operations).* *MobiTel.F2) "For the past 8 years that I have been in this company, I have had to decide constantly by myself - there has been nobody to discuss these ideas with. I would have wanted to discuss the ideas with somebody. It is now great that this forum provides us with the opportunity to step in, use the other members of this team as a sounding board, and see how to improve on the ideas of our unit." (M9 - a top Technology manager).* *Mobitel.F3) "Growing the technology department 2.5-fold increased the quality of our service delivery in a remarkable manner. This decision combined with a full investment plan made it certain that now the independent measurements of our network quality across the country will show that we are on a par or even better than both of our competitors." (M2 - a top Development manager).* *Mobitel.F4) "[On launching a new service] It took SeriousMobile more than half a year before they had to react. By that time, we had succeeded in tricking over more than 20,000 phone numbers from them. When we made our next moves, their reactions were somewhat faster." (M4 - a middle manager in Sales).*
G) Efficiency silos vs collaboration in the middle	**MobiTel - activating practices to introduce regular interactions between Marketing, Technology and Development to handle new business opportunities and increase the number of development projects**

MobiTel.G1) "The result of the discussions is that we have started receiving more feedback from marketing on what our customers want. The previous situation, when engineers were trying to make decisions about customers was frequently flawed. Previously the usual approach was 'Hmm, this customer has a problem. Let's send the problem to technology division and ask them to sort it out for the customer.'" (M9 - a top Technology manager).

MobiTel.G2) "We have previously had a constant conflict between the technology and marketing divisions. Our people attempt to make the world rational, but our marketing team is very creative. Hence, it has been difficult to sit down together and work on the joint problems as a team. We should understand the problem of our customer jointly." (M9 - a top Technology manager).

| H) Coordination vs autonomy | **MobiTel - activating practices to introduce bottom-up collaboration for network development initiatives to replace centralized procurement systems** |

MobiTel.H1) "Our engineers started suggesting collaboration with our competitors to agree upon sharing their antennae. In a number of locations where the companies had already erected three towers side by side we decided to dismantle some to save on costs and combine the equipment from three towers into one." (M10 - middle Technology manager).

4.2.3 Qualitative data analysis.

Already during the process of data collection, I conducted a preliminary analysis to begin the conceptualization and generalization of the data. Following data collection, I performed a rough categorization of concepts. Those categories first spread the information about the practices of strategy making across two primary domains: 1) temporal (i.e. whether the informants referred to practices at different phases of cyclical ambidexterity) and 2) structural (i.e. whether the practices were individual-, group- or organization - focused). Based on these broad categorizations I established coding schemes in order to structure the data collected in the above-mentioned categories to detect any patterns of interest.

After the categorization, I commenced coding individual data snippets to determine which meanings to apply to the data. During the first phase of research, I used the categorizations of Crossan et al. (1999) to analyze the possibilities of categorizing the construct elements under the four multi-level categories of organizational learning (intuiting, interpreting integrating and institutionalizing). However, after numerous encounters with the data I arrived at new semantic themes using the *axial coding* toolkit, a term in qualitative analysis referring to the "act of relating categories to subcategories along the lines of their properties" (Strauss & Corbin, 1998, p. 123).

I first identified different summary practices that appeared as the core framework for handling cyclical ambidexterity within case organizations. I recognized that I could divide the practices temporally into primarily two main types:

1. Practices used during the periods when the case organizations were predominantly focusing on either exploration or exploitation, which I called "Practices during relative inertia" and
2. Practices used during the periods when the case organizations were actively engaged in cyclical ambidexterity and redefining their strategic orientation. I called them "activation and deactivation practices".

During the periods of relative inertia in case organizations, three types of practices were actively at work. These were the practices that were associated with: confirming existing practices; reflecting on existing practices to look for triggers for revising the work; and handling of latent practices.

A. **Positive reinforcement of active practices**. First, there were practices that were associated with retaining the existing strategic orientation.

B. **Practices of reflection and triggering**. At times there arose a practice where managers checked whether there was a need to revise strategic orientation - hence I called them *reflecting practices*. Some of those practices were influential enough to initiate or trigger upcoming ambidexterity shifts, which I therefore called *triggering practices*. As reflection and triggering practices appeared together in the dataset, I coded the two under the same umbrella category.

C. **Handling of latent practices**. There was a third core practice linked to managing readiness to begin a shift in cyclical ambidexterity. On frequent occasions, the informants referred to strategy practices within their organization that they had used during earlier periods. Usually those practices were associated with the opposing strategic orientation - if the organization was presently primarily exploratory then the managers talked about past exploitive practices and vice versa. When the company was in the exploitive mode then the informants referred to some exploratory practices that had been used during a previous period. This did not mean that those practices rendered the organization ambidextrous. Those practices received little attention because people dealing with them had left the organization or had transferred their focus elsewhere. In other instances, those practices were set aside because other priorities had rendered them secondary. Given that the practices were still on the back burner and people were referring to them as having potential for being used again, the properties of those practices demonstrate a certain *incubation* or *hibernation* period during which these practices are not actively in use. I decided to label these sorts of practices *latent practices,* given that the Merriam-Webster dictionary defines *latent* as "present and capable of emerging and developing, but not clearly visible." (*lt. latere* - "to lie hidden").

However, I also identified other types of practices that kicked in during an active cycle of ambidexterity shift. I labelled them *activation practices* and *deactivation practices*. Data analysis demonstrated instances where strategy practitioners engaged in activating certain latent practices that were present in the organizations. As a byproduct of this activation, other actively-existing practices were deactivated into a latent state.

After encounters with the data, I realized that activation and deactivation practices occur across five main dimensions:

D. **(De)activation of reactivity vs proactivity practices**. The first dimension emerged from informant interviews wherein the representatives of the case organizations described being reactive to outside events and refining internal actions to react to those external stimuli.

Reactive practice was associated with an exploitative context. The other extreme of this dimension was a practice of being proactive and defining one's own agenda, associated with exploratory context.

E. **(De)activation of efficiency vs creativity practices**. The second dimension emerged as a continuum between an orientation of efficiency (associated with exploitation) and creativity (associated with exploration).

F. **(De)activation practices of a single vision vs multiple agendas at the top of the firm**. The third dimension entailed either a single focused vision and associated practices held by the top-management team (associated with exploitation) or a set of multiple, often conflicting, agendas at the top level (associated with exploration).

G. **(De)activation of efficiency silos vs collaboration practices at the middle levels of the firm**. The fourth dimension demonstrated either efficiently organized, but silo-like, practices among the middle managers (associated with exploitation) or idea-focused collaborative practices at the middle levels of the organization (associated with exploration).

H. **(De)activation of coordination vs autonomous decision-making practices**. The final dimension involved practices that were either coordination-focused - rules-based, systematic and procedure-driven throughout the organization (exploitative practices) or practices that promoted autonomous decision-making and freedom to act (associated with exploratory practices).

I will describe the data structure for the empirical findings in the two tables below. Thereafter I will elaborate on the detailed findings in the subsequent chapter in the present dissertation.

4.2.3.1 *Qualitative data structure at FixTel.*

First-order concepts. Practices described by informants	Second-order themes	Aggregate dimensions
• High degree of autonomy and freedom to deal with ideas • Innovation funnel up to TMT, resource allocation using just EBITDA • Competition between individual TMT members • Self-organized collaboration at middle-management level • External competitors unimportant, focusing on getting own things done	A) Positive reinforcement of active practices	
• Rationalizing developments referring to earlier ambidexterity shifts • Pressure to become ambidextrous - retaining exploration despite upcoming exploitation shift • Efficiency working groups turning partly exploratory	B) Handling of latent practices	1) Inert strategic orientation and triggering practices
• Financial indicators of revenue decline and pressure from the board • Saturation of strategic orientation and understanding internal myopia • Identification of need to observe competitors • Starting to think about sorting out "messy business"	C) Practices of reflection and triggering	
• Introducing system to scan environment and business situation	D) Proactivity vs reactivity	
• Setting 14 strategic topic areas and balanced scorecard to revise strategic priorities and track organizational efficiency • Collective cost cutting • Identifying and harmonizing shared vision • Structuring strategy process with deadlines and responsibilities • More analytical and coherent annual strategy process at the top management level	E) Creativity vs efficiency F) Single vision vs agendas at top	2) Activation of latent and deactivation of active practices

• Making efficiency working groups actively operational • Changed management style with stronger focus on short-term management efficiency goals	G) Efficiency silos vs collaboration at the middle	
• Responding to changed authoritarian management style of the board • Freezing innovative activities and increasing bureaucracy • Introducing tracking mechanisms to analyze cost cutting success	H) Coordination vs autonomy	

4.2.3.2   *Qualitative data structure at MobiTel.*

First-order concepts. Practices described by informants	Second-order themes	Aggregate analytical dimensions
• Structured, bureaucratic strategy making with limited autonomy • Efficiency mantra with diverging understandings about efficiency, which is handled contextually by managers • Thorough competitor scanning and reactive decision-making practice	A) Positive reinforcement of active practices	
• Firm's IT development unit's exploratory moves in exploitative situation • Retaining analytic strategic planning system with 18-month rolling financial forecasting mechanism	B) Handling of latent practices	1) Inert strategic orientation and triggering practices
• Saturation of exploitation strategy displayed by setbacks from excessive efficiency and threats of aggressive price-focused moves of competitors • Reasoning the need to revise strategic position e.g. by getting rid of rigid planning system, becoming more innovative and less reactive, insourcing customer service • Tapping on internal capabilities for success of IT development unit's exploration to become more exploratory	C) Practices of reflection and triggering	
• Redefining reactions to competitors to a more structured and proactive approach • Insourcing customer service function to increase proactivity	D) Proactivity vs reactivity	
• Establishing idea generation and initiative-building mechanisms • Increased investments in network to increase service alternatives • Establishing creative problem-solving and idea generation system	E) Creativity vs efficiency	
• Introducing clearly-defined new business segment and creating the organizational structure to deal with this new business • Bringing new talent to the organization for development functions • Changing retail concept to serve new customer groups	F) Single vision vs agendas at top	2) Activation of latent and deactivation of active practices
• Introducing weekly interaction between marketing, technology and IT development departments on development projects • Increasing the number of development projects managed collectively by in-house developers	G) Efficiency silos vs collaboration at the middle	
• Efficiency mantra replaced with challenge mantra • Introducing bottom-up collaboration with competing firms for network development initiatives	H) Coordination vs autonomy	

4.3   Inert Practices

4.3.1   Positive reinforcement of active practices.

4.3.1.1   *Existing practices at FixTel.*

Prior to starting the shift towards exploitation in 2008, FixTel had been largely in exploratory mode for 4 years. For this purpose, the company had set up strong managerial practices that relied on the exploratory mode, but which were about to be deactivated.

However, in-depth analysis of the practices also demonstrated remnants of the previous exploitative mode from the period of 2001-2003, making their practices partially ambidextrous. For instance, they had a permanent working group consisting of the sales and after-sales service teams, who held, depending on the issues at hand, either biweekly or weekly meetings to discuss quality issues and possibilities for increasing the efficiency of after-sales service. After starting the shift towards exploitation, this working group increased its meeting frequency. It also expanded its scope to support setting up two additional working groups in the Technology division as well as at the Top-Management level.

Lack of Structure for Strategy Making during Exploratory Inertia.

As could be predicted based on the earlier literature on strategy making (Hart, 1992), during exploratory inertia almost all respondents interpreted the predominant strategy practices in terms of a lack of a systematic approach to determining how strategy should be made. We were surprised, as we had expected a much more rational approach to strategy making in a heavily investment-laden dominant-market player with a strong multinational parent company.

> *"If I think about it - the ideas about the priorities of our company probably were somewhere. I suspect that they simply were in the heads of [...] and [... - referring to two members of FixTel management team] and they made us moving towards the priorities." (F11 - a middle manager in Development)*

A number of informants referred pointblank to the strategy practices in use during the exploratory inertia period by using words such as "mess", "disarray", and "lack of order". It was possible to see the disconnect between the people working in Finance and Administration and their colleagues who were working on innovative ideas, when they described their creative colleagues in terms of: "some people were doing nothing", "not adding value", and "are not useful". They also pointed out the lack of sanctions in those cases when somebody who had taken on a responsibility did not deliver appropriately based upon their promises by the agreed deadlines.

Autonomy and Free Idea Generation during Exploratory Inertia

The examples above well describe FixTel' practices during an exploratory period. In terms of Hart's (1992) framework, the company used a rather pure "generative" mode of strategizing, patterned with examples of an *ad hoc* or "no mode" approach to priority setting and planning activity.

Still, when probed during interviews, even those respondents who had responded negatively concerning the general lack of structure and lack of priorities in the company as a whole found that positive aspects of the freedom that working with new business ideas gave to FixTel outweighed the negative aspects related to lack of structure. Most interviewees pointed out that they enjoyed it when the group of developers had been able to bring out "hit of the year" products that customers received well.

The other respondents said that freedom of individual action was something they enjoyed personally, as it gave them both autonomy and an advantage in achieving their objectives inside the organization, such as illustrated by this informant:

> *Opinions from the grass-roots level are mostly taken into account by top-level managers. (F13 - a line manager in Marketing)*

Confirming the Hart (1992) generative framework further, during exploratory inertia the respondents described the existing system through a variety of examples. In principle, the companies that are in an exploratory mode of operation should allow a significant amount of time for a variation of ideas to emerge through free discovery, experimentation and playfulness. The evolutionary approach gives the organizational actors the chance to nurture their ideas to appropriate maturity so that these can move through the subsequent stages of selection and retention. This is necessary to make sure that well-developed ideas will grow into initiatives, and that organizational capabilities will provide the company successful future products and services (as theorized by Bower-Burgelman, Floyd & Wooldridge, 2000). The approach was well-exemplified during the exploratory inertia period at FixTel and most of the informants were positive about the freedom that this mode of strategizing gave to individuals in the organization:

> *I really like it that here, if you believe in your idea, then you can really do it. That was not the case in [the previous company where the informant worked, which was acquired by FixTel] (F15 - a line manager in Service)*

No Attention to Competitors during Exploratory Inertia

Interestingly, when asked about the competition situation during that period, not many of the respondents referred to the competitors. It appeared as if during exploratory inertia competitive pressures did not exist for FixTel as only three of the interviewed informants out of 20 acknowledged any significant consideration about the competitors. Most informants spelled out three or four names of companies who were direct competitors of FixTel, but when we inquired about how the moves of the competitors were tracked, most informants said that they do not pay attention to them:

> *We do not regularly observe their actions. (F11 - A middle manager in Development).*

Some of the informants were downright arrogant. It was further more surprising given the fact that those informants were part of the top Management Team, whose attention quite possibly should have been fixed on the minute details of their competitors' businesses. However, their replies told a different story:

> *We only have two, but they are at the cheap end and don't impact us (F1 - A top Marketing manager).*

> *We purchase data about the market share of our key brands in our country from [an international market research firm], who asks everybody about their revenue data and provide feedback about sales figures across the key brands of the main players on the market. (F7 - a top manager in Sales)*

This lack of attention towards competitors was surprising and we asked them to comment further about this. The answers shed some light on the potential reasons behind this unexpected finding (e.g. using a "helicopter view", focusing on customers rather than competitive pressures, and pointing out the indirect nature of competition):

> *We do not observe our competitors in detail to report on their activity. We only observe global figures – for example, whether the market is rising or falling (F2 - A top Finance manager)*

> *We should not focus on competitors. Our primary focus should be on our existing customers. We have developed a rather elaborate CRM, which helps to identify patterns of customer behavior a few months before they give up on our service. Hence, our key priority in our direct sales is those potential departing clients, and making attractive offers for them before they decide to leave us. (F14 - a representative of the operating core)*

The nonchalant attitude towards competitors may be explained by FixTel having operated as a strong former monopoly, without much competition from strong challengers. Indeed, even recently its primary competitors have been alternative service providers - mobile telecom firms, digital television providers and retail electronics sellers. However, direct competition to its core services – broadband internet and voice connection – had remained relatively weak.

Modes of Cooperation during Exploratory Inertia

During the period of exploratory inertia there were no structured ways of managing ideas, apart from expecting a pre-specified rate of return from all development projects. All projects had to show the top management team that the product or service reached an NPV threshold promising a break-even point within 2-3 years. It was a public secret that the business developers had created their own methods of "packaging" or "window dressing"[25] their new business proposals. They had started to process the ideas in such a manner that would help sell them to the top managers. According to theory, a purely autonomous or generative manner of idea building could result in a cutthroat competition between business ideas that must compete for the scarce resources of money and top Management attention.

In reality, at FixTel it was quite the opposite. Business managers and product managers at the middle-management level had created their own modes of cooperation with each other and with their colleagues from other divisions in order to improve their half-produced ideas and to increase the likelihood of top managers' approval of the projects. One of the informants who was leading the entire development function in the company at the time described the process in the form of the following anecdote, which appropriately summarizes the attempts of all individuals working in product development:

> *Of course, we have a system to measure the quality of business ideas. It is based on the NPV calculations. But the product developers are geeks. We don't know about finances. We know which product is cool, but for the [top management] selection committee we would have to accompany it with a business plan that would make the NPV look promising. We started our*

---

[25] The term "window dressing" was suggested by Claus D. Jacobs.

meetings with [business analysts in the finance department] to help us with that. (F11 - a middle manager in Development)

The example describes a high degree of self-organized coalition building and cooperation between business units, which models the generation of interactive mutual adjustment systems. The top management did not create these systems consciously and neither were their operations prescribed from the top. Hence, this may be categorized as autonomous strategic behavior on the part of middle managers and the operating core, which was in reality significantly shaping the actual strategic context of the firm (Burgelman, 1983).

A number of informants described the "funnel" approach to selection of viable investment projects. Unlike many other companies where the product developers or business managers would be forced to pitch their new business ideas in a highly-competitive manner, the informants described the cooperative nature of handling the funnel for business ideas. When the development projects were discussed all the members of the group try primarily to contribute to improve the suggested projects. Even when the prioritizing selection is made, the projects that will either be rejected or postponed are set aside on the basis of consensus to make sure that less developed, but potentially promising ideas might also be nurtured. One of the informants described the approach in the following manner:

We have introduced a system whereby four times a year we sit down with our development team [referring to a group of 20 middle managers from Product Development, Marketing, IT and Networks] and we make a long list of business ideas which we have cooked up somewhere in our departments. I remember how last time we had about 120 of them articulated. We just did their screening and chose 15-20 that looked the most promising. Those were elaborated further to present to the management team for immediate financing. It is mostly up to product managers to make their ideas look good and work with analysts from the Finance Department, to make sure that also their business projections would look good. (F11 - a middle manager in Development).

Low Top Management Cooperation during Exploratory Inertia

While there was a strong sense of collaboration in the middle, the situation at the top Management level was exactly the opposite. The Management Team members confirmed that during this period they did not discuss either the plans or results between themselves in a way that would be considered sharing mutual understanding among the Management Team members. The relations between the Management Team members seem to have taken place in a primarily competitive scenario. This proves that compared with middle managers and operating core personnel, who so surprisingly demonstrated their cooperative approach to getting their ideas sold to higher ranks, the top Management Team itself was much less uniform and consensus-driven than Hart's (1992) generative mode description might have suggested, as confirmed by all the interviewees. Some of them were pointing to the problem in a neutral manner, simply describing the situation:

I think that our management team still has to learn how to work as a unified team that is after the same thing. There are still lots of discussions at our meetings that focuses on "you vs. me" instead of "us". (F8 - a top Operations manager)

The other members of the Management Team were pointing their fingers at the CEO, complaining counter-intuitively that he was "too soft" or was looking for "too much consensus" instead of deciding on matters in a more decisive manner. However, irrespective of the roles of individual members of the top management team, the dynamics observed during the strategy sessions also pointed to a more competitive atmosphere, which was described by one of the TMT members:

> *I guess that our top management is just "boys playing men". At meetings, they go "uh-uh-uh-uh" [gesturing and imitating a large gorilla]. They stand up and speak about their achievements instead of really discussing what matters. (F20 - a top HR manager)*

It was also confirmed that no unified understanding existed about the priorities of the company among the top Management Team.

It is interesting to observe that even though the strategy-making mode during exploratory inertia largely followed the typology of Hart (1992) in its description of the "generative" mode, there were still some inconsistencies with the model. Hart (1992) specified that the "generative mode of strategizing" operates where the strategy process is "driven by organizational actors' initiative", where the role of the top management is primarily "sponsoring - endorsement and support" and the role of organizational members is "entrepreneurial - by taking risks and experimenting"; the full description of generative mode also presumes various levels of cooperation.

Hart (1992) points out that in generative mode the ideas emerge through evolutionary selection processes, where organizational members act as small entrepreneurial ventures who compete for resources at the top of the organization. However, as noted, in FixTel the organization's members engaged much more frequently in collaboration than competition to sell the ideas to the top Management Team.

In a similar manner, Hart (1992) points out that in generative mode, the top management team encourages experimentation and adjusts its strategy to reflect the promising business ideas that would have emerged from below. Innate to this description of the role of the top Management Team is a high degree of cooperation and mutual adjustment between the top Management Team members, which acts as the selection and retaining mechanism for the new initiatives.

However, contrary to what Hart's model would predict, at FixTel the top Management Team agreed that there was a low degree of cooperation among their members. There was, in fact, a high degree of competition between the TMT members to facilitate the smooth selection of ideas and nurture them into well-functioning businesses. Hence, *survival of the fittest ideas* at FixTel was primarily translated into the *survival of the fittest idea salespeople* appearing before the top Management level.

Resource allocation at management board level

During the exploratory inertia phase, FixTel had introduced and institutionalized a loosely-built annual strategy-making process. One of the informants described the annual meeting in the following manner:

We wanted to organize our planning activity in such a way that at the beginning of the year we identify some long-term goals in [the management board group + 30 business leads], and thereafter assign responsibilities and deadlines. It worked for a while but after some time, the responsibilities started to become vague and some initiatives simply disappeared or become of secondary importance. During the past couple of years, it has been more of a "tick-the-box" exercise rather than a well thought-through activity (F2 - top Finance manager)

The exploratory mode allowed the organizational actors a great degree of flexibility to work on their new business ideas. This was supported through structural means as FixTel had two strong Development units. One Development unit was working under the auspices of its Network business development unit, and the other in the IT business development unit. While there were also some elements of strategy making that were associated with the exploitative mode - i.e. top-down command or a rational-analytical approach (Hart, 1992; Hart & Banbury, 1994), as described above, these were also loosely structured.

Summary of Practices at FixTel during an exploratory inertia phase

To summarize, FixTel had institutionalized three practices that drove their strategy process during the period of exploratory inertia:

- *The practice of resource allocation to large-scale investments and major acquisitions* drove strategic priorities. The management team was obliged to report to the supervisory board on their plans concerning large-scale financial investments and making sure that the financial investments plan and the acquisitions plan would be associated with resource allocation measures that would help to operationalize their long-term growth goals

- *Ensure achievement of the targeted earnings rate*, primarily checked via earnings before interest, taxes and amortization – the EBITDA rate - by the supervisory Board. The Management Team followed up their financial results on a monthly basis and reported to the supervisory Board on a quarterly basis concerning the achievement of its EBITDA goals.

- *The innovation funnel* that selects the most viable new business ideas generated by a group of 20 middle managers from the Product Development, Marketing, IT and Networks units who will thereafter authorize individual product managers to sell the most viable business ideas to the top Management Team for financing decisions.

4.3.1.2   *Existing practices at MobiTel.*

In a similar manner, we analyzed the strategy practices of the exploitative case firm MobiTel. For the sake of full disclosure, I need to inform the reader that our data collection started at a moment when the company representatives had already initiated the first moves in the ambidexterity shift towards exploration. This means that, unlike with FixTel, we did not witness in first-person the full unfolding of a completely exploitative firm – the first analysis is based on the interviewees' interpretation of the recent past (looking back ca 1 year) rather than on the actual present situation.

The Efficiency Mantra

When we started our interviews with the representatives of MobiTel and asked them about their strategic priorities, something that still strikes us as peculiar was the number of times people used the word "efficiency" in both their mutual interactions and interviews with us. They repeated the phrases "efficiency", "cost effectiveness", "value for money", "cutting waste", "getting the best price from our suppliers" with such an intensity that it took us some time to get used to it. After a while, we even decided to code it humorously as the "efficiency mantra", because it appeared that the phrase was repeated as if it were a religious prayer which affirmed the feeling of belonging to the company and valuing those statements as a sacred priority.

We reflected the extensive use of "efficiency" phrases back to them and asked why they had taken their quest for efficiency to such an extreme that it had an impact on their daily behavior and the use of language. Two diverging answers emerged.

- One reinforced that people working at MobiTel had been discussing the issues of efficiency in detail and were attributing great importance to it as the core source of their competitive advantage. A typical answer to this question, echoed by many, observed that: *They exactly understood the causal links between the strong bargaining power that they had with their suppliers and how this allowed them to provide the products and services at a cheaper price than their competitors.*

- Another was more revealing. Three informants (including the CEO) said that discussions about efficiency were not ultimately necessary to reinforce being efficient, but to "*give an image of being efficient in the eyes of its customers and its competitors*". They said that when comparing the actual prices of their services in many instances "*MobiTel is not really the cheapest option among the competitors*". However, as they were spending millions in advertising, which transmitted only the one message to attract and retain more customers, they had no other choice but to also constantly reinforce the marketing message in their everyday interactions.

The Paradox of Efficiency

At this point, we decided to dig deeper. We asked a follow-up question on what constitutes efficiency, to understand how people perceived the building blocks or antecedents of efficient strategic orientation. We tried to understand whether the company was exploitative or whether it simply was a mere marketing ploy. The follow-up answers led to a series of interesting observations. We first identified that while the informants spoke about being efficient, people had divergent opinions about what "efficient" means. In some cases, the responses were even contradictory to each other, for example:

- Some said "*We have to keep down personnel costs by paying lower salaries*", while others said "*We should pay higher salaries than the competitors to make sure that we can attract those people who are smarter, more cost conscious and act more responsibly towards the common good".*

- Some said, *"We should not buy the latest technologies and we need to be careful about new ideas to keep the costs down".* The others said exactly the opposite - *"The latest technologies provide the cheapest servicing and unit costs, which allows keeping the systems running in the most efficient manner to make sure that the old and outdated mechanisms would not be too expensive to maintain".*

- Some were of the opinion that *"centralized procurement systems provided by the parent company of MobiTel helped to reduce the costs of purchases through the stronger bargaining power of the large multinational compared to a single national company".* Others thought that bulk purchases were *"much slower and had frequently provided obsolete solutions".* They believed that the mistakes of these purchasing decisions were more expensive to handle than the benefit of getting the goods cheaper by a couple of percentage points.

While there were contradictory answers to many questions about the business model that MobiTel managers were running, these answers did not necessarily demonstrate that the managers were "whitewashing" being efficient.

Hence, when posing the same questions during strategy discussions to the full group of Top Managers, a consensus appeared. The given answers seemed contradictory at first sight, but they portrayed a view of the context-specificity of the efficiency construct. When the managers were contemplating the identified paradoxes, they said that in certain instances, as in the case of some breakthrough technologies, they had consciously waited for their competitors to test them before deciding on procuring them for themselves. With other technologies in which they had more confidence, they had been the first on the market. They concluded that, as with salaries and central procurement, *"it depends"* on the particular issue.

There did indeed appear to be conscious choices behind taking steps towards efficiency. However, while the company Managers unanimously affirmed their willingness to start working with new ideas, they did not consider efficiency and working on new ideas to be mutually exclusive - still, the question remained about the building blocks of efficiency. One of the Managers summarized their discussion at the strategy session in the following manner:

> *It does not matter what our source of efficiency is. What matters is that in order to retain our strategy as a price leader and our flexibility for being ready to lower the prices at any point, our cost base must be 20% below competitors at all times. We cannot cut in sales nor in marketing, because these will have an immediate effect on our growth. The only things that remain are stronger bargaining with our suppliers, keeping our personnel costs down and delaying our investments (M7 - a top Marketing manager).*

No Frills, No Nonsense Management Style

Associated with efficiency, when we inquired about the efficiency issues in more detail then the managers gave us another dimension by talking about "efficient management". Due to the small company size most decisions had to be taken by a small group of people and the decision-making style was one that encouraged personal responsibility and personal risk taking:

> *I guess that MobiTel is more a company that consists of a group of small entrepreneurs rather than employees. Everybody tries to take initiative, find like-minded colleagues who can help and then struggle for resources from the headquarters (M9 - a top Technology manager).*

Many respondents described the style as "*taking personal responsibility for the well-being of the company*". This was something that was considered carefully during recruitment decisions:

> *When we are looking for new employees then yes, we look for content knowledge and experience, but usually there are two criteria, which are decisive. The most important is that the person is pleasant. We ask ourselves whether I would like to spend my weekend camping with this person at a remote destination. The second criterion is that the applicant would be able to take care of the company as if it was their household. If the candidate makes us feel uncomfortable or if we get a feeling of inability on the applicant's part for taking personal responsibility, then we will decide "no". (M3 - a top HR manager).*

This collegial style was reflected in everyday decision-making. As the number of employees is kept to a minimum, there is no room for slack - the operations are lean and all those who have been recruited to the company are expected to constantly think, decide and act. One of the managers said:

> *I have 20 direct subordinates, but they all have direct sales responsibilities and daily tasks. Hence, when I am struggling with something out of the ordinary that needs to be done, I really cannot act as a Dilbert manager and just delegate it. I need to do it. When I am in doubt about something, then I usually just have a chat with some of my colleagues, then go ahead and sort it out myself. (M4 - a middle manager in Sales).*

Some of the other members of the management team confirmed this. Decision-making style at MobiTel was jointly agreed to be a dynamic and fast-paced conversation, which was punctuated with prompt actions:

> *The conversations in our team are so intensive that we focus on only a small number of topics. If something needs to be discussed, then we conduct a prompt meeting, do it briefly, conclude with a decision and then we simply go ahead and do it. (M9 - a top Technology manager).*

During strategy meetings that we facilitated and attended, we witnessed the same. While the company was financially successful, its everyday management approach was not "corporate style", rather it was reminiscent of a group of friends at a start-up firm, having interesting discussions and taking quick decisions on the issues that they agreed upon.

Problems with the bureaucratic committee-based decision-making process

This no-nonsense management style at the organizational level at MobiTel itself, however, was in stark contrast with the management style imposed on the corporation by their parent company. This required MobiTel management to obtain approval for a number of their decisions.

One of the most radical examples was the requirement to seek approval for all expenses and investments where the contract size exceeded the threshold of 5,000 EUR. This requirement rendered the MobiTel branch effectively into the position of a tiny department within a large corporation. This requirement applied to all new product development ideas, service ideas, contracts signed with larger suppliers, investment decisions and major recruitment decisions for managerial positions.

All those decisions about the expenses above 5,000 EUR had to be discussed first at the national level, which was usually a rapid process, managed within a day. After national approval, a formalized request had to be submitted to an international committee, which reviewed the proposals once a month and decided whether to accept or reject them. The scope and composition of the committees varied depending on the topic. Some had 4-5 members, but the largest consisted of a dozen representatives.

For example, in the Product Development area the group consisted of 12 people. The group included all regional product managers and a couple of top Managers from the parent company. The group met through virtual channels once a month and reviewed all product development proposals submitted during the month.

This meant that in deciding about the Network investment ideas to be implemented in Estonia, the Network managers of neighboring countries also participated in the decision-making and vice versa - Estonian MobiTel Technology managers had the role of reviewing the investment proposals of their neighbors. The assessment of MobiTel Managers about these groups were:

> Sometimes we also get interesting insights from the other members of the committee, but if I would need a different opinion then I could simply pick up my phone and call one of them. Now we just wait for weeks and then waste my entire afternoon and the phone conference discussing a bunch of ideas from the other countries that are completely irrelevant to me just to get approval to buy a new replacement server that we badly need (M8 - a top manager in IT).

> They are just a waste of time. (M2 - a top Development manager).

In other instances, the established idea might morph in those group discussions into something that does not resolve the issues immediately, taking up a lot of time and ending up as something completely different, which no longer has any value:

> For example, we need a faster solution to sell the post-paid services. We do our preliminary design, establish our investment proposal, and put it forward to the committee, where somebody says: "What a good idea! We heard that Croatia and Norway also need it! Let's do a joint project!" Instead of a quick solution for our sales department we will waste the next months just discussing the needs of others, we will complete the system in 2 years instead of 6 months and by that time the outcome has become useless for us here (M8 - a top manager in IT).

The only exceptions to the 5,000-EUR rule were the decisions taken in the field of Marketing. Countries were considered too different in terms of what marketing campaigns to use. Only major campaigns were discussed with the parent company. In general, the Marketing managers of MobiTel had relative freedom in deciding on the use of various approaches to take. Informants agreed unanimously that the 5,000-EUR ceiling had led to rigidity in competing with other firms:

Our ideas do not move fast enough in the list of priorities of our owners. For example, SeriousMobile could create a solution for watching TV over the mobile connection. If we would like to do the same we would need some resources, but in our case, we cannot convince our owners and the committees. As Estonia is the most innovative in the region then our local competitors are constantly running ahead of us because we are unable to persuade the committees of the need for those investments (M4 - a middle manager in Sales).

Other interviewees accepted the rigidity:

It is certainly annoying, but still a manageable obligation. The only downside is that sometimes we might be in a hurry, but paperwork, together with waiting for the next meeting, consume our time. So far so good. We have managed to work around these procedures, which are quite different from the approach that we take here among ourselves (M9 - a top Technology manager)

Some also suggested coping mechanisms to handle the situation pragmatically and reduce bureaucracy by bending the rules and using the marketing label as a loophole:

If we are in a hurry, then we have sometimes sliced our expenses up to smaller segments to make sure that they are below the 5,000-EUR threshold. In other cases, we have relabeled certain things as "marketing related", because this field is not subject to such a high level of scrutiny by the parent company (M2 - a top Development manager).

Competitor Scanning

Efficient management style was reflected in a very thorough approach to competitor scanning activities, which were carried out with the purpose of prompt reaction. Unlike at FixTel, MobiTel had very elaborate systems for tracking the activities of its competitors. MobiTel was an aggressive player and had likewise communicated to its customers that they are the cheapest provider in all product segments. To deliver upon this promise it had to be able to respond very rapidly to any pricing challenges that the other two mobile firms brought to the market. As a result, they had created capabilities for both scanning the market and deciding quickly upon client marketing and sales offers.

For market scanning, MobiTel employed two full time people whose job it was to review the marketing offers of the competitors and to organize regular blind purchases of the competitors' products and services. Additionally, 20 business Sales Managers also gathered the offers of the competitors indirectly. They brought the news to the attention of the Sales, Marketing and Service Director, who then had the opportunity to review the situation and make immediate decisions.

It was peculiar to observe that in some relatively minor cases even the CEO of the firm was actively engaged in discussions about reacting to certain moves of the competitors. We witnessed a situation when the Marketing Director was deciding about the placement of certain advertisements that were supposed to be displayed as counter-responses to some of the competitors' billboards. The entire top Management Team was engaged in the debate: what kind of messages should they formulate on particular billboards? They discussed amongst themselves how best to place them next to competitors' advertisements to generate, for example, a comic effect.

In the case of minor pricing questions, the power for bargaining was delegated to line managers of the Sales Department, who were authorized to make offers to larger clients up to certain thresholds. Some more substantial issues related to the competitors' offerings were discussed at weekly sales meetings. In the case of major pricing updates from the competitors, they would bring it to the attention of top Management, and their global prices would be reviewed within a month. Part of the reason why major pricing upgrades took a bit longer was related to the billing system, which made it difficult to upgrade the prices except at monthly cutoff points. However, the pricing upgrades of all the competitors had actually been stalled in the wake of business downturn:

I guess we have all realized now that we are cutting off the branch that we are sitting on. Immediately after the introduction of number-transfer legislation [in 2005] all three competitors got into an active price war, and during the last year nobody has reduced their prices. (M4 - a middle manager in Sales).

The decision style was also much faster for larger product and service updates. During the interviews at FixTel, the Managers said that the absolute minimum time for introducing new substantial products would be 9 months, but more realistically, it would be 1.5-2 years. MobiTel Managers mentioned that product and service updates would usually take approximately 6 months of preparation. The Managers pointed out that this long interval was a problem:

We are slow and inflexible in our development processes. Some problems are related to the limited number of people we are recruiting, but a great deal of it is related to the long lead-times for decisions from our committees (M2 - a top Development manager).

The foregoing response illustrates a problematic aspect of the exploitative strategic orientation, which was pointed out by all the respondents from MobiTel Management.

Strategy making during exploitative inertia.
The strategy making process at MobiTel was highly structured, rules-laden and analytical. Hence, it was closely associated with "rational" mode as suggested by Hart (1992). The following description is provided primarily by (M1 - a top manager in Operations):

A number of important topics for our strategy process are delivered by our headquarters. They go through their annual process of defining the business at the beginning of the year and they deliver to us the core statements in February, explaining what business we are in and why we are doing this. They also deliver some core priorities, which act as a framework for our national strategy for the upcoming 3 years. Our work as the management team of MobiTel Estonia is to translate this framework via our own needs and possibilities into a strategy that would be implementable.

There are certain aspects in strategy making that are outside of our scope. These are the decisions that are completely centralized at this point, for example:

- *what the core underlying technology that we are using is,*
- *who the primary large suppliers for the entire group of enterprises are,*
- *the use of centralized IT systems (e.g. billing, financial reporting).*

However, apart from the core priorities and given centralized services, the other discussions and decisions about our strategy are open for our own interpretation.

Twice a year we organize our strategy meeting where we take the core priorities delivered by the headquarters, we look at the market situation in Estonia and set forth our plans for the upcoming two years. These plans are subsequently turned into individual goals and actions. Every person will formulate six personal priorities that will be followed on a monthly basis and discussed at personnel review meetings twice a year.

If the personal goals are not going to be fully met then there will be a discussion about the reasons, but it would also mean that the person would not get his or her bonus. Usually the maximum semiannual bonus would add between 10-20% extra to this person's salary for the respective month. As we are part of a Swedish multinational then it means that our salary system is egalitarian and bonuses are basically a sign of compliments rather than a source of a major extra earning.

The formal strategy process is appended with a separate process for large investments:

Four times a year we have a meeting with the MobiTel consortium top Managers, which take place in February, May, August and December. At those meetings, we present our summary investment plans. We present our ideas about different investment projects, which vary in scope and scale. For example - when we plan to set up an MBT in the center of Tallinn, and it earns back the investment within a month, nobody asks questions about it. However, we had conversations about investing in 3G technology for more than a year, because it is likely that the full investment will only become profitable after a decade. (M9 - a top Technology manager).

The strategy review combines a regular review of financial results, where the entire Management Team discusses the outcomes of the past month's work, analyzes any shortcomings and sets new plans for the upcoming period:

Once a month we print out the financial results, our CFO will run a number of different queries relating to his budget in his huge excel sheet, and review what needs to be done next to please our owners (M1 - a top manager in Operations).

4.3.2 Handling of latent practices.

In both case organizations, informants described practices that were completely or partially inactive. In some instances, specific departments of the organization handled those practices primarily without enjoying the full support of the company Management Team.

4.3.2.1 *Latent practices at FixTel.*

Some interviewees took a longer-term view of the past and described the practices based on how the situation had changed during the years. As FixTel had gone through a number of cycles between exploration and exploitation, it was also possible to reflect upon the previous periods when the company had a more structured approach towards its priorities, to strategy work, to new product development and the management of its existing businesses.

Before [i.e. 3-4 years earlier, during the exploitation period] we had a better system [for screening the most profitable initiatives], but at that time we did not have much content. The business ideas were then copied from some competitors from western countries. All that mattered was whether they met the NPV requirements and were profitable. Now it is exactly the opposite. We have become a lot smarter - we have many original ideas, we know what to do, but we have completely forgotten how to get them properly executed! Some guys at the Development Department make up fictional NPV figures that look reliable and nobody challenges them. (F14 - A representative of the operating core)

What this interviewee further points out refers to "islands of exploitation" within an otherwise exploratory organization. This essentially refers to partially ambidextrous properties of the case organization that can be later activated across the organization.

A few years ago, one top manager thought that it would be a good idea to start introducing metrics based on the Balanced Scorecard methodology. It was when BSC was a hot topic, but they agreed upon metrics only for our sales team. The others were left out of this initiative. (F14 - a representative of operating core)

Several people pointed out that in order to handle the unstructured patterns of organization they had to create their own personal structured approach. This is well-exemplified by the following story from one of the informants at the top Management level, who had joined the company at about the same time that the company started its last shift toward exploration:

It was mostly "management by hope" - most people whose help I needed were situated in random structural units, some people were to be outsourced, one was located in the Network department, another in the Service department. It was all a result of the decisions that were made [during the previous exploitative period] when we decided to sack our entire IT department. Most of my work was about negotiating and convincing other people to join my efforts to do something that would be worth doing. (F6 – top IT manager)

This personal story exemplified coping mechanisms in an unstructured environment. However, its retrospective link to the previous period was also highly significant from the point of view of managing the following upcoming shift towards exploitation, because it pointed out the lesson that the management team had learned during the previous shift. The problems of having to look around for talent to implement exploratory initiatives, although the existing talent had been outsourced by FixTel just a couple of years earlier, was mentioned by several top Managers.

The previous shift from exploration to exploitation was an all-encompassing cost cutting, which had reduced the headcount over the period from 2000 to 2003 by 46% (from 2,535 employees in 2000 to 1,354 employees in 2003).

A number of top Managers pointed to this decision retrospectively as a mistake, which was made following the burst of the dot-com bubble. The negative perception about retaining the IT function in-house coincided with two loss-making months in 2001, which had apparently killed their illusions of the potential of IT solutions as a moneymaker. As a result, cost cutting led at the first stage to outsourcing Network management and maintenance functions in 2001 - then to full outsourcing of IT function in 2002. However, the Managers also confirmed that they had not realized the core business nature of IT and Network management functions. They realized only in retrospect that those functions should have been kept inside FixTel, because it would have allowed the development of core services in-house by people who would have been well familiar with its all core systems. The informants openly labelled them as "lessons learned for the future".

4.3.2.2 Latent practices at MobiTel.

In a similar manner - MobiTel also had its examples of latent practices. In their case, an island of exploration existed within an otherwise exploitative organization. It was the IT development department, consisting of eight people. The head of the IT department (informant M8)[26] elaborated further in a detailed historic account on this subject, summarized below.

In the early phase of MobiTel in 2001, when it was still an independent company, a group of enthusiasts working in the IT department of MobiTel programmed their own billing system, which was based on the architecture of Cerillion. The system was built on a modular basis partially using freeware software, which allowed the system to be set up within a short timeframe and with minimal resources.

When the system was created, it was considered a landmark and it satisfied the needs of MobiTel in Estonia adequately. However, a year later an MNC bought MobiTel Estonia and started expanding. At that moment, the parent company realized the strength of the system built in Estonia as well. They introduced it in neighboring markets where the MobiTel Estonia IT department was responsible for localization.

A few years later, the MobiTel Corporation had already expanded into 28 countries across Europe and they looked at the possibilities for introducing a new unified billing system. There were two alternatives to consider - one produced in Sweden, and another in Estonia, but neither measured up. After a series of deliberations in 2005, the top IT managers from the company headquarters said that they would build a completely new fully centralized billing system for the entire corporation. They gave the IT department employees in Estonia an early warning saying that they would still be needed for another year to keep the present systems up, but when the group-wide billing system would be finalized, they should find another job.

Since MobiTel had just acquired another mobile firm in Croatia, it needed a prompt solution. Hence, the Estonian IT Department developers were sent to Zagreb to localize a temporary solution for a year, but they completed the most successful project ever. The localization won several local and international awards. The Estonian MobiTel IT team itself felt like a phoenix risen from the ashes.

At the same time, the investments in a centralized billing system were humongous, but the preparations did not go according to plans and MobiTel Headquarters decided to abandon their project. Concurrently, the MobiTel Corporation had realized that their recent acquisitions in 28 markets had become unsuccessful and they started selling off their businesses one by one. During 2007-08 they divested from all major European markets and focused primarily on Northern and Eastern Europe. As a result, within 2 years they reduced the number of their home markets from 28 countries to merely 11.

Based on MobiTel Estonia's billing system success story, which coincided with MobiTel Corporation's failure, the group IT bosses concluded that the billing system built in Estonia was now "a strategic platform for MobiTel", which would be introduced in all countries.

---

[26] The Head of the Department himself had joined MobiTel just four months prior to this interview, which means that this information primarily relies on tertiary data. To confirm its reliability, we also discussed the same case with another top Manager (M9 - top Technology manager) who confirmed the accuracy of the account.

However, this strategic decision was not followed up with resourcing. And so the IT team in Tallinn, which was previously servicing MobiTel branches in only four countries, had just received orders to start working on development projects for the entire corporation. This is the wider cultural issue - with a company-wide freeze on recruitment, whenever new duties are assigned, the ones already working are expected to simply work harder.

The result led to a situation where the local IT development team started dealing with interesting development projects for the other national branches. (M8 - a top Manager in IT).

There are several lessons that MobiTel Managers learned from this complex narrative of dealing with corporate-level decision-making, which all have provided confirmation of the importance of latent practices and their potential to serve as triggers to activate subsequent exploratory practices:

- First - the result of this project reinforced the fact that there was a substantial exploratory capability in-house, which was capable of producing award-winning development projects and implementing them in an international setting. Hence, MobiTel Estonia Managers understood the existing potential for additional tasks.

- Second, "doing your own thing" led to substantial feelings of empowerment. The Management Team of MobiTel Estonia realized that they might now have a much stronger voice in the entire MobiTel Corporation. The team had understood that although there had been successful in-house initiatives that the parent company was killing with their authority and much larger resources to invest in alternative solutions, local solutions might nevertheless successfully outlive the ones who criticize them.

- Third, it was obvious that there was a difficult balance between managing the needs of a single country and handling the requirements for the entire group. There were periods in company history where the local companies had autonomy for deciding what to do and how, in terms of development. At other times, there had been stages in which all decision-making systems were completely centralized.

- Fourth, in dealing with the resourcing issues of the newly-tasked IT department, they saw that it would be necessary to negotiate for more resources for development and maintenance activities to satisfy MobiTel Estonia needs.

4.3.3   Looking for triggers to revise existing practices.

In the following data category, the informants described different triggering events or insights that informed them about the saturation of their present strategic orientation. They also described different signs that suggested an upcoming shift in the orientation. In each of the two case organizations, the triggering practices were slightly different. However, in both cases the underlying reasons were either directly or indirectly associated with the pressure on the bottom line. In both instances, the company management felt the need to initiate the shift in cyclical ambidexterity because of the falling profitability of their firm.

4.3.3.1 Triggering practices at FixTel.

The interviewees pointed out that during that phase the managers started feeling an upcoming threat and that this resulted in a revised approach to the identification of their business domain as well as their understanding of how they need to rationalize their work on future planning.

Saturation of strategic orientation as a trigger of shift in strategic orientation

We first asked the respondents to identify when they first sensed that the situation was about to change. We asked two related questions: "Can you remember an exact moment that triggered the change for the company?" and "What triggered change for you personally?" The respondents were generally ambiguous in their answers. Most middle-level managers and operating core representatives referred to the internal memos that were sent around by Management about new practices. Hence they referred to external triggers in describing various stimuli that they had responded to.

However, there were also examples that demonstrated the ability of the informants themselves to identify triggering practices. One of the vivid examples given clearly referred to what might be called the "saturation of the present strategic orientation" - reasoning that it had become "as good as it gets". This indicated a situation where the people observing the market were able to deduce that the existing strategic orientation was no longer viable, from comparison with the markets in neighboring countries:

> *We came out with [a new and expensive high-end product] at the peak of the economic boom [during exploratory inertia] and in a matter of three days, our entire stock was sold out. Estonia is a country where the GDP per capita is less than a third of Finland's and [a similar product] sold in Helsinki received just a lukewarm reception during the same period. I remember thinking about this and telling my colleagues that this is insane. It is 'as good as it gets' and from now on we should brace ourselves for the worst (F6 - top Manager in IT).*

Alternatively, respondents referred to difficulties that they were sensing in the new market segments, even as the old segments where FixTel had monopolistic power were drying up. In a similar manner, the informants used analytic reasoning to suggest that the present strategic orientation and the practice of ignoring the competitive situation, prevalent throughout the period of exploratory inertia, was no longer viable. While people working in the finance area pointed this out, others also mentioned it as it had been a topic for discussion at the top management level for a while:

> *We had already observed for some time that the market for fixed calls had been shrinking. Now we had to come up with new hits, which were in competitive business areas like cable TV and video rental services, where there were already substantial competitors in place and we were also fighting with media piracy. We realized that it was not so simple any more to simply push something to the market and then start milking the opportunity with yet another aggressive marketing campaign. We had to revise our approach. (F1 - top Manager in Marketing)*

It was interesting that while just less than a year before, these same informants were arrogant about the competition, they had now revised their opinions and started to pay closer attention.

Feeling of internal weaknesses as a trigger to shift.

While the above-mentioned triggers were externally-driven, there were also issues pointed out by informants inside the organization that were mentioned as triggers. One respondent referred to weaknesses inside the organization, which also could have been categorized as a saturation of the existing strategic orientation - an orientation that had been considered by the informants to be ineffective given the market situation. The respondents had uniformly agreed that the company had paid strong attention to its customers, and by implementing numerous customer-focused initiatives it had ensured itself constantly higher customer satisfaction with both its products as well as with its service. Still, some informants pointed out the internally-driven myopic focus as a potentially threatening factor:

> We are a technology-oriented firm. Engineers playing with cool toys. While we have slogans about being customer-focused, we did not know much about customer needs. Our product development people thought primarily about the toys we wanted to see in our own houses. Just an example - [referring to a recently sold ADSL Modem] required the client to read a 20-page manual or have our help desk guide the clients for 5 minutes on installation. At the same time, Apple sells gadgets that only have a single button and come without a manual. (F4 - top Manager in Service)

Given the history of FixTel, which was a company run by communications engineers, part of the history was still haunting the firm. Even though the company had put lots of energy into bringing the customers to the core's focus, there were still problematic issues on how to revise the mindset of many people.

Moves of competitors as triggers. While in the phase of exploratory inertia, respondents rarely ever mentioned external issues. During the triggering phase people started to talk more about the upcoming external threats, which included both technological as well as market-related threats. One of the topics, raised several times, was the need to start paying attention to the moves of the competitors. It is interesting that while during the exploratory inertia period the informants either ignored the competition or were not attributing due importance to it, during the triggering and reasoning phase the significance of the competitors became more important. One of the informants elaborated on this:

> It has become easier to compete with us. You no longer need a cable to use internet like a couple of years ago. The customers needed a significant investment and to go through quite a hassle to switch the internet provider as building new connection lines is expensive. However, now that a relatively high-speed internet connection can be provided via mobile solutions, we cannot be so comfortable any more (F5 - a top Manager in Technology).

In addition to the technology push, price was also a contributing factor to why the competition had to be observed more carefully. FixTel had positioned itself as a high-quality service provider, whose price was either the highest or relatively high. They were able to create their position due to their first-mover advantage and network effect in a high-entry-cost market. To retain this position, they had focused on constant product and service development in order to be steps ahead of the competition. However, given that the technology in this area had become good enough for customers, the additional pioneering innovation no longer provided the justification for a higher price. While the competitors started entering the market with low-cost alternatives, and in the light of the higher price sensitivity of the customers in a contracting economy, FixTel was also for this reason forced to pay attention to the moves of the competitors:

> *Our wakeup call was that people were no longer willing to pay such a high price for our products and our growth rate slowed down. Our mobile competitors started offering internet service for a cheaper price. Their quality was not so good, but it was good enough for many clients. Also [a local energy company] had started competing with us and introduced cheap low-speed over-the air internet solution that started eating up our market share. (F9 - A middle manager in Operations)*

All these arguments contributed to contemplation on why the company might have started its shift toward exploitation.

Stronger pressure from the Supervisory Board as a trigger of shift.
During the phase of exploratory inertia, the Supervisory Board of FixTel had been largely hands-off. The informants said that the company Supervisory Board had started to apply stronger pressure on the Management Team, which indicated the need to push the company's strategic direction onto a different course. Some respondents simply pointed out the push of the Board as a source of a potential problem for the company, thereby identifying this as an outside trigger:

> *Our owners were very satisfied with FixTel in the past because we have been able to show results. Now world trends and the Estonian economic environment are both getting tougher. However, the Board seems to continue to think that we must be able to show the same profitability nevertheless. (F10 - a top Technology Manager)*

> *During the past few years, we have always had a 'hit of the year'. When the economic downturn started affecting us, and it was obvious that we would not be able to come up with something new, then the Board required us to cut costs. (F2 - a top Finance Manager).*

> *The board demands that the EBITDA rate should be at a minimum rate of 30%. If our revenues fall, then we would have to cut costs immediately. (F8 - a top Operations Manager)*

4.3.3.2 Triggering practices at MobiTel.

Saturation of exploitation strategic orientation.
Triggering practices at MobiTel were associated with the early-warning signs, which demonstrated that efficiency goals had started stretching people of the organization. The years 2004-05 were noted as the period when MobiTel was had become overly efficient. During those two years, as many functions were outsourced as possible, all the managers were forced to identify the opportunities to cut down on each employee's position to a maximum extent:

> *If there was even a faint possibility that one person could do the work of two - we had to get rid of the second person. We then increased the salary for the one remaining 1.5 times and asked him or her to work harder and smarter. The situation was very difficult in terms of managing risks - if somebody was sick or had to be away then some work simply stopped. (M12 - a top Manager in Operations)*

One of the informants provided an interesting anecdote about how the company had become over-the-top in its efficiency focus, and which acted as a reminder that perhaps the exploitation strategy in its extreme was inappropriate. The case that he described identified well how achievement of one objective to an extreme might ultimately turn out funny:

> *It was a standard practice that we had to get at least a 20% discount on every agreement. We negotiated with a number of advertisers for all-in-one Christmas Card service to our business and VIP customers. We only realized two weeks before Christmas that due to our tough negotiation stance the company had put its priorities elsewhere and was planning to postpone delivering our Christmas cards until just shortly before Easter. We then decided to instead start talking about "smart efficiency" - that we have to be efficient, but not cheap (M12 - a top Operations manager)*

Saturation of the exploitation orientation had manifested itself also in other ways. Several informants pointed out that the minimal investments of MobiTel during 2003-05 had resulted in short-term good financial results, but had an adverse impact on their ability to provide good coverage of their network, which led to customer dissatisfaction.

> *During that period, we had conflicting goals between the owners and the Management Team. While the Swedes were looking for the possibility of investing the bare minimum, we convinced them that if we continue according to the same strategy we would no longer be able to attract new customers. Fortunately, they bought our arguments and for the past 2 years, we have been able to invest reasonably well in improvements to network quality. Impartial measurements now demonstrate that we are on a par with SeriousMobile and LoveMobile (M4 - a middle manager in Sales).*

From 2006, MobiTel started recruitment again and started looking at the possibilities for insourcing the functions that were previously outsourced.

Threat of aggressive low-price counter moves of competitors.
One of the major triggers of exploratory action was an attack by two competitors of MobiTel. The competitors released aggressive marketing campaigns with cheaper prepaid phone cards. SeriousMobile released their prepaid card called Cheap Deal with a pricing offer that was not at the same price level as the MobiTel offering, but still significantly cheaper than its comparable subscription-based packages. LoveMobile released shortly thereafter a hostile marketing campaign on cutting costs and produced a new prepaid card branded "MobyTel", so that it sounded very similar to the trademark of MobiTel and was priced the same. Both competitors disconnected the branding of their prepaid cards from their company brands and initiated marketing and PR campaigns where they conveyed the following message:

> *They claimed, "SeriousMobile and LoveMobile are high-quality service providers, but MobiTel, MobyTel and Cheap Deal are cheap and lower-quality service providers." It was a wicked, but very effective campaign. In a way, they downgraded their own prepaid products, but by doing this, they strengthened the differentiation and image of their core services. What was worse was that they also conveyed the message to price-sensitive customers that there are alternatives out there. As they had now provided the alternatives, they took a large piece of the cake that was until that time only ours (M2 - a top Development Manager).*

The strong PR campaign, which pointed out the problems with network quality and reminded them of the early days when MobiTel only had a handful of transmission stations erected, had an adverse effect on MobiTel's image. MobiTel company Managers were able to deal with price competition, but were taken by surprise by the aggressive PR campaigns, which resulted in a loss of image for them and a number of their customers switched to other providers:

> We still have to deal with the jokes about "providing a shuttle bus service to an area where you can use MobiTel phone" (M1 - a top Manager in Operations).

Due to inadequate reaction by MobiTel managers, the PR damage of this campaign was significant and a customer survey pointed out a few months later that a substantial number of customers were identifying MobiTel as a mobile telephone provider with "poor network quality".

Consequently, the managers of MobiTel realized that while both ethically and legally the campaigns of their competitors were questionable, their unique low-cost position was threatened if both competitors start attacking them simultaneously. This triggered numerous discussions about the adequacy of the low-cost strategy and contemplation of possible alternative strategies for MobiTel, which would also convey the messages that the network quality was constantly improving and so was their customer service.

4.4 Activation of Latent and Deactivation of Active Practices

In the following subchapter, I will point out the findings in the data that demonstrate activation and deactivation of various practices during cyclical ambidexterity. Based on data analysis, I have described activation and deactivation practices across five dimensions:

A. Activation and deactivation of reactivity vs proactivity practices.
B. Activation and deactivation of efficiency vs creativity practices.
C. Activation and deactivation practices of single vision vs multiple agendas at the top of the firm.
D. Activation and deactivation of efficiency silos vs collaboration practices at the mid-level of the firm.
E. Activation and deactivation of coordination-focused vs autonomous practices.

4.4.1 Practices across reactivity and proactivity dimension.

4.4.1.1 Activation practices of reactivity at FixTel.

Introducing the system to scan the environment and competitors.
The only practice associated with greater reactivity to outside stimuli activated at FixTel was the system for more appropriate scanning of the external environment, in particular the competitors. As noted in the previous stages by several informants, FixTel had not been paying enough attention to the activities of competitors during the exploratory inertia phase. However, in the changed circumstances another dimension was worth regular review:

> *In the new situation, we had to start thinking about how to manage in a competitive environment. How to constantly count money, how to constantly observe competitors' positions, how to be competitive as a flexible service provider. (F3 - a top Manager in the regulatory area)*

One of the departments that was responsible for dealing with interactions with the state regulatory body also had the responsibility of interacting with potential cooperation partners and competitors in order to handle the agreements for the use of the company's optical network to provide other services. While their role to date had primarily been administrative and legal cooperation, the management of FixTel allocated to them the responsibility of collecting the data related to competitors' moves and reporting on this issue of importance to company management and other departments. The aim of this move was to become quicker and more efficient in handling the decisions-making practices by the top Management of the firm.

4.4.1.2   Activation practices of proactivity at MobiTel

Revised reasoning on speedy reaction to competitors.
It was interesting to observe that the MobiTel Management Team activated the opposite practices. As a background: the participants of strategy discussions were very critical about their reactive approach to the actions of competitors and pointed out how it made it more difficult for them to prioritize:

> *It bothers me that we are sometimes almost twitching to act. When SeriousMobile does something on Monday then we have to respond by Wednesday. I don't know if this is the best approach - we might earn some extra money with the fast response, but I am sure that we are also losing a lot because of our overly reactive approach. Perhaps we should be focusing more on our own way of doing certain things. (M4 - a middle manager in Sales).*

Many informants pointed out during the interviews that they would like to activate practices that would help to make the company work in a proactive and systematic manner:

> *Most of the changes to our processes have been made because of some sort of a problem. So far, we have not had anybody to deal with our business processes on a systematic basis. People have defined the processes within their departments, but there is nobody cross-departmental, who would have led discussions on a systematic review of all the processes. Part of the reasons is that our business is becoming more complex and it has become more difficult to define the processes. On the other hand, the market is becoming more saturated, which means that we should try to utilize all the possibilities for serving our clients better than before. For that reason, better understanding of the big picture would be essential. (M1 - a top Manager of Operations).*

The ideas pointed out in the interviews were further elaborated in strategy meetings. During strategy discussions, MobiTel Managers subsequently specified a set of simple guiding principles, which helped them determine what types of moves would deserve an immediate reaction. They also specified the extent of an adequate response.

At the same time, they realized that it might be a good idea to agree upon smarter ways to react, referring back to the problem that they had had when competitors started attacking them in the prepaid segment. They realized that until that time they had primarily relied on traditional marketing tools, while some things could be resolved with public relations tools, whereby instead of strategic reactions, the company management would provide public comments through PR means, which would not bring about major changes across the organization.

> *If we were to use the PR tools better, then we could replace the war of businesses with a war of words. While the differences in product and service quality are just minor, the main deciding factor is reputation. As the public image is very crucial in our business, it would make a big difference in the eyes of the customer (M7 - a top Marketing Manager).*

Insourcing the customer-support function for business clients.
Another important issue that was pointed out by a number of respondents during analysis was related to the outsourcing of the customer support function. While the Managers realized that in the early 2000s it was "fashionable" to outsource non-core functions to cut costs and to try to focus instead on "real" management, by 2008 this was re-labeled as a past mistake.

The Management of MobiTel learned the hard way – and they finally acknowledged that the most promising customer segment was the small business client, who tended to be loyal and stable customers, but who needed somewhat more customized solutions than their one-size-fits-all outsourced client service approach allowed.

> *In one instance, we had a very patient business customer. We had managed to convince the representative of their firm about our prices and they decided to transfer the phone subscriptions of their entire firm - around 600 numbers to us. However, when they started communicating with our call center about the transfer - their application was rejected four times because of various problems that our outsourced client representative was unable to solve. The customer was my friend who finally called me and I had to interfere myself to get things done. If it had not happened, we most probably would have lost the client. (M4 - a middle manager in Sales)*

This story was shared during the next strategy discussions among the management and it led to a number of action points, among which the most important was the subsequent insourcing of the customer support function:

> *We discussed this amongst ourselves for a long time. While it does not matter to small household customers who answers their questions about their latest phone bill, we cannot use the same approach with our larger business customers. There are two problems. First, our outsourced partner can never be as flexible as our customers would need. Second, we look unreliable in the eyes of our customers when they realize that the service to them is not provided in-house. (M4 - a middle manager in Sales).*

Less firefighting and a more proactive approach.
The first reply that all Managers gave was related to reducing the reactive management style and improving the practice of delegating their functions, which provided some further time for planning and reflections. This was something that they all pointed to as the most substantial change compared to the previous phase:

It might be interesting that despite all the dramatic changes that were carried out during those two years, the most dramatic change is that it has become more peaceful. Two years ago we were only firefighting, but now we've got much more time for discussing amongst ourselves and for thinking ahead. In part it is because we have agreed upon our priorities much better (M9 - a top Technology manager).

This approach was indirectly related to a number of other initiatives implemented at MobiTel. For example, one of the informants described their approach to planning their network. Partially this plan was facilitated by the increase in the number of people who worked in the Network Development department and hence they had much more time to proactively plan for the next stages of their network development:

Our proactive approach has certainly improved. For example - whenever some large construction projects are begun, they have an impact on the mobile network quality of the neighborhood. Earlier we found out about the "connection holes" when many of our customers called us and said that their connection dropped out at the place where a new skyscraper was built. Now, whenever somebody starts building a new business center or expands an airport, one of our technicians will get in touch with them, carry out the necessary measurements, and make the appropriate adjustments to our network. (M1 - a top Manager in Operations).

4.4.2   Practices across the efficiency and creativity dimension.

4.4.2.1   Activation practices of efficiency at FixTel.

Efficiency practices activated due to pressure from the Board.
While efficiency practices were triggered partially by internal forces, the strongest reason to activate them was the pressure from the company Supervisory Board. The owners of the company managed FixTel via what they considered the most important financial ratio: the EBITDA ratio to revenues. The requirement of the supervisory board was to keep this indicator above 30% at all times. In 2008, the ratio dropped to 28.3%. The Board considered this a sign that company profitability might be dropping. The FixTel Management Team had to deliver a concrete action plan to revise their approach to a changing market situation that was no longer favorable.

Respondents perceived the pressure from the Board in different ways. One of the informants tried to explain that the top-down pressure was debatable. In parts of the organization, the pressure was not experienced as a real trigger of change:

The situation was not so bad. Yes - the business was shrinking, but we were not about to start having losses. Why do we have to achieve 30% EBITDA? Our bosses could have easily explained to the Board that we might also have continued with our development business and survived just a few years with slightly smaller margins - and that's all (F11 - a middle manager in Development).

It is interesting that even informants whose statements (responding to the previous question on personal coping) reflected an openly negative personal view concerning the pressure applied by the Supervisory Board, became more pragmatic over time and focused on achieving these results:

Of course, we discussed the change events. If our Board gives us a profitability goal and the market is falling then the only way of making sure what do we need to do is to discuss where we should cut and how much (F1 - a top Manager of Marketing).

Simplifying strategy content - focusing on a few core priority areas.

Hence, the representatives of the top Management referred to the push by the Supervisory Board as an opportunity to rethink their present business model and come up with an alternative course of action:

The company strategy was no longer simply identifying new cool ideas to try out and market - we had to start coming up with ideas on how to survive. While we were nowhere near bankruptcy, the push from the Board was so strong that we were forced to start identifying new solutions on how to make our living in new ways. (F1 - a top Manager in Marketing)

The result of this thought process forced the top Management Team to revise their thinking and start focusing at the top on a single vision instead of multiple conflicting agendas. During the first year that the newly-structured annual strategy was carried out, in 2009, the company's top Management Team identified the priorities for the 3 following years. This included indicators, objectives and functional action plans. The priorities were divided into four core areas based on the perspectives of the Balanced Scorecard methodology, which were further divided into 14 sub-areas. Those were labeled the "14 strategic pillars". The Management Team started constantly observing results across those pillars at their meetings and asked their departments to translate them across the entire company according to the principles of the Balanced Scorecard's classic 4 perspectives:

- The customer satisfaction index, including the areas of: 1) product quality, 2) customer service quality, 3) customer contact net promoter score and 4) assessment of the FixTel company brand;
- Operational efficiency, including 1) the adequacy and 2) the profitability of the product portfolio;
- Managing people, including 1) employee commitment, 2) employee competencies and 3) managerial competencies;
- Business results, including 1) ARPU growth and 2) the EBITDA of the current year.

When we observed strategy discussions on revising priorities, a few core issues were worth noting. One of the reasons behind revising the priorities was to simplify management and the overview of the core areas. While previously the company had a flexible approach to priorities - the Management Team was primarily focused on overall company EBITDA and NPV figures of individual products - there were some business units (e.g. Sales and Service) that had established a detailed indicators system, which had started to create local optimal solutions inside the organization. People said in strategy discussions that, for example:

Our Service Department has for a long time had a rather detailed approach to the core nature of customer service. They have used a myriad of quality-management tools - 6sigma, lean management, NPS, the 5S-technique, dealing with repeat complaints, minimizing client contact time and so on.

The result is that our customer service is relatively over-streamlined. We could have invested our energy and money somewhere else with better results (excerpt from a strategy meeting - April 2009).

The revised strategy discussions were trying to look at the big picture, create a unified agenda and prioritize it top-down. This lead to the most important 14 core areas that were implemented across the whole organization.

Efficiency practices activated at regular meetings.

Another informant described particular working groups whose main role was to lead discussions and thereby lead the change processes across the entire firm, and handle part of the reasoning behind the shift toward exploitation:

> *We set up a couple of working groups at different levels that were discussing the efficiency initiative. At our regular Friday meetings with our management board, we spent hours discussing the possibilities of cutting costs and seeking best practices from other companies on how to achieve some immediate results. Second - we created two working groups on efficiency. One in technology and another in the Service division, who also met on a weekly basis to discuss the options for cutting costs (F2 - a top Finance Manager).*

Reflecting upon the need to retain employees despite cuts.

Some informants described the need to involve a larger group of people for a particular reason – for instance, to look for ways to reduce the need to cut personnel. We can conclude from the example that people were actively trying to avoid the negative consequences of cutting back in personnel. From another angle though, this behavior also demonstrated that by retaining employees, it is possible to also retain needed competencies for the upcoming shifts back to the exploratory mode:

> *In a training, we heard about the Japanese management model, whereby organizations discuss their difficulties with their employees. Frequently it helps them to take a long-term view and, for instance, leads to a situation whereby people decide to reduce their salaries to retain their long-term employment. We discussed this among the management team and thought that it might be an alternative (F7 - a top Manager in Sales).*

The issue of retaining the number of employees and thereby keeping the talent in-house despite difficulties is probably one of the most important conscious management practices during the shift. As already described above, in the section on exploratory inertia, the Management Team reflected upon this as a significant mistake during the previous shift toward exploitation. During that shift, they outsourced IT and Network functions, which they later confirmed were part of the core development function. Hence – during their explication of the upcoming shift - several managers explicitly stated that they wanted to make sure that they would not significantly cut back the headcount in the development businesses.

As a follow-up, let me present here an excerpt from another interviewee (interviewed 1.5 years later - in May 2010), who reflected upon the same topic as a follow-up of the change processes. This interview confirmed that the method had proven to be effective and had only lessened the workforce 3% (i.e. 30 employees out of 1,332 people working at FixTel in 2007) during the year that saw significant efficiency initiatives and cost cutting:

> *Discussing this among the core employees, we only lost 30 people in 2008 [at the start of the exploitation cycle] and already in 2009 we managed to employ more people even though we were substantially cutting our costs (F20 - a top Manager in HR).*

It was also interesting to study activities targeted towards avoiding cuts in personnel and retaining the employees who were dealing with exploratory activities also in house. It may be concluded that part of the reason behind this conscious decision was related to a participative management culture, which attempted to preserve the people in a family-like manner. Another reason is probably related to the historic practice of carrying out shifts in the exploration-exploitation continuum, which had taught the company to retain the talent in-house, because otherwise it would be difficult to attract new talent for upcoming shifts back to exploration.

Referring to earlier shifts.

As the interviews progressed, some more respondents made observations about historic events referring to earlier shifts. This allowed it to be pointed out that the upcoming change was nothing surprising. It also demonstrated ways of reasoning and rationalizing the upcoming change initiative for efficiency:

> *In the service side, we are rather used to efficiency cuts. We have implemented a number of initiatives already before [referring to earlier shift toward efficiency] - during this period we re-engineered our process management, created smaller and more focused profit centers, benchmarked our activities with more than 20 other telecommunications firms in the world and introduced an ISO 9001 - based quality management system. All these systems have been in operation with service scorecards ever since and hence they were very natural to our division (F4 - a top Manager in Service).*

Ambidextrous pressure during efficiency activation.

The informants said that during the first phase of change events in fact nothing much changed in terms of existing work. This was less prevalent in support functions (Finance, Administration and IT), but most informants who were working in core operating business departments (Technology, Operations, Marketing, Sales and Service) said that in terms of their daily routine then did not think that much had changed. They confirmed that, yes, efficiency measures had been added to their plate. However, they still considered it to be an important part of their daily routine to continue working on exploratory activities, especially in those areas that were related to large investments. So in essence, most of them, in reflecting upon their daily routine, said that their workload had grown in some cases to double what it was previously. When we asked why that was the case, one informant explained:

> *The telecommunications business requires large-scale investments and most decisions have a time lag of 2-5 years. Larger investments are earned back in 5-10 years; with small-scale new services it takes between 1-2 years to get the service off the ground. If we were slow during this year, then during the following we would have to work our butts off to meet our targets because the competitors would not be waiting. (F15 - a Service line manager).*

4.4.2.2   Activation practices of creativity at MobiTel.

While FixTel activated a number of practices that increased the efficiency of their operations, we observed how MobiTel worked on the opposite agenda and instead activated the practices leading to more creativity and more exploration.

Riding an opportunity for a good reputation in development by developing more.

One of the first issues that was pointed out during the activation practices of creativity was the billing case study that was mentioned in the previous sub-chapter as an important trigger for upcoming change. The managers of MobiTel used the accidental success story of that exploration island as an example that they repeated in every possible instance in order to solicit the attention of people at the headquarters and negotiate additional resources for local development projects and to increase staffing in IT development, product development and network development teams in their firm:

> *Given that our IT development team in Estonia created the billing system for the entire Corporation, we have created a strong reputation among the group companies and we could build on this reputation to move ahead with innovation projects (M8 - a top Manager in IT).*

These opportunities were elaborated further in interviews where the Managers suggested a number of ideas to develop services, which could provide them with revenues for improving network quality and investing in future technologies to provide fast mobile internet through the means of 3.5G and 4G.

Increasing network investments.

The Managers in the fields of IT, Technology and Development elaborated in detail on the chain of events that followed the strategy discussion from the year earlier. Their discussions pointed out the need to embody "the cutting edge technology" in order to be able to compete with the other two players in the market.

MobiTel managers said that they had prepared an investment plan, supported with a package of materials for their mother company, which outlined:

1. Present differences in network quality between them and their two competitors,
2. Results of a customer satisfaction study that pointed to the ratio of dropped calls and lost connections compared with two competitors and
3. Earnings forecasts to highlight the potential increase in revenues that the investment promised.

The Managers said that, as before, their bosses at headquarters gave them a difficult time by scrutinizing the investment plan in detail, but given the changed circumstances, they managed to convince the top brass of the importance of the planned investment:

> *Luckily, it was much easier this time compared with the discussions that we had when we fought for the 3G network license. We were asked to provide some additional supporting materials and our plan was approved after a two-month debate. We managed to keep our purchase costs down by joining our forces with the Russian MobiTel branch. In Russia, they constantly build*

new MBT stations. They put up 10 MBTs every day. Hence, they helped us to procure new network stations for a much cheaper price. (M9 - a top Technology Manager).

The planned investments coincided with the introduction of a number of innovations on the customer side - the popularity of the use of mobile internet had skyrocketed since the introduction of the iPhone across the world. The increasing popularity of 4G modems promised up to 100 Mbit per second connection over the air, which introduced the opportunity for the mobile companies to reach the internet speed of fixed-phone operators for the first time.

Because of developments in technology, we started installing new network stations that already had 4G-ready systems in place. You only had to install an additional chip that provided the final boost of the network speed. (M9 - a top Technology Manager).

Those global developments of technology handed MobiTel the possibility for establishing new stations and upgrade many of their existing stations with a newer setup, which led to the situation that, by early 2010, MobiTel had equalized network quality across the country. Indirectly, those investments also increased the motivation of people working at MobiTel, because of the inferiority complex that their lagging systems had created:

It makes all the difference now - our connection quality changed like night into day compared to before those changes. I think that if the [representatives of headquarters] would not have agreed with our investments plan then it would have been highly likely that I would have resigned. (M9 - a top Technology Manager).

Increasing the number of development projects and new services.
MobiTel in Estonia had previously managed a limited number of applications projects that were allocated to them by the headquarters. They had also dealt with a limited number of improvement projects of existing services. However, starting from 2009 the number of development projects had multiplied:

Now the number of product development projects has grown substantially. While before we managed 3-4 projects concurrently, at this moment there are 31 development projects in the pipeline, which is an exponential growth compared to 2 years ago. Some of them are related to improvements of existing products, the others are completely new services that we are about to bring to the market. (M2 - a top Development Manager).

As a result of these initiatives, MobiTel launched a number of services for their mobile clients during the exploratory period of 2009-10. The notable releases were:

- A mobile gaming portal
- A mobile music purchase portal
- A mobile ID certification service allowing digital signature over mobile phone
- A mobile TV and
- A digital newspaper subscription service.

4.4.3   Practices across single-vision and multiple agendas at the top.

The third dimension where activation and deactivation practices started unfolding in both case organizations during cyclical ambidexterity was the aspect that related to competition vs collaboration at the top of the organization. Whereas FixTel had many conflicting agendas at the top and the managers were constantly competing for priority for their items, the MobiTel top Management shared a single efficiency-focused vision. Both case organization started deactivating their existing practices and activating the types of practices associated with the opposite strategic orientation.

4.4.3.1   Single-vision activation practices at the top by FixTel Management.

Harmonizing shared vision on efficiency at the top and using company "Think Tanks".

The informants shared their views on the need to harmonize the revised vision of their organization in order to carry out change processes. The informants pointed out that the upcoming shift had forced them to carry out a considerable change across all business areas and some of these changes could have been embraced by the participative culture of FixTel, which had enabled them to handle these changes in the past. This participative approach is a notable feature in the culture of FixTel, which in my view allowed making the transition between shifts of strategic orientation considerably smoother than it might have been otherwise. Hence, the informants described in great detail different meetings that were held at the managerial level, at the middle-management level and in various working groups.

A number of issues had been discussed at "Think Tank" meetings of FixTel key personnel on a regular basis at least twice a year. The Think Tank was a group of 50 FixTel employees that included its top Management, key people from its middle management but also a number of bright people from various parts of its organization who had demonstrated their interest in wider trends in society and cared about the future of FixTel's ability to contribute beyond their everyday role. This group included people from all its core departments, but also from product development, quality management and the in-house training division. The Think Tank normally gathered twice a year – during the spring it took a long-term view, discussed future trends for two full days, as well as existing problems related to them, such as different new product ideas and ways of expanding businesses. During the fall, it spent a full day focusing primarily on operational issues and on the plans and priorities for the next year. The CEO of FixTel admitted his confusion over not knowing "if they had found a good role for the Think Tank, which could also be a more structured part of company strategy discussions". However, the participants themselves were positive about the work that they had done in the Think Tank and pointed out that they appreciated the inclusive and egalitarian nature of this large forum of people:

> *We have had very participative management. We have held at least twice a year in spring and autumn thorough discussions on various important issues. For a full day, we brainstorm on overall trends and for another day what to improve in our activities. Hence, it was only natural*

that in face of difficulties we can gather them again and discuss all together how to revise our approach (F8 - top Manager in Operations).

It is interesting that while during individual interviews the informants were openly critical about the changes, which considerably revised their approach to doing things, it was exactly those activation practices during the creation of a single vision at the Think Tank and related working groups that made the change processes easier.

The informants rationalized and ultimately willingly accepted change and described how they attempted to make the efficiency cuts work. One of the informants (interviewed in May 2010) took the ex-post view and described the result of the involvement process:

As we discussed the difficulties that our company was facing in 2008, the core people all together then also agreed the cost cuts in 2009 came much more easily. I guess that when we managed to resolve the metaphysical issues then all the individuals understood more easily what had to be done. I would say that it was not that the cost cutting killed motivation. As a result of these extensive discussions, perhaps the positive emotions were reduced, but they did not go so far as becoming negative emotion (F23 - a line manager in Service).

Streamlining strategy process at FixTel during activation of a single-vision creation.
During the strategy discussions I observed, one of the core topics that was analyzed in depth was the streamlining of strategy work itself. During the exploratory inertia phase, most people complained about the lack of structure in strategizing. It often happened that people complained that the priorities of their business unit were identified either late or were not identified at all. Some of the respondents also continued to face a similar situation during the change events, and referred to an increased workload during the change events:

The process of setting the goals for our unit is not working. It is already April and we haven't agreed in our department on what our annual target for this year should be. I suppose that during the next two weeks I should take the time, go through a view of the year, and establish the proper plan for sales and revenues (F7- a top Manager in Sales).

However, a more clearly-structured top-down driven strategy process was being designed and managed by the CEO of the company himself, which led to an agreement on an annual process, with clearly-specified deadlines, during which certain activities were carried out. The plan also included clearly-specified responsibilities.

The company Think Tank of 50 key personnel, which focused twice a year on wider discussions, took part in the streamlined strategy process. The added annual strategy process was structured across three levels of organization. 1) strategy discussions among top Management, 2) discussions among three cross-departmental groups (a customer-focused group, a technology-focused group and a development-focused group) and 3) discussions at the departmental level. In a classic manner, the discussions at the beginning of the year reviewed the results of the past year, identified long-term scenarios and deliberated on a need to renew the business model. The discussions during the second half of the year were primarily focused on short-term goals, on efficiency metrics and the investment decisions for the next year. The year was punctuated first by company-wide meetings for goal setting, and thereafter by occasions for individual goal setting for the next year.

Figure 9. Exploitation-focused annual strategy process (from FixTel strategy slides)

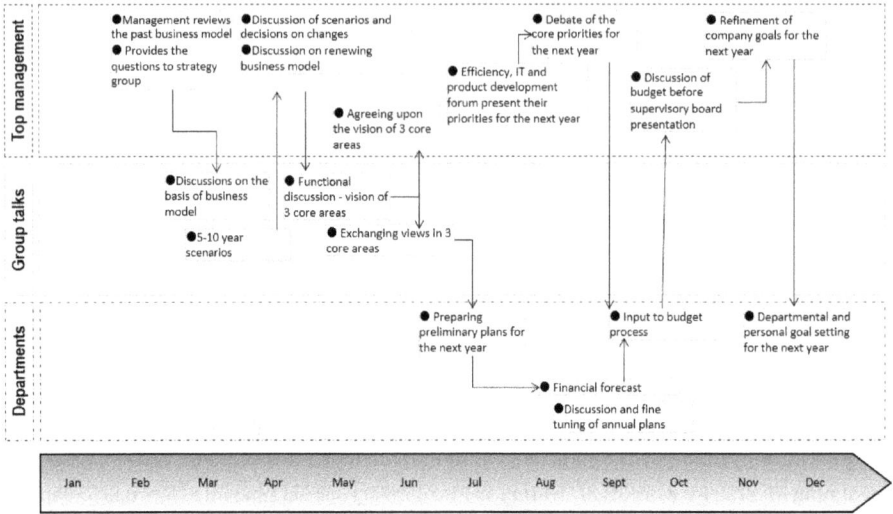

Figure 9 displays the most important elements of the annual strategy cycle. The graphical representation displays the importance of the top Management discussions about strategic issues, which was not the case during the prior phase of exploratory inertia. The newly-established strategy process hence provided analytical tools, but also highlighted the responsibility of the top Management to keep the strategy in the limelight continuously throughout the year. This was the case during the exploratory criteria period only during the fall, when the next year's investment budget was being prepared for the Supervisory Board. At other times, the Management deliberated upon strategy reactively on an ad hoc basis - when the issues of importance were raised at Management Board meetings or when the parent company requested some data.

Putting in joint business metrics system based on Balanced Scorecard.
While the Balanced Scorecard metrics system has already been mentioned previously in the section on activating efficiency practices, it will also be elaborated in the section associated with creating a single vision. The respondents described their activities in structuring their efficiency initiatives, whereby they reintroduced Balanced Scorecard-based metrics systems for managing their activities:

> *This year we started discussing "cleaning our house". In essence, this means introducing a traditional BSC-style metrics system, which is not exactly using BSC terminology, but what is important is that it has started to work (F8 - a top Manager in Operations).*

The structured metrics system was put in place together with concrete tracking mechanisms, which allowed FixTel managers to discuss the business results across 14 core topic areas on a monthly basis. The Management Team used the framework to then also report further to the Supervisory Board on the generic outcomes of this, primarily focusing on the financial indicators.

While the Supervisory Board was still mainly interested in EBITDA figures, the Management Board also managed to convince it of the usability of the ARPU-based (Average Revenue Per Paying User) measurements to refocus thinking from generic financial performance to a measure that would be more appropriate for a telecommunications firm. It was clear that the home market was already saturated - it had become very difficult to sell new subscriptions. However, due to corporate policies the parent company had forbidden FixTel from entering the neighboring markets so as not to cannibalize the revenues of the other companies belonging to the same group. Hence, instead of intensive market growth, people discussed the need to identify possibilities for increasing profitability per customer:

> *Due to saturation of our market, we reprioritized our indicators. Hence, instead of overall-growth EBITDA figures we focused more on ARPU, which reflects our present possibilities much better (F8 - a top Manager in Operations)*

ARPU is a generic indicator, frequently used by infrastructure firms. During strategy discussions, one representative of FixTel did an elaborate presentation about the business model of French municipal utility firms, which in the absence of any other possibilities for market expansion use the strategy of intensifying services to its existing customers, for example, even providing undertaker services[27]. This presentation created an intensive debate about additional services that may be provided to the existing customer groups, based on the company's core competencies. However, the core of the message that the participants discussed again and again was the need to simplify the customer offering, which had become too complex during the previous period when the Product Development department was given the opportunity to ship too many new products to the market, some of which were poorly linked and created conflicting demands for employee competencies.

4.4.3.2 *Activation practices of multiple agendas at the top by MobiTel management.*

At MobiTel, the interactions were the opposite. While FixTel had too many conflicting agendas at the top, MobiTel was restrained by their strategy-creation approach. Hence, their Management Team contemplated activating practices that would allow multiple agendas at the top.

Revising the approach to strategic planning.

During strategy-making discussions, managers referred to weaknesses associated with rigid ex-ante approvals-based management committees and rigid planning systems, which were strongly linked to quarterly investment forecasting, monthly reviews of financial indicators and semi-annual personnel review discussions.

> *We have paid rigorous attention to minuscule detail. Our plans are scrutinized by the managers and committees and all the potential expenses that could be slashed in half have been cut.*

---

[27] The case study that was used in this presentation referred to Grenoble *Société de Services*, which handles municipal water, transport, gas, electricity, hospitals and funerals services under a single management structure.

However, at a certain point when looking at our competitors we would have to acknowledge
that by continuing like this we are going to miss some very important opportunities. We should
start discussing how to revise our approach and allow more flexibility. (M6 - a top Manager in
Sales and Service)

While the planning systems were clearly defined, most decisions still landed on the desks of three
key people in the organization: the CEO, the CFO and the Head of Business Development. The other
members of the top Management Team acted primarily as a source of ideas, but they did not have
ultimate decision-making authority. The Managers deliberated on these issues and pointed out that
the company had moved to much more complex business areas that were too multifaceted for just
three people to handle.

I guess that at a certain moment we realized that too much was going on to make it possible for
the three of us [referring to the Head of Business Development, the Head of Finance and the
Head of Operations] to be able to oversee it all. We realized that the only way to achieve our
goals would be to involve as many people as possible from our company to be able to tap into
the opportunities and test out the ideas that we were unable to absorb. (M1 - a top Manager of
Operations).

Bringing in new talent and increasing the number of personnel.
Following from this, the most important point that the Managers described related to their
negotiations for increasing the in-house talent pool in several core areas.

Because of discussions between the MobiTel Estonia Management Board and the corporate Head
Office, concerning the strategic nature of the billing work done in Estonia, a part of its IT
development function was considered so important for the development of the MobiTel Corporation
that, while it was centered in Estonia, its reporting responsibilities were shifted to Head Office. It
hence became responsible for developing and maintaining IT billing solutions for the entire group
in 11 countries.

At the same time, the Management convinced the owners about the need to revise the strategic
orientation of MobiTel Estonia to be able to bring to the market a series of new products and services
and to establish a competence center that would allow bringing these products to the market. Due to
these background explanations, the Product Development unit grew from two persons to six persons
by 2010. In a similar manner, the Technology Development Department grew during 2010 from
three persons to eight:

Growing the Technology Department 2.5 times increased the quality of our service delivery in
a remarkable manner. This decision - combined with a full investment plan - made it certain
that now the independent measurements of our network quality across the country allow us to
be on a par or even better than both of our competitors. (M2 - a top Development Manager).

Idea generation delegated from the top of the organization.
As a result of the shift, the Managers confirmed that the newly-staffed Product Development
Department, the larger IT Development Department and the Technology Development Department,
hand in hand with the idea funnel, had provided them with an increasing ability to deal with

innovation. This had brought about particular results in terms of actual services that had been brought to the market (as described above), but it also created permanent systems to help develop dynamic capabilities within MobiTel to handle those issues in the future.

> *For the past 8 years that I have been in this company, I have had to constantly make decisions by myself - there has been nobody to discuss these ideas with. I would have wanted to discuss the ideas with somebody. It is now great that this forum provides us with the opportunity to step in, use the other members of this team as a sounding board, and see how to improve on the ideas of our unit. (M9 - a top Technology Manager).*

Strengthening a new segment by insourcing business service.

While previously customer service at MobiTel was fully outsourced, one of the first changes in practice was to insource the Business Sales Department. The top Manager in Sales (M6) provided us with statistics that showed information about household customers. According to the data 53%t of households used the on-line web self-service platform to interact with MobiTel, 22% were using their interactive voice response (IVR) solution, 16% called their Customer Call Center, 9% came in person to the service centers and less than 1% sent regular e-mails. For prepaid phone cards, 90% of them used IVR and the remainder chose either to come to Customer Service in person or to call the Customer Call Center. However, they had analyzed the segments and realized that unlike private customers, who were satisfied with automated service, business customers required an approach that was more personal.

> *You cannot tell the automated answering machine that you would like to install five mobile modems for the shop surveillance systems. To tackle requests like this - it is an area where our outsourced service providers were as incapable as automated answering machines. We just could not afford to have somebody else talk to our customers on our behalf, because the requests that our business customers put forward were simply much more complex and customized than our standard packages could deliver. (M4 - a middle manager in Sales).*

Hence, MobiTel recruited 20 salespeople and made them actively responsible for expanding the small business segment. MobiTel started this change with an aggressive marketing campaign that no other mobile providers had matched prior to that – in 2009 they started offering free calls between callers registered to the same firm.

> *It took SeriousMobile more than half a year before they had to react. By that time, we had succeeded in tricking over more than 20,000 phone numbers from them. When we did our next moves, their reactions were somewhat faster. (M4 - a middle manager in Sales).*

This was one of those decisions where even the representatives of the parent company were shocked by the outcome.

> *They had also done similar aggressive campaigns in Sweden, but it never brought such dramatic results. Since then, our sister companies in Latvia and Lithuania have copied the same - obviously, it works better in the Baltic than in the Nordic countries. (M4 - a middle manager in Sales).*

Become an innovative challenger to handle more complex business.

MobiTel strategy to date had been that of a traditional "price challenger", which used a set of predetermined rules to move reactively and aggressively in the market and try to always attract the price sensitive customers by its agile operations and efficient management of resources. In strategy discussions, the Managers came to the following conclusion: price no longer provided a sustainable competitive advantage and there were new and untapped opportunities in segments that were not covered by the two competitors. In the changed circumstances, the Managers thought about the possibility of revising their strategy and becoming an "innovative challenger" to start servicing more complex business segments. The first underlying argument for revising their approach stemmed from their previously very limited in-house product development ability.

> *We have had two rules. First: "invest as late as possible". This means that we should try to see first how others have managed with this technology. The second rule: "use what you have got", which means that we have to be inventive in trying to get things done with as low costs as possible. Because of those two rules - with the exception of billing development - most of the IT activity has been outsourced and internal IT function within the house primarily focuses on the planning and coordinating function of the outsourced activities. (M8 - a top Manager in IT)*

These discussions led to a revision of the approach for new product development and the participants of the strategy discussion were unanimously for reorganizing their investment planning and development approach in order to come up with value innovation possibilities creating value for customers in the areas they had not thought about until this date.

4.4.4   Practices across efficiency silos and collaboration at mid-level.

I observed that the fourth dimension where the activation and deactivation practices had their impact related to collaboration practices at the mid-level of organization. It was another dimension where the two case organizations demonstrated activation and deactivation practices of an opposing nature. FixTel departments and middle managers had their collaborative approach broken down due to a stronger focus on efficiency goals. MobiTel, on the other hand, activated more energetic co-operation.

4.4.4.1   Activation of efficiency practices at mid-level in FixTel.

Managing cost-cutting and making efficiency working groups operational at mid-level.

The cost-cutting and single-vision creation at the top of the organization under the previous dimension, discussed above, led to the pragmatic mindset quickly permeating the entire company. When we subsequently interviewed the middle managers, only two of the respondents referred to difficulties in accepting the changes. Most respondents among the middle managers confirmed that they had actively participated in respective meetings to discuss the upcoming changes and started cutting costs. They also confirmed that they had introduced meetings on similar topics in their own departments, too:

> *I introduced monthly meetings in my department where we discuss residual income in detail. For half the day we focus on the issues of business revenues and in the second half of the day*

we contemplate our expenses and discuss the possibilities for cutting back. (F15 - a line manager in Service).

The first element of cost cutting was related to making a number of project groups operational to discuss cuts. People working in the Finance Department facilitated those meetings:

We established several new groups to discuss issues related to efficiency. The Technology Division runs one of them - they look into possibilities of cutting costs in existing and new investments. The Services Division runs another, which analyses the possibilities for cutting the costs of client contacts and make daily interactions more efficient by resolving or standardizing some issues. This forum is closely interrelated with another forum – the quality forum of the Service and Sales Division, which primarily tackles quality incidents that have arisen out of client contacts. Finally, we also discuss efficiency issues every second week at our top management level (F5 - a top Manager in Technology).

When we asked what the subject of discussions in these working groups was, we received interesting insights about the nature of the business. One of the respondents replied in the following manner:

You have to invest in cost cutting. For example - old copper cables. Technically, they would not be obsolete for 20 more years, but their maintenance is more expensive than fiber optics. Optics is more expensive to install, but it can serve more services. In the end, it is more profitable to install new technology rather than to maintain the old. This means that to cut our maintenance costs we need to make constant investments in technology that is more expensive (F10 - a middle manager in Technology).

This reply conveys the message that the discussions in those working groups were not just simple nor simplistic. The groups were not only focusing on the cost-cutting task as a chainsaw exercise – or how to technically or administratively cut any expenses that exceeded particular thresholds. Instead there were intensive debates, which focused on the long-term promise of certain technologies, which might have been at that time more expensive options, but promised to either cut costs or increase profitability in the end. Some discussions that started with cost-cutting lead to more strategic debates about the nature of the business FixTel was in:

We have to decide if we are providing services or cables. The exponential development of the quality of broadband service means that a service provider in New Zealand can easily provide services to customers located in Estonia over our cable. The same applies to us - do we want to create services that we only sell via our own cables or can we sell the same services in other markets? (F5 - a top Manager in Technology)

Furthermore, some discussions in the efficiency working groups were clearly exploratory as they focused on a wider range of subjects related to how to use the existing capabilities to increase revenues. Those two examples demonstrate that while the groups were labelled "efficiency groups", their scope of discussion was mostly wider and they primarily helped to instigate strategy discussions across the entire organization and thereby increase the participation of a wider group of people in defining the company future.

Reallocation of responsibility at mid-level.

A great deal of the responsibility for new product development was transferred to the Marketing and Sales Departments. It was no longer the technology push that dominated the agenda of what new products would be worked on. In the new situation, the Marketing, Sales and Service Departments were in charge of observing the customer interaction and putting forward most of the ideas on what types of new trends would be worth pursuing. While this certainly had a positive influence on satisfying the existing customers, it also created additional stress for the Technology and Development Departments:

> *If I were to joke, in the past our innovative activity was run primarily by the Technology Department. Then we were dealing with innovation. However, now the Marketing Department leads and I would say that what they are doing is just "improvements" (F12 - a middle manager in Technology).*

Competing for resources at the middle-management level.
The product development function introduced a number of practices to enable the most efficient choices among investment ideas. In the new situation, the idea had to be presented to a number of departments first. After going through the funnel, and only once the top management team had approved the idea as having strong potential for their existing customers, the product developers could start working on the prototype. In comparison with the previous situation where they first developed the prototype and then had much more discretion to take the first steps, this approach significantly cut their initiative:

> *Before, we had an approach that was based on "key people" - every project idea, every new initiative had somebody identified as a key person who was responsible for it. If this person had a vision which matched the top management's, then he had all the resources in hand to just go ahead and do it. In the new situation all those projects were frozen, hence most people who were taking responsibility and acting responsibly simply stopped doing anything at all (F11 - A middle manager in Development)*

While previously the ideas were implemented on a freeform basis, there were a number of people who simply profiled themselves differently. They took the revised strategy process as a "change in the rules of the game" and rationalized it, as illustrated by such comments during strategy workshops, as:

> *Before we were playing basketball - if you got the ball then all you had to do was to get close to the basket and then take a shot. If you were successful then you got your points. Now we are into bridge. You have to carefully plan and think with whom you are playing in pairs and contemplate what the other's hand might be (an informant during a strategy workshop).*

However, despite these critical notes and references to the rules of the game, while the situation remained largely the same, a large group of people did note that the revised approach to strategy had brought about a revised quality for FixTel in general.

4.4.4.2   *Activation of collaboration practices at mid-level in MobiTel.*
While during the exploratory inertia period FixTel had been an organization where middle managers were collaborating to get their development projects approved by a top Management with competing agendas, MobiTel individual departments were much more at odds with each other. Despite being a smaller firm in terms of its headcount, the individual departments operated more like small fiefdoms,

which was mostly due to competition for resources in a rigid and bureaucratic resource allocation process. As could be observed, those departments activated a number of collaboration practices during the ambidexterity cycle towards exploration and started to work together more.

Cross-departmental discussion groups on new products and customer problems.
Interaction between the Marketing, new product Development and Technology Departments had continued on a regular basis. The three Departments organized their weekly meetings where they discussed the problems of existing customers, ideas about improving existing products or the development of completely new products:

> *The result of the discussions is that we have started receiving more feedback from marketing on what our customers want. The previous situation when engineers were trying to make decisions about customers was frequently flawed. Previously the usual approach was "Hmm, this customer has a problem. Let's send the problem to the Technology division and ask them to sort it out for the customer." (M9 - a top Technology Manager).*

All parties who participated in these discussions pointed out the value of the interactions, which helped to solve customer problems and come up with new product ideas. However, one of the managers pointed out another reason why the interactions had become useful:

> *Previously, we had a constant conflict between the Technology and Marketing divisions. Our people attempt to make the world rational, but our Marketing team is very creative. That's why it has been difficult to sit down together and work on the joint problems as a team. We should understand the problem of our customer jointly. (M9 - a top Technology Manager).*

Hence, as a result of these discussions, the two Departments who had previously held different perceptions about each other's functions and capabilities had the chance to regularly discuss and develop joint understandings of both issues at hand as well as their roles in handling those issues.

Interaction between Marketing and Technology Departments led to customer solutions.
Some of the development projects were related to the simplification of several customer solutions. Namely, Marketing and Technology spent a considerable amount of time together discussing appropriate sales packages by market segments. Earlier, the mobile firms had sold their subscriptions by identifying a price per minute of calling, a price per text message, a price per MB of data and a price for a monthly subscription. The result was that the competition was straightforward, but did not take into consideration the differing communication needs of various customers.

MobiTel's products were among the first on the market to segment the customers into straightforward groups. Family members valued the option of free calls within their family; the elderly placed more value on the option of a lower monthly fee; the youth valued communication via cheaper text messages; businesspeople wanted cheaper data connection.

The Marketing, Product Development and Technology Departments worked together to identify the most appropriate customer segments, identified the most appropriate pricing strategies for those segments and the IT developers provided programming for the billing solution to make sure that it would allow the correct pricing for those segments. As a result, the company developed 10 packages for household users, 11 packages for business users and 3 packages for prepaid phone cards, which were all launched in 2010 with an intensive marketing campaign.

Guided evolution mechanisms that rely heavily on the development function.
In purely exploratory firms, idea generation would have been carried out based on managerial principles that support creation, selection and retention mechanisms of new business initiatives. The approach taken by MobiTel was more comparable to the systems suggested by the model of "guided evolution" (Lovas & Ghoshal, 2000), which had a specific twist to it. While Lovas and Ghoshal had suggested that all the employees create a variation of ideas, MobiTel had two primary sources for new business ideas:

- One of them was structurally facilitated by the individuals whose function was to work on development projects (i.e. the Product Development Department, the Network Development Department and the Marketing Department), who started to come up with new business ideas;
- Some ideas were transmitted through the discussions with the representatives of other branches of MobiTel in other countries.

The group of people who work on development projects thereafter scrutinizes those ideas. The selection process continuously follows the selection methods set forth by MobiTel Corporation centrally, and people working on the development projects will work until the very end to complete them as part of the retention mechanism.

4.4.5   Practices across coordination and autonomy dimension.
Finally, the fifth dimension across which the case organizations activated and deactivated their strategy-making practices was related to coordination and autonomy. Autonomous FixTel activated more coordination-associated practices, while MobiTel, which was overloaded by the bureaucracy introduced by their parent firm, took a number of steps to activate a higher degree of autonomy-associated practices.

4.4.5.1   Activation of coordination-oriented practices at FixTel

Tracking mechanisms - practice of review.
One of the first practices worth mentioning during the activation of coordination-oriented practices, was introducing a tracking mechanism. While during the exploratory inertia phase, the people working at FixTel were primarily interested in sales results, and "being Number One" was considered to be important by a number of employees, there was also an innate need to keep track of how the efficiency goals were being met. This posed a challenge for the Finance Department as the company had previously established information systems to keep good track of sales figures, but there was no such simple-to-use solution for keeping track of and answering the constant question of other departments: "how much have we saved already?".

Hence, the Finance Department came up with a customized financial reporting solution that allowed focusing on unit costs and aggregating them into user-based revenues in term of ARPU figures where the departments could drill in and see what their particular contribution to the savings was. When the middle managers introduced a routine in their weekly meetings to discuss cutting costs in their field, they also had the chance to refresh this information once a month and see how they were progressing with the cost-cutting.

In a similar manner, people reflected during the interviews that this had created the practice of assessing the achievement of milestones during their discussions, an observation that was frequently repeated among the people working across departments. A business analyst who participated in almost all these meetings summarized the experience in the following manner:

> *I remember that when we discussed the monthly results there was a recurring theme. Habitually, either one of the department leaders or some other participant at the meeting asked me at a certain point in the discussion the crucial question: "Is what we are doing now good enough?" or "Are we pleasing the Supervisory Board already?" or "How much further do we still have got to go?" At first, it was a difficult question. After a while, it became funny. Finally, I started preparing my presentations in such a way that I anticipated this question and tried to get to this upfront (F14 - a representative of operating core).*

This question "are we pleasing the owners already?" - given that it was repeated a number of times - reflected the mindset of the FixTel employees, and showed that in their opinion they were dealing with a temporary situation. They were working hard in order to achieve a certain minimum threshold to bring the company to a new qualitative stage and they were hoping that once this was achieved it would become easier for them.

Putting in place a metrics system for efficiency.
When we clarified with a follow-up question about the systems, procedures or models that were put into use during the analyses leading to the shift toward exploitation, then the only item that was clearly pointed out was in reference to discussions held with the help of financial analytics tools. One of the informants referred to basic tools to help complete this phase:

> *We created a simple Excel table for analyzing project profitability. A product manager can just enter the core data and get in a matter of 30 minutes the reply on whether their planned project will meet our target efficiency goals or not (F14 - a representative of the operating core).*

Centralizing and bureaucratization of strategy making.
A number of informants reflected upon their dissatisfaction with the degree of inflexibility that the newly-established practices had created for them. One of the informants described the dissatisfaction with formalized and bureaucratized strategy process at FixTel in our interview held in June 2010:

> *Planning has now become too theoretical. The business ideas don't just occur to us in November when we are working on the investment budget [for the next year] (F10 - a middle manager in Technology)*

The management team had focused on their Balanced Scorecard approach whereby the core areas of the company were divided into 14 themes of importance. The informants who had been with the company for a longer period took this with a sense of irony.

> *I remember the good old Swedish times [referring back to the period prior to 1996, when the company was run by Swedish expats]. Every year they brought out another wheel of fortune where they had divided strategy into colorful segments - here we plan, here we implement, here we check and here we correct what has gone wrong. They also set dates and deadlines, which never worked in practice because of turbulent changes in the environment. (F12 - a middle manager in Technology)*

Part of it might be explained by a down-to earth Estonian management style, where people tend to despise management fads and buzzwords. However, partially this also relates to the mindset of engineers who prefer to just "go ahead with it and get it done" instead of planning and forecasting.

Freezing of exploratory activities leading to loss of innovative edge.
It was a uniformly held view that FixTel had substantially reduced its innovative capabilities during the shift towards exploitation:

> *In terms of innovation, we can say that there have been two periods where we have been really innovative. One period was 1996-99 at the height of the dot-com boom and the second was just when we finalized the launch of Digi-TV in 2005-07, when we also received a number of innovation awards. Nowadays we tend to be tail joggers[28]. We don't do anything particularly innovative, instead we mostly have stayed with copying innovative services from other companies in the group (F19 - a middle manager in Service).*

> *Now the strategy is mostly being made by the business planning work group. It is driven by Marketing and Finance. They only know about customers and numbers, but they don't have a clue about what can or what cannot be built [referring to lack of engineering know-how]. (F12 - a middle manager in Technology)*

As the company focus shifted to simplification of services and products and trying to make sure that the existing customers would be well served in order to increase the ARPU indicators, a number of people who were working on new product development were rather vocal in displaying their dissatisfaction with the changed situation. They were mainly concerned about the fact that their initiative had been reduced and that the budget for exploratory initiatives had been substantially cut. The employees in the Development Department mainly retained their positions, however, due to the priority held by the Management Board of guaranteeing that they would not lose their best talents.

From a related angle, the added bureaucracy had also created additional hurdles, as the financial projections of the planned developments had to be much more elaborate than before. This was also pointed out by some informants:

> *The newly revised NPV methodology has also had adverse effects. Have you heard about the advertisement with the theme of good ideas becoming reality? In our case, when we are so*

---

[28] Literal translation of the colloquial "sabassörkija" - "tail jogger" indicating somebody who is lagging behind others.

deeply stuck in the financial analysis then ultimately the good ideas only turn into snails![29] (F6 -a top Manager in IT)

The third negative consequence of this move was the increasing competitiveness of the development function. Less was invested, hence a lesser number of initiatives were financed, which also meant that while previously whenever a developer wanted to work on a cool new product or service it was relatively easy to get going - in the new situation, however, the developers had to compete much harder for the scarcer resources. Some of this competition was for investment funds, but a significant part of the competition was for a set of scarce resources that were badly needed in order to complete development projects:

We might have worked on a business idea for 6 months, and ultimately at the end of the 6-month period we face the IT resource committee, and then we are simply told that "your project is not a priority, forget it - we first have to finalize programming the other four large things here!" (F11 - middle manager in Development)

This reduced the motivation of the group of people whom FixTel management had nurtured as their talents. As a result, four developers ended up leaving the company in the period 2008-10. A few informants reflected some of this frustration:

Before we talked about network, now we only talk about the customer. But the customer does not necessarily know what he wants. (F16 - a representative of the operating core)

4.4.5.2   *Activation of autonomy-oriented practices at MobiTel*

Similarly, activation practices developed at MobiTel, which had become more autonomous resulting from a number of practices introduced during the shift in ambidexterity.

Cooperation with competitors.
During the exploratory shift, MobiTel managers also started to revise their approach towards competitors. Instead of aggressive competition, the company started to cooperate with them in a number of areas. One of the areas of cooperation also had a mutual benefit for cutting costs in the field of network building. While during previous years, the expansion of the network and building new MBT towers was the source for competitive rivalry, the companies now started agreeing upon sharing their resources:

Our engineers started suggesting collaboration with our competitors to agree upon sharing their antennae. In a number of locations where the companies had already erected three towers side by side we decided to dismantle some of them to cut the costs and consolidate the equipment from three towers to one. (M10 - middle Technology manager)

The "efficiency" mantra replaced with the "challenge" mantra.
An interesting observation that I made during my last discussions with the managers in August 2010 was that there was a significant change in the vocabulary that they used. If in 2007-08 the most used words were "cutting costs" and "efficiency", then in the last interviews those two phrases were almost

---

[29] Word-play in Estonian language: "Hea mõte saab teoks" means both "Good idea becomes reality" and "Good idea turns into a snail".

absent. Instead - the words that tended to recur throughout the interviews were "challenges", "accomplishing", "trying harder" and "revising our approach", which demonstrated that the managers had been through considerable changes in their mindset.

5 Discussion and Conclusions

In this final chapter, my task is to reflect upon the findings and to interpret the results in the context of existing theory.

Case analysis followed an iterative process whereby I first explored the qualitative data according to a set of predetermined frameworks. I developed interview questionnaires following theories of cyclical ambidexterity - such as the conceptualization of Siggelkow and Levinthal (2003), Gupta et al. (2006) and Raisch and Birkinshaw (2008). In my attempt to capture the essence of strategy work across multiple levels of organization I primarily relied on the work of Hart (1992), Crossan et al. (1999) and Burgelman (1983; 1991). At a later stage, I elaborated my conceptualizations with the notions of cyclical ambidexterity articulated by Simsek et al. (2009) and with a wider perspective of strategy as practice (Johnson, Melin, & Whittington, 2003; Johnson, Langley, Melin, & Whittington, 2007). Following this approach, I created a multi-level model of the organizational learning involved in cyclical ambidexterity and analyzed whether the data from the two case organizations would confirm or disprove the theoretical frameworks. This quasi-deductive approach arrived at a dead-end.

Thereafter I revised my approach to make it more of an interpretive case study where results would be interpreted through the principles of in-vivo coding, leading to first- and second-order coding as suggested by Van Maanen (1979). As a result, I was able to develop an iterative conceptual model, which formed the foundation of this dissertation. The following sections are dedicated to reviewing the results of this convoluted process.

In my first subchapter below, I will focus on the conceptualization of the theoretical model and its individual components and their interlinkages. In the following subchapter, I will concentrate on the contribution of this study to the previous literature. I will determine my first set of conclusions by concentrating on the study results through the lens of previous literature on cyclical ambidexterity and strategy as practice. Thereafter I specify the managerial implications of those findings. Finally, I will conclude the chapter with a discussion on limitations and potential future research avenues.

5.1 Conceptualization

In addition to identifying the contents of the generic dataset and after coding the data from interviews and strategy discussions, I analyzed the transcripts to identify any other consistent patterns across the themes – either within or between the cases studied. I started to combine those conclusions into a holistic model to demonstrate a generic pattern of cyclical ambidexterity in the strategy practices of the two case organizations. There were individual differences in two case firms due to their size differences and especially since one was shifting from exploration to exploitation while the other moved in the opposite direction. However, I detected a pattern, which can be used to make sense of and systematize the events and practices in both organizations. The analysis unveiled two overarching themes and eight sub-themes that described practices associated with the unfolding of cyclical ambidexterity in these particular cases.

Figure 10. Conceptual model of the practices of cyclical ambidexterity

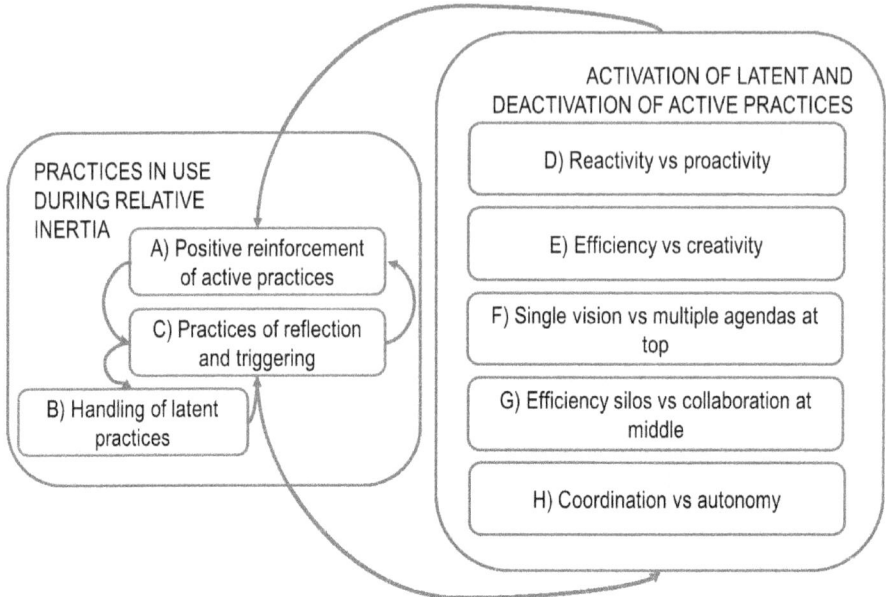

As the figure above illustrates, the analysis revealed a set of two main practice categories related to cyclical ambidexterity: 1) a category primarily associated with continuing "the current *modus operandi*", or "practices during relative inertia", as stated in the model. 2) The second category is about the process of "activating" and "deactivating" strategy practices within the organization, which relates to the legitimization and de-legitimization of one or the other set of practices. Due to the underlying dynamics, which entail activating and deactivating the practices that are in "sleeping" mode, I have labelled them "activating latent practices and deactivating active practices ". In the subchapter below, I will describe each of the practices.

5.1.1   Practices during relative inertia

Three themes emerged when I synthesized the practices during the period of relative inertia in the case organizations. A) **Positive reinforcement of active practices**. First, there were practices that were associated with retaining the existing strategic orientation. B) **Handling of latent practices**. Second, the managers referred to the practices used during the previous period, which were in a latent state, waiting for reactivation during the upcoming shift in cyclical ambidexterity. C) **Practices of reflection and triggering**. The managers occasionally reflected and checked the need to revise the strategic orientation.

All three practices combining together operated as a single-loop learning mechanism, which reinforced the situation of relative inertia and was periodically intermingled with a search for signs in the environment to check whether it would be an appropriate moment to start a shift in cyclical ambidexterity by activating some latent or non-existent practices or deactivating some of the existing practices.

5.1.1.1   *Positive reinforcement of active practices.*
The data showed that practices used for strategy making during the phase of relative inertia strongly confirmed the earlier theory linked to strategy-making frameworks, as suggested by Hart (1992).

As FixTel managers were engaged in strategy making during the period of exploratory inertia, it was mostly executed in *generative-organic* mode (Hart, 1992), whereby the top Management did not have a particular agenda for strategy making. They were just keeping their eye on whether the company was able to meet the 30% EBITDA-to-revenue ratio. The top management team focused primarily on endorsement practices of new business ideas that were sold to them by the employees working within the organization. The product and service developers had been given a high degree of autonomy to deal with ideas and they had self-organized to collaborate between individual departments to prepare the most appropriate business cases for top Management approval.

Working on strategy during the exploitative inertia phase, MobiTel Managers organized the process according to the *rational-analytical* approach (Hart, 1992), whereby strategy was driven by a formalized structure. MobiTel's parent company had assumed the strong role of "boss", who had the task of evaluating and controlling the strategy creation and implementation properties. The middle managers at MobiTel, as well as most top Management, had to follow the system (Hart, 1992, pp. 337-8). MobiTel Managers had largely copied these highly-structured and bureaucratic strategy-making practices and agreed to the limited autonomy provided to them by the parent firm. Assisting the efficiency-oriented mindset was a strong culturally-rooted discursive practice (Clarke, Kwon, & Wodak, 2012), whereby the informants in this case organization engaged in an "efficiency" mantra by constantly talking about "having to be efficient", "having to increase efficiency", "having to choose between A and B on the basis of which one is more efficient in the short/long term".

It was interesting to observe that during the relative inertia phase, the case organizations demonstrated polar practices for reacting to the moves of competitors. While FixTel did not place any strategic importance on the acts of competitors, MobiTel followed their each and every move and was occasionally even over-reacting. An example of this was when the top management team discussed erecting new billboards, within a day, next to their competitors' advertisements on one of the main roads in the capital city.

5.1.1.2   *Handling latent practices.*
Representatives of both case organizations referred to past ambidexterity cycles. The lessons of those cycles provided a source for discussions and analysis in the light of upcoming shifts in strategic orientation. In the case of FixTel, the history of cycling was longer and hence the informants referred

to a number of occasions as "past mistakes" or to "what we learned". MobiTel representatives pointed to a single practice of the firm's IT development unit, which was able to demonstrate successful exploratory initiatives in a firm that was otherwise biased towards exploitation.

Perhaps the greatest importance of the latent practices - occasionally "brought out" for further scrutiny - related to the possibility of surfacing alternative agendas or rebellious approaches meant to challenge the existing practices for doing things. The middle managers or management teams of the respective organizations both did this. In those instances, the core message that those latent practices carried was exemplified by:

> Look, there are some people in our firm who can do it differently than we are doing it at the moment. It seems that the different practices provide positive results. Perhaps it would be worthwhile to try the same elsewhere as well." (An extract from a MobiTel strategy session, a generalization of the statement by informant M9, Top Technology Manager).

In other instances, the latent practices referred to past events where the managers concluded that while they were responsible for previous decisions, they had learned the lessons and were willing to revise the practices in the same or similar circumstances in the future. At both case organizations, this argumentation was used with reference to overly active previous outsourcing campaigns. The managers in both case organizations referred to past mistakes that had created the situation whereby either IT developers or the customer handling sections of the respective firms seemed unimportant at first sight, but proved to be essential later. Given their strategically vital importance to the core functions of the firms, they had to be "repatriated" to the appropriate location under the auspices of the firm during the upcoming ambidexterity cycle.

5.1.1.3   *Looking for triggers to revise existing practices.*

In line with the competence modification processes suggested by Floyd and Lane (2000, p. 156), whereby the managers recognized the need to change, the first triggers to revise existing practices manifested themselves in both case organizations as signs of the saturation of the existing strategic orientation.

At FixTel the managers came to the conclusion that the generative mode of strategy making had lead them to suboptimal solutions driven by too many conflicting agendas at the top, which they felt did not allow them to make effective decisions. At MobiTel, humorous instances of extreme efficiency led the management team to envisage that it might be a good idea to revise the aim of achieving efficiency at any cost.

However, the primary triggers for revising existing practices in both case organizations were the indicators of falling revenues and the associated pressure to start changing the prevalent approach. In the case of FixTel, the Supervisory Board members who insisted that the EBITDA-to-revenues ratio must be at least 30% took the pressure. In the case of MobiTel, middle managers, who had become tired of the excessively rigid planning approach that did not provide them with enough autonomy, felt the immediate pressure from competitors who started attacking the low-cost position of the firm.

Ensuing from those triggers, both case organizations engaged in a sequence of practices to activate some latent practices, which were associated with the opposite end of the cyclical ambidexterity continuum, and to deactivate the other practices that had become obsolete.

5.1.2 Activation of latent practices and deactivation of active practices.

I also identified other types of practices that kicked in during active shifts of ambidexterity. I labelled them "activation practices" and "deactivation practices". Data analysis demonstrated instances where strategy practitioners engaged in activating certain latent practices that were present in the organizations. As a byproduct of this activation, other practices were deactivated into a latent state. Based on the data, I synthesized activation and deactivation practices occurring across five main dimensions (see the full list of practices in the segment **Qualitative data analysis** above). D) Activation of reactivity vs proactivity practices. The case organizations described either being reactive to outside events and refining internal actions to react to those external stimuli (exploitation) or being proactive and defining their own agenda (exploration). E) Activation of efficiency vs creativity practices. The second dimension emerged as a continuum between the orientations of efficiency (exploitation) and creativity (exploration). F) Activation practices of single vision vs multiple agendas at the top of the firm. The third dimension entailed either a single-focused vision and associated practices held by the top Management tTeam (associated with exploitation) or a set of multiple conflicting agendas at the top of the firm (associated with exploration). G) Activation of efficiency silos vs collaboration practices at the mid-level of the firm. The fourth dimension demonstrated efficiently organized, but silo-like practices among the middle managers (exploitation) or idea-focused collaborative practices at the middle of the organization (exploration). H) Activation of coordination vs autonomous decision-making practices. The final dimension demonstrated either practices that were coordination-focused - rules-based, systematic and procedure-driven throughout the organization (exploitative practices) or practices that promoted autonomous decision-making and freedom to act (associated with exploratory practices).

5.1.2.1 The reactivity - proactivity dimension.

One interesting generalization from the data on the dimension of reactivity-proactivity prompted a return to the definitions of exploration and exploitation. By the definition of organizational ambidexterity building blocks, one might consider a shift towards exploitation as an introspective shift, that is, "becoming more centered on the sensory and perceptional experiences of one's own organization". Likewise, the shift toward exploration might be considered an extrospective shift - meaning "consideration and observation of things external to the self-examination; study of externals"[30].

However, in practice the case organizations demonstrated exactly the opposite managerial behavior during the inertia of their strategic orientation. It was also interesting to observe how the focus of managerial attention was revised during the process of shifts.

---

[30] Definitions *introspection* and *extrospection* from Merriam Webster online dictionary: merriam-webster.com

- Exploration-focused FixTel was almost ignorant of the behavior of their competitors during the period of exploration (i.e. they were introspective). However, changed circumstances in the economic climate forced them to start changing their focus of attention and pay more heed to the actions of the competitors. It was possible to observe during the unfolding of the shift how FixTel managers became much more open towards the actions of competitors than they were at the outset.

- Exploitation-focused MobiTel was overly occupied by the actions of their competitors and they even had established and institutionalized internal processes, which required them to intensely observe and promptly react to any activities that might have an adverse impact on their competitive position. During the shift toward exploration, the company managers consciously revised their approach and became less concerned about the external impact posed by competitors, started managing their own agenda with a more proactive and self-oriented manner.

In the case of FixTel we were surprised about their lack of attention to competitors, which could have been explained partially by the fact that it was formerly a monopoly, but there are also two alternative explanations:

- While the company was in exploratory mode, their focus was indeed primarily self-centered. In other words, the company was mainly interested in staying at the forefront of competitive pressures by focusing on continuous innovation that mattered to its customers and by focusing on their needs and not so much on competitive rivalry with the other players on the market.

- During the period of exploratory inertia, the market was growing fast and this gave FixTel enough resources to continue its exploratory activities. Only once the economy started contracting was the company forced to start closing its businesses and the moves of the competitors became more important for FixTel to observe. The latter observation is confirmed also during the data collection below in the next stages of the shift, which demonstrates that when FixTel started its shift towards exploitation, its managers activated practices for observing the actions of competitors as well.

Deactivation and activation of practices across the first dimension - reactivity and proactivity - manifested in applying attention to the moves of competitors. FixTel, who during exploratory inertia had almost completely ignored the behavior of the competitors, realized that the competitive situation had changed. The mobile providers had started offering cheaper internet services that were not so good in terms of quality, but still good enough to start threatening its competitive position. Likewise, MobiTel whose reaction speed to the actions of the competitors had been overly dynamic, had started to experience the performance implications of their excessively agile behavior. This had led to suboptimal managerial practices and organizational myopia fixating on short-term quick solutions that had not allowed the Management Team to focus properly on new business creation.

During activation of reactive practices, the FixTel Management Team introduced internal practices for observing and scanning the situation regarding the competitors. The department that had thus far focused on regulatory issues was also tasked with handling the data gathering about the moves of competitors and bringing those issues to the attention of the top Management Team. As a byproduct of this activated scanning practice, the top Managers at FixTel started regularly discussing issues regarding the situation in the changing environment, which in turn reinforced the other dimensions of cyclical ambidexterity.

MobiTel, on the other hand - spelled out an approach during their strategy meetings, which included a smarter way to react. Furthermore, the departments dealing with investment planning set out to describe a better-structured forward planning system for future network coverage. This was complemented by strategy discussions that relied on "Blue ocean" methodology, which assisted in rethinking the core services that company was providing from a novel angle.

5.1.2.2 Efficiency - creativity dimension.

The following dimension of activation of latent practices in the field of efficiency and creativity was clearly observable in both case organizations. The theory on ambidexterity suggests that efficiency and creativity are two core constructs associated with exploitation and exploration (Gibson & Birkinshaw, 2004), and this was easily observable in both case organizations.

At FixTel, internal forces originally triggered efficiency practices, but soon the Supervisory Board took up their activation agenda. The Supervisory Board requested the Management Team of FixTel to come up with an action plan to demonstrate how they will ensure the continuous achievement of a minimum 30% EBITDA ratio to revenues level. While the company was not in difficulties, such strong pressure from the company Board created a chain reaction. The top Management Team engaged in actions to first simplify strategy content and focus on 14 strategic core areas that were implemented with the assistance of the Balanced Scorecard methodology all across the organization. The byproducts of these practices were a reduction of new business generation and all-encompassing cost cutting throughout the firm.

At MobiTel, the activation practices attempted to generate new ideas and initiatives to come up with new businesses. As a result, the managers in the firm activated a creativity practice by establishing idea creation and initiative building mechanisms. They recruited additional developers, insourced customer support and made additional investments in network development. As a result, some good initiatives followed. MobiTel launched a number of services during the shift to exploration: mobile gaming, a music purchase portal, mobile TV and other innovations. During activation of creativity-focused practices, MobiTel Managers also tapped into the capability of their IT developers, who had created an earlier isolated "pocket of exploration" and based their associated practices on empowering this unit and expanding the lessons of the unit to the rest of the company.

5.1.2.3   The single vision vs multiple agendas dimension at the top.

Two dimensions in the dataset can be categorized under the heading of collaboration vs competition. One of the dimensions is associated with strategy practices at the top of the organization. The other reflects the strategy practices of middle managers. Across both dimensions, the case organizations demonstrated polar practices during relative inertia and opposite shifts during activation of new practices.

Lubatkin et al. (2006) suggested that behavioral integration at the top of the firm, their unity of effort and capacity to create coordinated efforts would be a vital predictor of their ability to create fully ambidextrous organization and thereby influence the success of the firm. However, O'Reilly and Tushman (2008) have proposed that in the case of cyclical ambidexterity, the top management teams may be capable of managing those inconsistencies in a fashion that would be feasible for a firm operating in dynamic environment.

The case organizations demonstrated the dual examples of handling this type of conflict vs collaboration. FixTel strategy practices at the top of the organization during exploratory inertia can be described as competition of multiple agendas at the top of the firm. At the same time, MobiTel's strategy practices during exploitative inertia at the top of the organization can be regarded as implementation of a single reactive, efficiency-targeted vision. During the ambidexterity shift, both organizations started revising their collaboration vs competition practices at the top of the firm. FixTel started unifying their top management agenda and MobiTel started creating a multiplicity of different initiatives at the top of the firm.

On another note, the practices of the top Management Team of FixTel provide reasons to reflect upon the properties of the generative mode of strategizing discussed by Hart (1992).

While the properties of the FixTel strategy process in general were fully in line with Hart's (1992) "generative" mode of strategy making, it had an interesting twist. Hart (1992) specifies that the "generative mode of strategizing" exists where strategy process is "driven by organizational actors' initiative", where the role of the top management is primarily "sponsoring - endorsement and support" and the role of organizational members is "entrepreneurial - by taking risks and experimenting".

Hart (1992) points out that in the generative mode the ideas emerge through an evolutionary selection processes, where organizational members act as small entrepreneurial ventures who compete for resources at the top of the organization. However, in FixTel the organization's members engaged much more frequently in collaboration rather than competition to sell the ideas to the top Management Team.

As another observation, Hart (1992) points out that in generative mode, the top management team encourages experimentation and adjusts its strategy to reflect the promising business ideas that emerge from below. This description of the role of the top management team presumes a high degree of collaboration and mutual adjustment between the top management team members, which acts as the selection and retaining mechanism for the new initiatives.

However, at FixTel, the top management team agreed that there was a low degree of cooperation among their members. Quite the reverse was true - there was a high degree of competition between the TMT members in the process of facilitating the smooth selection of ideas and nurturing them to well-functioning businesses. Hence, the *survival of the fittest* ideas was primarily translated into *survival of the strongest idea salespeople* at FixTel top management level.

5.1.2.4   The silos vs collaboration dimension at the mid-level

The penultimate dimension of activation and deactivation practices was also related to the choice between competition and collaboration, concerning the middle management of the organizations. In both instances, the firms engaged in practices of activating the opposite phase during cyclical ambidexterity.

It was interesting to observe that in both case organizations the middle management solved some of the shortcomings in cyclical ambidexterity that the top management teams were unable to handle. At FixTel, the middle managers had initiated collaboration practices to manage product development, whilst the top Management Team was engaged in multiple agendas.

Likewise, at MobiTel a "pocket of exploration" dealt with IT development projects. The top Management Team was unable to integrate effectively into other exploratory moves at the outset. In both case organizations, it took some time and triggering practices by the other stakeholders until the top Management Team was able to activate respective exploratory practices across the board. Hotz has suggested in his dissertation that due to intra-level balancing, the middle managers taking a strongly exploratory role may be balanced out by a strongly exploitative orientation in the top management team (Hotz, 2010, pp. 60-4).

5.1.2.5   The coordination - autonomy dimension.

Finally, the last dimension of the activation and deactivation of practices was associated with the dimension of coordination vs autonomy. Our case organizations displayed rather typical states during relative phase inertia on this continuum. FixTel, as an exploratory firm, enjoyed a high degree of autonomy throughout the ranks of the firm. MobiTel, as an exploitative firm, was subject to a higher degree of coordination and control, which was applied to them by the bureaucratic requirements of the parent company.

Puranam et al. (2006, p. 275) have argued that the tug-of-war between coordination and autonomy is one of the most important ambidexterity tradeoffs. They suggested that an exploratory firm is faced with a substantial loss of autonomy with disruptive consequences to its practices. Likewise, Jansen et al. (2006, p. 1670) tested the inverse hypothesis between the degree of centralization and exploratory innovation, demonstrating that it reduces non-routine problem-solving ability.

I concluded that compared with the other five dimensions, the change across this dimension was the least impactful for the strategy practitioners within the case organizations.

When the case companies started their shift in the cyclical ambidexterity continuum, it was possible to observe activation of the respective opposite type of practices and deactivation of present practices.

FixTel witnessed an increasingly control-focused approach that intensified bureaucracy and coordination requirements. This was illustrated by tracking mechanisms to analyze the success of efficiency initiatives and to understand the progress of cost cutting. As expected, some FixTel employees complained about lost autonomy and an increasingly rigid decision-making approach that had resulted in suboptimal solutions.

On the other hand, MobiTel activated the practices associated with a higher degree of autonomy. The efficiency-related discursive practices were replaced with talk of individual and organizational challenges, a reflection of which, when translated into the respective terminology, meant: "challenge" is connected to a higher degree of autonomy, whereas "efficiency" links to a higher degree of coordination.

5.2   Implications for Theory

There have been calls in the ambidexterity literature for upcoming studies to seek an integration of the exploration and exploitation concepts, to find out whether a better understanding of the internal structure of the exploration-exploitation paradox can inform ambidexterity literature on how to balance ambidextrous duality more effectively (O'Reilly & Tushman, 2008). The present dissertation attempted to fill the gap by providing some insights into this black box.

At the outset of this thesis I posed a question concerning whether the firms engaging in cyclical ambidexterity vacillate between rational (exploitation-oriented) and generative (exploration-oriented) modes during the times when they create their strategies and go through shifts. Or do they rely on an adaptive mode of strategy making - as suggested by Andersen (Andersen, 2000; 2004; Andersen & Nielsen, 2009), whereby middle managers enjoy a great degree of autonomy and participate actively in strategic decision-making, while supported by existing strategic planning systems?

The data collected from the case organizations supported both claims. In the case of FixTel, the organization that had the longer history of cyclical ambidexterity, the properties of strategy work were closer to the "adaptive mode" throughout the cycle from the inert strategic orientation in exploratory mode through to the exploitative strategic orientation phase. However, the case of MobiTel, which had a shorter history of ambidexterity cycles, and where the cycles were relatively longer, confirmed a more discrete vacillation between rational (exploitation-oriented) and generative (exploration-oriented) mode of strategy making. Hence, we might conclude that the data suggests that more frequent cycling might lead towards a more adaptive mode of strategy making, whereas less frequent cycling success more discrete strategy-making modes. However, further studies on this subject would definitely be needed to confirm this suggestion.

5.2.1   Implications for ambidexterity literature.

The aim of this research was to describe which practices are used by organizational actors involved in strategy making in the context of cyclical ambidexterity. We managed to clarify that while undergoing cyclical ambidexterity cycles, companies keep multiple capabilities for strategy making in-house, activating the practices that are deemed appropriate with the associated upcoming shift in strategic orientation and deactivating the practices that become redundant.

Stemming from this conceptualization, I managed to identify five dimensions of practices that were activated during cyclical ambidexterity. Doing so helped to conceptualize the constructs of ambidexterity further.

While the ambidexterity literature has relied strongly on dynamic capabilities theory, which defines exploration and exploitation duality as a potential source for managing organizational tradeoffs to increase managerial capabilities (O'Reilly & Tushman, 2008), present-day studies on ambidexterity have not touched upon the concept of latent capabilities within cyclically-ambidextrous organizations. When observing cyclical ambidexterity unfolding within the case organizations, I witnessed how the informants frequently looked back and reflected upon past practices or capabilities that had been purposefully or accidentally deactivated.

Helfat and Peteraf (2003) have conceptualized various life cycles of organizational capabilities and in the terms of their typology, I refer to "capability renewal" or "capability redeployment". However, Helfat and Peteraf suggest that capability renewal normally occurs in situations where the capability is actively in use. The data collected from the case organizations also suggest that occasionally the upcoming activation of certain capabilities may be preceded by a completely latent state whereby certain functions and practices within organizations were completely deactivated for a certain period.

5.2.2   Ambidexterity shifts may be incremental and can take time.

Tushman and Romanelli wrote in their landmark paper on punctuated equilibrium that shifts into exploration occur in most cases as "short bursts" while companies frequently stay in the permanent mode of exploitation (Tushman & Romanelli, 1985). Simsek et al. (2009) and Gersick (1991) also referred to "sporadic exploration" - sporadic episodes of exploration (change) during a longer period of relative stability. They refer to the "radical change" that shifts bring about, usually regarding technological discontinuities, created by those radical shifts that would redefine the rules of the game in a particular industry or revise the competitive landscape of the particular market.

While the specificity of the industry or case context may have been the reason behind this finding, when analyzing through the shifts of ambidexterity at the two case organizations featured here, the data from the present study does not necessarily confirm these arguments.

First, in the case of both organizations, I could not identify a radical shift in the companies' strategic orientation. The ambidexterity cycles did not bring about substantial revisions. Instead of "transformation", I would therefore rather call these moves "adjustments" of strategic position.

Second, in both cases the firms did not witness rapid exploration transformations. Instead, they progressed through a continuous period of change process during which certain practices were activated, while other practices were deactivated. As a result, the cyclical ambidexterity occurred via a series of relatively minor and smooth actions by organizational players, which took longer than suggested by Tushman and Romanelli (1985), Simsek et al. (2009), and Gersick (1991).

Obviously, the limitations of the present study do not allow for a generalization of these findings. The data might be subject to the properties of a competitive environment, the pace of change in markets and technology, and even the particular history of the company. However, the observed nature of the shifts would call for further research initiatives that would look in more detail into the subject of the duration and rhythm of ambidextrous shifts in other industries and geographical locations. Still, the results of the study provide an intriguing impetus towards rethinking the theory of how we understand cyclical ambidexterity and the individual shifts that unfold in its practice.

5.2.3   Earlier shifts may result in more effective practices.

As the context of the cases was different (size, strategic orientation, direction of ambidexterity shift, autonomy of operations), it is impossible to generalize cross-case findings. However, it is possible to draw one interesting conclusion. When analyzing the case data, it became clear that FixTel demonstrated better overall capabilities for ambidexterity shifts:

- Overall satisfaction with the outcome of the shift was higher among the respondents;
- Informants spoke with higher readiness to undergo a shift in strategic orientation;
- The shift in strategic orientation was a more conscious choice, as reflected by the statements of the managers of the organization.

During its 17-year history, FixTel had gone through seven ambidexterity shifts, averaging a shift every 2.5 years. At the same time, during the 15 years of its history MobiTel had gone through three shifts, averaging one shift every 5 years. In terms of relative intensity of ambidexterity (the sum of relative exploration and relative exploitation of the case organizations), the data indicated that FixTel scored higher on relative ambidexterity.

As a result, it was possible to generalize that, compared to MobiTel, FixTel had stronger internal capabilities for carrying out shifts. During interviews, managers of FixTel referred multiple times to lessons from their experience of past shifts and suggested that they aim to avoid the same mistakes in the upcoming anticipated shift.

At the same time, at MobiTel the managers referred only to a single incident as a past mistake (i.e. overly-active outsourcing, also labelled as a "past mistake" in the coding of FixTel interviews). In the MobiTel case, the reasoning processes of Managers during the unfolding of the ambidexterity shift were not as elaborate as at FixTel, where the Managers were "keeping in mind" that a similar mistake must never happen again. At MobiTel, the Managers were primarily focusing their attention simply on "undoing the past mistake". However, at FixTel the Managers were going beyond the undoing of the mistake - they were generalizing a pattern of behavior from their experience and hence they were attempting to institutionalize a rule to make sure that the past mistake would not be repeated.

Klarner and Raisch have analyzed the impact of regularity and frequency in cyclical ambidexterity shifts and concluded that firms with regular cycles outperform those that change irregularly (Klarner & Raisch, 2013). The data of the present study confirms this finding. Analysis of patterns across the cases led to the proposition that intensity and repetition of ambidexterity shifts lead to path-dependent learning, which enables the managers to create and institutionalize better practices to guide them through future shifts.

5.2.4   (De-)Activation of practices informing the strategy-as-practice literature.

The activation of latent practices and deactivation of active practices in these case organizations can inform the strategy-as-practice literature from different angles. In this particular data set, the interesting aspect was related to the discursive practices associated with shift.

When the entire MobiTel staff was engaged with discursive practices in 2008, which invoked in them a constant repetition of the "efficiency mantra", they used the word "efficiency" in different contexts all the time. As the practices associated with efficiency were gradually rooted out, the shift in discursive practices was remarkable. It was possible to witness how within 2 years the key personnel had managed to deactivate the word "efficiency" from their mental maps and instead activate another discursive practice that engaged them in a revised concept: "challenge". Due to the exploratory shift, the participants in the conversations had managed to effectively revise their discursive practices and come up with new vocabulary that shaped their behavior. While I did not engage in deep context-specific discourse-historical analysis (Clarke, Kwon, & Wodak, 2012), the noted verbal practices in strategy discussions were evident.

5.2.5   Methodological contribution.

Ultimately, this study also provides a modest methodological contribution to the study of ambidexterity. As I pointed out in the previous chapter and detailed further in *Annex 2 - Summary of Studies Measuring Exploration and Exploitation*, there is considerable variation in ways of measuring and calculating ambidexterity. These range from one-dimensional tools that facilitate summing up exploration and exploitation, their multiplication, balance, and absolute differences - to studies taking a multi-dimensional view in calculating the relative degree of exploration and exploitation. A recent review paper by Junni et al. (2013) took a meta-analytical stance and shed light onto this methodological multiplicity of available approaches to measure ambidexterity.

I decided to take a pragmatic stance. I wanted to understand the extent of both exploratory and exploitative initiatives in the case organizations, with the aim of understanding when and how shifts in ambidexterity happen, and how I could witness cyclical ambidexterity when I see shifts occurring. Hence in my dissertation, I decided to measure the exploration and exploitation constructs independently of each other. I therefore mapped the two aspects longitudinally on a timeline. The associated measurement protocol was described in Chapter 3 and may be worth replicating in future longitudinal studies.

It seems worth pointing out that the multi-level analysis provided interesting insights. There were a number of occasions where observation of strategy discussions or interviews revealed exploitative practices in exploratory firms, which were not identified in the official list of initiatives. In one case, a unit called the "Efficiency Group" in a case organization discussed as many exploration-related initiatives as exploitation issues in practice. If the analysis would have remained at the company level, these observations would not have been so rich in detail and in one particular instance, the conclusion about the extent of exploitation would have been downright wrong.

5.3   Managerial Implications

For managers, the findings can provide two interesting insights. First, recently there have been a number of books written for a popular audience, which touch upon the subject of organizational ambidexterity and its effect on individuals or organizations (O'Reilly & Tushman, 2002; McGrath

& Macmillan, 2009; McGrath R. G., 2013; Birkinshaw, 2013). In addition, a number of articles have been written in The Harvard Business Review, The California Management Review and The MIT Sloan Management Review, which are popular among managers. In those books and articles, the eminent authors have suggested that managers cultivate ambidexterity. As a result, the topic is gradually becoming a more popular discussion subject in many global organizations.

I demonstrated in this thesis how managers in two case organizations had engaged in a particular type of ambidexterity - cyclical ambidexterity. While many organizations could set up an ambidextrous design based on structural choices, practicing managers might also contemplate the cyclical nature of their own environment and their organization. While cyclical ambidexterity is not necessarily the most optimal design for handling the conflicting demands of exploration and exploitation in all contexts, managers could review the theory that suggests where cyclical ambidexterity could entail higher performance returns. The theory suggests that in industries where the subject domain is tight or narrow (Gupta, Smith, & Shalley, 2006), businesses are subject to an intense competitive rivalry (Jansen et al. 2005), R&D intensity is higher (Uotila et al. 2009) and there is a high propensity for product innovation that formulates core technologies or dominant designs, this agenda could be effective (Simsek, Heavey, Veiga, & Souder, 2009). Should a company be active in one of those industries, managers might learn from these two case studies and reflect upon the implications of their successes and failures.

Second, a number of factors - internal triggers, the external impact of a changing economic environment - determined how and when ambidexterity shifts started unfolding in those particular case organizations. However, it could also be observed that while top managers had information about the company's past, they were not always in the driver's seat in initiating the shifts. In one case the shifts were initiated by the Supervisory Board. In the other case, the middle managers partially triggered the shift when they pointed out untapped opportunities. It is understandable that the top management teams might become the victims of their past successes given that they constantly try to find ways of reinforcing existing strategic orientations and well-established strategy practices that have proven their worth. However, the managers might want to think about their ability to observe changing environmental conditions, spot the appropriate time for initiating the shifts and be proactive in carrying out the change initiatives.

5.4   Limitations – Boundaries

The limitations of the study are related to the study design and sampling. First - selecting two in-depth case studies always imposes limited generalizability in terms of theoretical contribution. The case studies frequently describe the phenomena in detail, but it remains to be seen whether the same generalizations could be applied elsewhere. Furthermore, selection of cases in one geographical region and a small market further limits generalizability. As Yin (2008) suggests, case study findings will not transfer statistically to a wide population. However, case study research promises analytical generalizations for developing new theory. In addition, given the small market and the small number of players in the market, the cases were more easily identifiable and better observable.

Second - the selection of cases in the telecommunications sector generates an industry bias. While other industries might have provided a different stance, I have attempted to reduce industry bias through briefly analyzing other major case organizations in the industry in order to identify what the overall industry trend vis-à-vis shifts in strategic orientation were. As other firms in the Estonian telecommunications industry were also going through a change towards exploitation during the observed period of 2008-2010, the case of FixTel most probably exemplifies the overall trends of this particular industry better. However, MobiTel was an outlier, but at the same time the company had a longer case history of consciously "*swimming against the current*" during other periods. When the competing organizations were primarily dealing with moves into new products and services, MobiTel managers were carefully observing their moves and only after other industry players had identified the products or services that worked well through trial and error, did MobiTel managers cautiously invest. At other times, when the other telecom firms were cutting costs, MobiTel managers carried out aggressive moves of expansion. Overall, both observed case companies followed their well-prepared strategic patterns.

The third limitation is the duality of the role of the researcher. In order to access the case sites, I had to provide the case organizations a return for the value of my participative inquiry. At the outset of the research initiative, I was a part of a two-person team that participated in their strategy sessions as consultants and facilitators. This role conflict may pose certain limitations with respect to the possible subjectivity of the findings. However, we negotiated the access to the case organizations with the provision that our role will gradually change from that of an active participant towards that of a more reflective researcher. In addition to reflecting upon my personal participation while writing the dissertation, I also allowed the representatives of the case organizations to reflect upon the process to increase the validity of the research findings.

The fourth limitation of this study is also methodological. In some instances, the interviews relied only on the retrospective account of the informants. The interviewees might have explained some aspects through the lens of retrospective rationalization, which can have an impact on the accuracy of some interview data.

5.5   Future research

This research endeavor was just a modest attempt to describe how cyclical ambidexterity unfolds in two organizations. As in every in-depth observation, it is difficult to conclude whether any of the practices in use are the best possible practices or whether some other companies could have handled the same series of change events in a better manner.

Future research may focus on observing some additional companies in a similar manner and try to identify dependent variables that would determine the success of company strategy and therefore continue with the narrative about which practices of cyclical ambidexterity are more successful for the performance outcomes of the firm. This may call for both qualitative studies and quantitative studies, where some of the constructs of the present dissertation can be analyzed among a larger panel of companies.

The second interesting question that could be answered by future research is related to the question of timing and motivation for the different phases. Both case organizations demonstrated that cyclical ambidexterity was part of their history. There are clearly-identifiable exploratory and exploitative periods in their past. A number of long-serving managers were well cognizant of those cycles. Still, in both cases management did not actively initiate the shifts. The company Supervisory Board exerted significant pressure on company Management, thereby largely being the most important trigger of strategic orientation. In both cases, the Supervisory Board members remained mostly hands-off during the period of the original inertia, but became concerned about falling earnings indicators, which led them to start demanding actions triggering the shift in ambidexterity. It would be interesting to analyze whether there are some managers who anticipate the falling trend of their business and thereby avoid being thrown into the situation of stressful and hasty change. It would further be very interesting to find out if those who time their shifts better also gain better financial results.

Bibliography

Adler, P. S., Goldoftas, B., & Levine, D. I. (1999). Flexibility Versus Efficiency? A Case Study of Model Changeovers in the Toyota Production System. *Organization Science, 10*(1), 43-68.

Agarwal, R., & Helfat, C. E. (2009). Strategic Renewal of Organizations. *Organization Science, 20*(2), 281-293.

Alexiev, A. S., Jansen, J. J., Bosch, F. A., & Volberda, H. W. (2010). Top Management Team Advice Seeking and Exploratory Innovation: The Moderating Role of TMT Heterogeneity. *Journal of Management Studies, 47*(7), 1343-1364.

Ambrosini, V., Bowman, C., & Burton-Taylor, S. (2007). Inter-team coordination activities as a source of customer satisfaction. *Human Relations, 60*(1), 59-98.

Amburgey, T. L., & Dacin, T. (1994). As the Left Foot Follows the Right? The Dynamics of Strategic and Structural Change. *Academy of Management Journal, 37*(6), 1427-1452.

Andersen, T. J. (2000). Strategic Planning, Autonomous Actions and Corporate Performance. *Long Range Planning, 41*(8), 1271-1299.

Andersen, T. J. (2004). Integrating decentralized strategy making and strategic planning processes in dynamic environments. *Journal of Management Studies, 41*(8), 1271-99.

Andersen, T. J., & Nielsen, B. B. (2009). Adaptive strategy making: The effects of emergent and intended strategy modes. *European Management Review, 6*, 94–106.

Andriopoulus, C., & Lewis, M. W. (2009). Exploitation-Exploration Tensions and Organizational Ambidexterity: Managing Paradoxes of Innovation. *Organization Science, 20*(4), 696-717.

Ansoff, I. H. (1965). *The concept of corporate strategy.* Homewood, IL: Jones-Irwin.

Arthur D. Little. (2011). *Disruptive Threat or Innovative Opportunity? Scenarios for Mobile Voice OTT.* Arthur D. Little - TIME. Retrieved 01 26, 2013, from http://www.adlittle.com/downloads/tx_adlreports/ADL_OTT_Disruptive_threat_or_inno vative_opportunity_v2_01.pdf

Auh, S., & Menguc, B. (2005). Balancing exploration and exploitation: The moderating role of competitive intensity. *Journal of Business Research, 58*, 1652-1661.

Barnes, B. (2001). Practice as collective action. In T. R. Schatzki, K. K. Cetina, & E. v. Savigny, *Practice Turn in Contemporary Theory* (pp. 25-36). New York: Routledge.

Benner, M. J., & Tushman, M. L. (2003). Exploitation, Exploration, and Process Management: The Productivity Dilemma Revisited. *Academy of Management Review, 28*(2), 238-256.

Birkinshaw, J. (2013). *Becoming A Better Boss: Why Good Management is So Difficult.* Jossey-Bass.

Birkinshaw, J., & Gibson, C. (2004). Building Ambidexterity into an Organization. *MIT Sloan Management Review*(Summer), 47-55.

Boumgarden, P., Nickerson, J., & Zenger, T. R. (2012). Sailing into the Wind: Exploring the Relationships among Ambidexterity, Vacillation and Organizational Performance. *Strategic Management Journal, 33,* 587-610.

Bourgeois, L. J., & Brodwin, D. R. (1984). Strategic Implementation: Five Approaches to an Elusive Phenomenon. *Strategic Management Journal, 5*(3), 241-264.

Bower, J. L. (1970). *Managing the Resource Allocation Process: A Study of Corporate Planning and Investment.* Boston: Harvard Business School Press.

Bradach, J. L. (1997). Using the Plural Form in the Management of Restaurant Chains. *Administrative Science Quarterly, 42,* 276-303.

Brown, S. L., & Eisenhardt, K. M. (1997). The Art of Continuous Change: Linking Complexity Theory and Time-Paced Evolution in Relentlessly Shifting Organizations. *Administrative Science Quarterly, 42,* 1-34.

Burgelman, R. A. (1983). A Process Model of Corporate Internal Venturing in the Diversified Major Firm. *Administrative Science Quarterly, 28,* 223-244.

Burgelman, R. A. (1991). Intraorganizational ecology of strategy making and organizational adaptation: theory and field research. *Organization Science, 2*(3), 239-262.

Burgelman, R. A. (2002). Strategy as Vector and the Inertia of Coevolutionary Lock-in. *Administrative Science Quarterly, 47,* 325-357.

Burton, R. M., & Obel, B. (2004). *Strategic Organizational Diagnosis and Design: The Dynamics of Fit* (3rd Edition ed.). Springer.

Cao, Q., Gedajlovic, E., & Zhang, H. (2009). Unpacking Organizational Ambidexterity: Dimensions, Contingencies, and Synergistic Effects. *Organization Science, 20*(4), 781-796.

Carter, C., Clegg, S. R., & Kornberger, M. (2008). S-A-P zapping the field. *Strategic Organization, 6*(1), 107-112.

Chakravarthy, B. S., & Doz, Y. (1992). Strategy Process Research: Focusing on Corporate Self-Renewal. *Strategic Management Journal, 13 (Summer Special Issue on Strategy Process),* 5-14.

Chandler, A. (1962). *Strategy and Structure: Chapters in the History of American Industrial Enterprise.* Boston, MA: Harvard Business School Press.

Chan-Olmsted, S. M., & Guo, M. (2011). Strategic Bundling of Telecommunications Services: Triple-Play Strategies in the Cable TV and Telephone Industries. *Journal of Media Business Studies, 8*(2), 63-81.

Chen, E. l., & Katila, R. (2008). Rival Interpretations of Balancing Exploration and Exploitation: Simultaneous or Sequential? In S. S. (ed), & S. Shane (Ed.), *The Handbook of Technology and Innovation Management* (pp. 197-214). Wiley-Blackwell.

Clarke, I., Kwon, W., & Wodak, a. R. (2012). A Context-sensitive Approach to Analysing Talk in Strategy Meetings. *British Journal of Management, 23*, 455-473.

Corley, K. G., & Gioia, D. A. (2004). Identity Ambiguity and Change in the Wake of a Corporate Spin-off. *Administrative Science Quarterly, 49*, 173-208.

Crossan, M. M., Lane, H. W., & White, R. E. (1999). An organizational learning framework: from intuition to institution. *Academy of Management Review, 24*(3), 522-537.

Cummings, S. (1995). Centralization and Decentralization: the Never-Ending Story of Separation and Betrayal. *Scandinavian Journal of Management, 11*(2), 103-117.

Daft, R. L., & Weick, K. E. (1984). Toward a Model of Organizations as Interpretation Systems. *Academy of Management Review, 9*(2), 248-295.

Dess, G. G., Lumpkin, G. T., & Covin, J. G. (1997). Entrepreneurial strategy making and firm performance: Tests of contingency and configurational models. *Strategic Management Journal, 18*, 677-695.

Donaldson, L. (2001). *The Contingency Theory of Organizations.* Sage Publications.

Duncan, R. B. (1976). The ambidextrous organization: Designing dual structures for innovation. In R. H. Kilmann, L. R. Pondy, & D. P. (eds.), *The management of organization design: Strategies and implementation.* (pp. 167-188). New York: North Holland.

Dutton, J. E., Walton, E. J., & Abrahamson, E. (1989). Important Dimensions of Strategic Issues: Separating the Wheat from the Chaff. *Journal of Management Studies, 26*(4), 379-396.

Eisenhardt, K. M. (1989). Building Theories from Case Study Research. *Academy of Management Review, 14*(4), 532-550.

Eisenhardt, K. M., & Martin, J. A. (2000). Dynamic Capabilities: What are They? *Strategic Management Journal, 21*, 1105–1121.

Elion Ettevõtted AS. (2009). *Company Annual Report.* Tallinn: Elion Ettevõtted AS.

Elion Ettevõtted AS. (2010). *Company Annual Report.* Tallinn: Elion Ettevõtted AS.

Farjoun, M. (2010). Beyond Dualism: Stability and Change as a Duality. *Academy of Management Journal, 35*(2), 202-225.

Fine, C. H. (1999). *Clockspeed : Winning Industry Control in the Age of Temporary Advantage.* Basic Books.

Floyd, S. W., & Lane, P. J. (2000). Strategizing Throughout the Organization: Management Role Conflict in Strategic Renewal. *Academy of Management Review;, 25*(1), 154-177.

Fredrickson, J. W. (1986). The Strategic Decision Process and Organizational Structure. *Academy ol Management Review, 11*(2), 280-297.

Fuentelsaz, L., Maicas, J. P., & Polo, Y. (2012). Switching Costs, Network Effects, and Competition in the European Mobile Telecommunications Industry. *Information Systems Research, 23*(1), 93-103.

Galunic, C. D., & Eisenhardt, K. M. (1996). The Evolution of Intracorporate Domains: Divisional Charter Losses in High Technology, Multidivisional Corporations. *Organizational Science, 13*, 547-566.

Gavetti, G., & Levinthal, D. (2000). Looking Forward and Looking Backward: Cognitive and Experiential Search. *Administrative Science Quarterly, 45*, 113-137.

Gazzaniga, M. S., Ivry, R. B., & Mangun, G. R. (1998). *Cognitive Neuroscience: The Biology of the Mind.* W. W. Norton & Company.

Geerts, A., Blindenbach-Driessen, F., & Gemmel, P. (2010). Achieving a Balance between Exploration and Exploitation in Service Firms: A Longitudinal Study. *Academy of Management Conference Proceedings*, (p. 8). Montreal.

George, A., & McKeown, T. J. (1985). Case studies and theories of organizational decision-making. *Advances in Information Processing in Organizations, 2*, 21-58.

Gersick, C. J. (1991). Revolutionary change theories: a multilevel exploration of the punctuated equilibrium. *Academy of Management Review, 16*(1), 10-36.

Gibson, C. B., & Birkinshaw, J. (2004). The Antecedents, Consequences, and Mediating Role of Organizational Ambidexterity. *Academy of Management Journal, 47*(2), 209-226.

Gilbert, C. G. (2006). Change in the Presence of Residual Fit: Can Competing Frames Coexist? *Organization Science, 17*(1), 150-167.

Gioia, D. A., & Chittipedi, K. (1991). Sensemaking and Sensegiving in Strategic Change Initiation. *Strategic Management Journal, 12*(6), 433-448.

Golsorkhi, D., Rouleau, L., Seidl, D., & Vaara, E. (2010). Introduction: What is Strategy as Practice? In D. Golsorkhi, L. Rouleau, D. Seidl, & E. Vaara, *Cambridge Handbook of Strategy as Practice* (pp. 1-20). Cambridge University Press.

Gomez, P., Raisch, S., & Rigall, J. (2007). Die Formel for profitables Wachstum. *Harvard Business manager*(Juli), 2-10.

Gupta, A. K., Smith, K. G., & Shalley, C. E. (2006). The Interplay between Exploration and Exploitation. *Academy of Management Journal, 49*(4), 693-706.

Hall, D. J., & Saias, M. A. (1980). Strategy follows structure! *Strategic Management Journal, 1*(2), 149-163.

Hannan, M. T., & Freeman, J. (1984). Structural Inertia and Organizational Change. *American Sociological Review, 49*, 149-164.

Hart, S. L. (1992). An integrative framework for strategy-making processes. *Academy of Management Review, 17*(2), 327-351.

Hart, S. L., & Banbury, C. (1994). How Strategy-Making Processes Can Make a Difference. *Strategic Management Journal, 15*(4), 251-269.

He, Z.-L., & Wong, P.-K. (2004). Exploration vs. Exploitation: An Empirical Test of the Ambidexterity Hypothesis. *Organization Science, 15*(4), 481-494.

Heil, S. (2009). *Strategy Creation in a Restructuring Environment: The Case of an Estonian Fixed Telecommunications Operator Transferring to a Competitive Market in 1993-2003.* Tallinn, Estonia: Estonian Business School PhD Dissertations. doi:978-9985-9824-0-2

Helfat, C. E., & Peteraf, M. E. (2003). The Dynamic Resource-Based View: Capability Lifecycles. *Strategic Management Journal, 24*, 997-1010.

Hines, T. (1987). Left Brain / Right Brain Mythology and Implications for Management and Training. *Academy of Management Review, 12*(4), 600-606.

Hotz, F. (2010). *Organizational Ambidexterity: A Multi-Level Perspective on Organizational Alignment.* St.Gallen: (unpublished). Retrieved from http://www1.unisg.ch/www/edis.nsf/SysLkpByIdentifier/3773/$FILE/dis3773.pdf

Huber, G. P., & Power, D. J. (1985). Research Notes and Communications. Retrospective Reports of Strategic-level Managers: Guidelines for Increasing their Accuracy. *Strategic Management Journal, 6*, 171-180.

Huff, A. S., & Reger, R. K. (1987). A Review of Strategic Process Research. *Strategic Management Journal, 13*(2), 211-236.

Huff, J. O., Huff, A. S., & Thomas, H. (1992). Strategic Renewal and the Interaction of Cumulative Stress and Inertia. *Strategic Management Journal, 13*, 55-75.

Hutzschenreuter, T., & Kleindienst, I. (2006). Strategy-Process Research: What Have We Learned and What is Still to be Explored. *Journal of Management, 32*(5), 673-720.

ITU. (2012). *Measuring the Information Society.* Geneva, Switzerland: International Telecommunications Union. doi:ISBN 978-92-61-14071-7

Jansen, J., Van den Bosch, F. A., & Volberda, H. W. (2005). Exploratory innovation, exploitative innovation, and ambidexterity: the impact of environmental and organizational antecedents. *Schmalenbach Business Review, 57*(4), 351–63.

Jansen, J., Van den Bosch, F. A., & Volberda, H. W. (2006). Exploratory Innovation, Exploitative Innovation, and Performance: Effects of Organizational Antecedents and Environmental Moderators. *Management Science, 52*(11), 1661–167.

Jarzabkowski, P. (2005). *Strategy as practice: An activity based approach.* London: Sage.

Jarzabkowski, P., & Spee, P. (2009). Strategy-as-practice: A review and future directions for the field. *International Journal of Management Reviews, 11*(1), 69-95.

Jarzabkowski, P., & Whittington, R. (2008). Hard to disagree, mostly. *Strategic Organization, 6*(1), 101-106.

Jarzabkowski, P., Balogun, J., & Seidl, D. (2007). Strategizing: The challenges of a practice perspective. *Human Relations, 60*(1), 5–27.

Jarzabkowski, P., Smets, M., Bednarek, R., Burke, G., & Spee, P. (2013). Institutional Ambidexterity: Leveraging Institutional Complexity in Practice. In E. B. Michael Lounsbury (editor), *Institutional Logics in Action Part B* (pp. 37-61). Emerald Group Publishing Limited. Retrieved from http://dx.doi.org/10.1108/S0733-558X(2013)0039AB015

Johnson, G., Langley, A., Melin, L., & Whittington, R. (2007). *Strategy as Practice: Research Directions and Resources.* Cambridge: Cambridge University Press.

Johnson, G., Melin, L., & Whittington, R. (2003). Guest Editors' Introduction. Micro Strategy and Strategizing: Towards an Activity-Based View. *Journal of Management Studies, 40*(1), 3-22.

Junni, P., Sarala, R. M., Taras, V., & Tarba, S. Y. (2013). Organizational Ambidexterity and Performance: A Meta-Analysis. *Academy of Management Perspectives, 27*(4), 299-312.

Katila, R., & Ahuja, G. (2002). Something Old, Something New: a Longitudinal Study of Search Behavior and New Product Introduction. *Academy of Management Journal, 45*(6), 1183-1194.

Khanaga, S., Volberda, H., Sidhu, J., & Oshri, I. (2013). Management Innovation and Adoption of Emerging Technologies: The Case of Cloud Computing. *European Management Review, 10*(1), 51-67.

Klarner, P., & Raisch, S. (2013). Move to the Beat - Rhythms of Change and Firm Performance. *Academy of Management Journal, 56*(1), 160-184.

Langley, A. (2007). Process thinking in strategic organization. *Strategic Organization, 5*(3), 271-282.

Lebraud, J.-C., & Karlströmer, P. (2011). *The Future of M&A in Telecom.* Singapore and Dubai: McKinsey & Co, http://telecoms.mckinsey.com. Retrieved from www.mckinsey.com/~/media/mckinsey/.../Telecoms/PDFs/M_A.ashx

Lechner, C. (2006). *A Primer to Strategy Process Research.* Göttingen: Cuvillier Verlag.

Lechner, C., & Floyd, S. W. (2012). Group Influence Activities and the Performance of Strategic Initiatives. *Strategic Management Journal, 33*, 478-495.

Levinthal, D. A., & March, J. G. (1993). The Myopia of Learning. *Strategic Management Journal, 14*, 95-112.

Levitt, B., & March, J. G. (1988). Organizational Learning. *Annual Review of Sociology, 14*, 319-340.

Lincoln, Y. S., & Guba, E. G. (1985). *Naturalistic Inquiry.* Beverly Hills: SAGE Publications.

Lovas, B., & Ghoshal, S. (2000). Strategy as Guided Evolution. *Strategic Management Journal, 21*, 875–896.

Lubatkin, M. H., Simsek, Z., Ling, Y., & Veiga, J. F. (2006). Ambidexterity and Performance in Small-to Medium-Sized Firms: The Pivotal Role of Top Management Team Behavioral Integration. *Journal of Management, 32*(5), 646-672.

Mantere, S. (2005). Strategic practices as enablers and disablers of championing activity. *Strategic Organization, 3*(2), 157-184.

March, J. G. (1991). Exploration and Exploitation in Organizational Learning. *Organization Science, 2*, 71-82.

Markides, C. (2007). In Search of Ambidextrous Professors. *Academy of Management Journal, 50*(4), 762-768.

Markides, C. C. (2013). Business Model Innovation: What Can the Ambidexterity Literature Teach Us? *Academy of Management Perspectives, 27*(4), 313-323.

McGrath, J. E. (1981). Dilemmatics: "The Study of Research Choices and Dilemmas". *American Behavioral Scientist, 25*(2), 179-210.

McGrath, R. G. (2001). Exploratory Learning, Innovative Capacity and Managerial Oversight. *Academy of Management Journal, 44*(1), 118-131.

McGrath, R. G. (2013). *The End of Competitive Advantage: How to Keep Your Strategy Moving as Fast as Your Business.* Harvard Business Review Press.

McGrath, R. G., & Macmillan, I. C. (2009). *Discovery-Driven Growth: A Breakthrough Process to Reduce Risk and Seize Opportunity.* Harvard Business Review Press.

Miles, R. E., & Snow, C. C. (1978). *Organizational strategy, structure and process.* New York: McGraw-Hill.

Miller, D., & Friesen, P. (1980). Archetypes of Organizational Transition. *Administrative Science Quarterly, 25,* 268-299.

Miller, K. D., Zhao, M., & Calantone, R. J. (2006). Adding Interpersonal Learning and Tacit Knowledge to March's Exploration-Exploitation Model. *Academy of Management Journal, 49*(4), 709-722.

Mintzberg, H. (1990). The design school: Reconsidering the basic premises of strategic management. *Strategic Management Journal, 11*(3), 171-195.

Mintzberg, H., & Waters, J. A. (1985). Of Strategies, Deliberate and Emergent. *Strategic Management Journal, 6*(3), 257-272.

Mintzberg, H., & Westley, F. (1992). Cycles of Organizational Change. *Strategic Management Journal, 13*(Special Issue: Fundamental Themes in Strategy Process Research), 39-59.

Mintzberg, H., Raisinghani, D., & Théoret, A. (1976). The Structure of "Unstructured" Decision Process. *Administrative Science Quarterly, 21,* 246-275.

Mom, T. J. (2006). *Managers' Exploration and Exploitation Activities: The Influence of Organizational Factors and Knowledge Inflows.* Rotterdam: ERIM Ph.D. Series Research in Management 79.

Mom, T. J., Bosch, F. A., & Volberda, H. W. (2007). Investigating Managers' Exploration and Exploitation Activities: The Influence of Top-Down, Bottom-Up, and Horizontal Knowledge Inflows. *Journal of Management Studies, 44*(6), 910-931.

Mom, T. J., Bosch, F. A., & Volberda, H. W. (2009). Understanding Variation in Managers' Ambidexterity: Investigating Direct and Interaction Effects of Formal Structural and Personal Coordination Mechanisms. *Organization Science, 20*(4), 812-828.

Nelson, R. R., & Winter, S. G. (1982). *An Evolutionary Theory of Economic Change.* Cambridge, MA: Harvard University Press.

Nelson, R. R., & Winter, S. G. (1982). *An Evolutionary Theory of Economic Change [Kindle DX version].* Cambridge, Massachusetts: The Belknap Press of Harvard University Press.

Nerkar, A., & Roberts, P. W. (2004). Technological and product-market experience and the success of new product introductions in the pharmaceutical industry. *Strategic Management Journal, 25*, 779-799.

Nickerson, J. A., & Zenger, T. R. (2002). Being Efficiently Fickle: A Dynamic Theory of Organizational Choice. *Organization Science, 13*(5), 547-56.

Noda, T., & Bower, J. L. (1996). Strategy Making as Iterated Processes of Resource Allocation. *Strategic Management Journal, 17*(Special Issue: Evolutionary Perspectives on Strategy (Summer, 1996)), 159-192.

Ocasio, W. (1997). Towards an Attention-Based View of the Firm. *Strategic Management Journal, 18*, 187-206.

OECD. (2013). Building Blocks for Smart Networks. *OECD Digital Economy Papers*(215), 30. doi:http://dx.doi.org/10.1787/5k4dkhvnzv35-en

O'Reilly, C. A., & Tushman, M. L. (2002). *Winning Through Innovation: A Practical Guide to Leading Organizational Change and Renewal.* Harvard Business School Publishing.

O'Reilly, C. A., & Tushman, M. L. (2008). Ambidexterity as a dynamic capability: Resolving the innovator's dilemma. *Research in Organizational Behavior, 28*, 185-206.

O'Reilly, C. A., & Tushman, M. L. (2013). Organizational Ambidexterity: Past, Present, and Future. *Academy of Management Perspectives, 27*(4), 324-338.

Patton, M. Q. (2001). *Qualitative Research & Evaluation Methods* (3rd Edition ed.). Sage Publications.

Pettigrew, A. M. (1992). The Character and Significance of Strategy Process Research. *Strategic Management Journal, 13*(Winter), 5-16.

Pettigrew, A. M., & Whipp, R. (1993). *Managing Change for Competitive Success (ESRC Competitiveness).* Wiley-Blackwell.

Pfeffer, J., & Salancik, G. R. (1974). Organizational Decision Making as a Political Process: The Case of a University Budget. *Administrative Science Quarterly, 19*(2), 135-151.

Puranam, P., Singh, H., & Zollo, M. (2006). Organizing for Innovation: Managing the Coordination-Autonomy Dilemma in Technology Innovations. *Academy of Management Journal, 49*(2), 263-280.

Raisch, S., & Birkinshaw, J. (2008). Organizational Ambidexterity: Antecedents, Outcomes, and Moderators. *Journal of Management, 34*(3), 375-409.

Rautio, T., Anttila, M., & Tuominen, M. (2006). Bundling of information goods: a value driver for new mobile TV services. *International Journal of Revenue Management, 1*(1), 45-64.

Reeves, M., Haanæs, K., Hollingsworth, J., & Pasini, F. L. (2013, February 19). *Ambidexterity: The Art of Thriving in Complex Environments*. Retrieved from BCG Perspectives: https://www.bcgperspectives.com/content/articles/business_unit_strategy_growth_ambid exterity_art_of_thriving_in_complex_environments/

Regnér, P. (2003). Strategy Creation in the Periphery: Inductive Versus Deductive Strategy Making. *Journal of Management Studies, 40*(1), 57-82.

Regnér, P. (2008). Strategy-as-practice and dynamic capabilities: Steps towards a dynamic view of strategy. *Human Relations, 61*(4), 565-588.

Rillo, M. (2008). Top Management Homophily Impact on Strategic Issue Selling. *Unpublished - Academy of Management Annual Conference Proceedings*, (p. 29). Anaheim, CA.

Romanelli, E., & Tushman, M. L. (1994). Organizational Transformation as Punctuated Equilibrium: an Empirical Test. *Academy of Management Journal, 37*(5), 1141-1166.

Rosenkopf, L., & Nerkar, A. (2001). Beyond Local Search: Boundary-Spanning Exploration, and Impact in the Optical Disc Industry. *Strategic Management Journal, 22*, 287-306.

Rothaermel, F. T., & Alexandre, M. T. (2009). Ambidexterity in Technology Sourcing: The Moderating Role of Absorptive Capacity. *Organization Science, 20*, preprint pages 1-22.

Rothaermel, F. T., & Deeds, D. L. (2004). Exploration and Exploitation Alliances in Biotechnology: A System of New Product Development. *Strategic Management Journal, 25*, 201-221.

Sanchez, R., Heene, A., & Thomas, H. (1996). *Dynamics of Competence-Based Competition.* Elsevier.

Sarasvathy, S. D. (2001). Causation and Effectuation: Toward a Theoretical Shift from Economic Inevitability to Entrepreneurial Contingency. *Academy of Management Review, 26*(2), 243-263.

Sasson, A., & Minoja, M. (2010). Banking on ambidexterity: a longitudinal study of ambidexterity, volatility and performance. In P. Mazzola, & F. W. (eds), *Handbook of Research on Strategy Process* (pp. 240-263). UK: Edward Elgar.

Sastry, A. M. (1997). Problems and Paradoxes in a Model of Punctuated Organizational Change. *Administrative Science Quarterly*(42), 237-275.

Scandura, T. A., & Williams, E. A. (2000). Research Methodology in Management: Current Practices, Trends and Implications for Future Research. *Academy of Management Journal, 43*(6), 1248-1264.

Schneider, B. (1987). The People Make the Place. *Personnel Psychology, 40*(3), 437–453.

Seo, S. (2007). Triple-Play Competition in the U.S. Telecommunications Industry: Exploring Cable Operators' Adoption Pattern of Triple-Bundled Services. *The International Journal of Media Management, 9*(1), 1-8.

Sidhu, J. S., Commandeur, H. R., & Volberda, H. W. (2007). The Multifaceted Nature of Exploration and Exploitation: Value of Supply, Demand, and Spatial Search for Innovation. *Organization Science, 18*(1), 20-38.

Sidhu, J. S., Volberda, H. W., & Commandeur, H. R. (2004). Exploring Exploration Orientation and its Determinants: Some Empirical Evidence. *Journal of Management Studies, 41*(6), 913-932.

Siggelkow, N., & Levinthal, D. A. (2003). Temporarily Divide to Conquer: Centralized, Decentralized, and Reintegrated Organizational Approaches to Exploration and Adaptation. *Organization Science, 14*(6), 650-669.

Simsek, Z. (2009). Organizational Ambidexterity: Towards a Multilevel Understanding. *Journal of Management Studies, 46*(4), 597-624.

Simsek, Z., Heavey, C., Veiga, J. F., & Souder, D. (2009). A Typology for Aligning Organizational Ambidexterity's Conceptualizations, Antecedents, and Outcomes. *Journal of Management Studies, 46*(5), 864-894.

Simsek, Z., Veiga, J. F., Lubatkin, M. H., & Dino, R. N. (2005). Modeling the Multilevel Determinants of Top Management Team Behavioral Integration. *Academy of Management Journal, 48*(1), 69-84.

Smith, W. K., & Lewis, M. W. (2011). Toward a Theory of Paradox: A Dynamic Equilibrium Model of Organizing. *Academy of Management Review, 36*(2), 381-403.

Smith, W. K., & Tushman, M. L. (2005). Managing Strategic Contradictions: A Top Management Model for Managing Innovation Streams. *Organization Science*, 522–536.

Strauss, A., & Corbin, J. (1998). *Basics of Qualitative Research: Techniques and Procedures for Developing Grounded Theory.* Sage Publications.

Taylor, A., & Helfat, C. E. (2009). Organizational Linkages for Surviving Technological Change: Complementary Assets, Middle Management, and Ambidexterity. *Organization Science, 20*(4), 718-739.

Teece, D. J., Pisano, G., & Shuen, A. (1997). Dynamic Capabilities and Strategic Management. *Strategic Management Journal, 18*(7), 509-533.

Teleography.com. (2009). *TeleGeography Report.* Washington D.C.: Teleography.com. Retrieved from http://shop.telegeography.com/products/telegeography-report

Tushman, M. L., & Anderson, P. (1996). Technological Discontinuities and Organizational Environments. *Adminstrative Science Quarterly, 31,* 439-465.

Tushman, M. L., & O'Reilly, C. A. (1996). Ambidextrous organizations: Managing evolutionary and revolutionary change. *California Management Review, 38*(4), 8-30.

Tushman, M. L., & Romanelli, E. (1985). Organizational Evolution: A Metamorphosis and Model of Convergence and Reorientation. In L. L. Cummings, & B. M. (eds), *Research in Organizational Behavior, 7* (pp. 171-222). Greenwich, CT: JAI Press.

Uotila, J., Maula, M., Keil, T., & Zahra, S. A. (2009). Exploraiton, Exploitation, and Financial Performance: Analysis of S&P 500 Corporations. *Strategic Management Journal, 30*(2), 221-231.

Van Maanen, J. (1979). The Fact of Fiction in Organizational Ethnography. *Administrative Science Quarterly, 24*(4), 539-550.

Venkatraman, N., Lee, C.-H., & Iyer, B. (2007). Working Paper: Strategic Ambidexterity and Sales Growth: A Longitudinal Test in the Software Sector. *Presented at the 65th Annual Academy of Management meeting in Honolulu, Hawaii.*, (p. 45).

Voss, G. B., & Voss, Z. G. (2013). Strategic Ambidexterity in Small and Medium-Sized Enterprises: Implementing Exploration and Exploitation in Product and Market Domains. *Organization Science, (forthcoming)*, Articles in Advance, pp. 1–19.

Weick, K. E., & Quinn, R. E. (1999). Organizational Change and Development. *Annual Review of Psychology, 50*, 361-386.

Whittington, R. (2003). The Work on Strategizing and Organizing: for a Practice Perspective. *Strategic Organization, 1*(1), 117-125.

Whittington, R. (2006). Completing the Practice Turn in Strategy Research. *Organization Studies, 27*(5), 613-633.

Whittington, R., & Vaara, E. (2012). Strategy-as-Practice: Taking Social Practices Seriously. *Academy of Management Annals, 6*(1), 285-336.

Wooldridge, B., Schmid, T., & Floyd, S. W. (2008). The Middle Management Perspective on Strategy Process: Contributions, Synthesis, and Future Research. *Journal of Management, 34*(6), 1190-1221.

Yin, R. K. (2008). *Case Study Research: Design and Methods (Applied Social Research Methods)* (4th ed.). Sage Publications.

Zajac, E. J., Kraatz, M. S., & Bresser, R. K. (2000). Modeling the Dynamics of Strategic Fit: A Normative Approach to Strategic Change. *Strategic Management Journal, 21*(4), 429-453.

Zollo, M., & Winter, S. G. (2002). Deliberate Learning and the Evolution of Dynamic Capabilities. *Organization Science, 13*(3), 339-351.

Analyzed Annual Reports of Telecom Firms in Estonia

Bravocom Mobiil AS annual reports 2003 - 2012 (10 reports reviewed and analyzed)

Eesti Telekom AS annual reports 2006 - 2012 (7 reports reviewed and analyzed)

Elion Ettevõtted AS annual reports 1993 - 2012 (incl. its predecessor Eesti Telefon AS and its former and present subsidiary firms: Connecto AS, Elion Esindus AS, Esdata AS, IT Koolituskeskuse OÜ, Microlink Eesti AS, Sertifitseerimiskeskus AS) (32 reports reviewed and analyzed)

Elisa Eesti AS annual reports 2003 - 2012 (incl. its predecessor Radiolinja Eesti AS and its former and present subsidiary firms: Elisa Andmesideteenused AS, Uninet AS, Unineti Andmeside AS) (16 reports reviewed and analyzed)

Eltel Networks AS annual reports 2004 - 2012 (9 reports reviewed and analyzed)

EMT AS annual reports 2004 - 2012 (including its predecessor Eesti Mobiiltelefon AS and former and present subsidiary firms: Voicecom OÜ, EMT Esindused AS, Mobile Wholesale AS and Serenda Invest OÜ) (9 reports reviewed and analyzed)

Levira AS annual reports 2000 - 2011 (12 reports reviewed and analyzed)

Starman AS annual reports 2005 - 2012 (including its former and present subsidiary firms: Eesti Digitaalringhäälingu OÜ, Eesti Digitaaltelevisiooni AS, Levi Kaabel AS, Tallinna Kaabeltelevisiooni AS and Taevakaabel AS) (12 reports reviewed and analyzed)

STV AS annual reports 2003 - 2012 (10 reports reviewed and analyzed)

Tele2 Eesti AS annual reports 1996 - 2012 (including its predecessor Ritabell AS and its present subsidiary Televõrgu AS) (19 reports reviewed and analyzed)

Telefant AS annual reports 2006 - 2012 (7 reports reviewed and analyzed)

Top Connect AS annual reports 2006 - 2012 (7 reports reviewed and analyzed)

Viasat AS annual reports 2003 - 2012 (10 reports reviewed and analyzed)

Annexes

Annex 1 - Original Interview Questionnaire

Two interviewers carried out interviews. The author of the dissertation and the second interviewer participated during the interview equally, changing roles regularly.

At the start of the interview, the two interviewers always described the background of their assignment, informed about the topic areas of the questionnaire and requested for the permission to use voice recorder during interviews. We confirmed to the respondents that the actual source data of the interviews remain anonymous.

One of the interviewers made immediate transcript of the discussion on laptop computer. The computer notes and audio transcript were compared at the later stage. The interviews were held at the company premises, usually either at the rooms of the interviewees or in specially designated small meeting rooms. The duration of the interview varied between 82 minutes to 143 minutes. In a few instances, the interviewees requested for a short pause, recorded in the interview transcript.

This semi-structured interview questionnaire outline was adapted for the specific interviewee - e.g. top management, middle management and operating core. It was also customized using snowballing technique - when a respondent had given an interesting reply, the interviewees frequently asked some additional follow-up questions to request for examples, confirmation or rejection of the claims of informant. In some instances, the interviewers also were referring to the claims of other respondents (anonymously) seeking for alternative views of some topic areas.

Introductory and operational questions

1.   Can you describe your background - your education, your tenure within this company, where else have you worked?
2.   Can you describe your daily work, your tasks and responsibilities?
3.   Who are your primary colleagues and counterparts inside your company? In which fora and how frequently do you interact with them?
4.   Do you have some regular meetings that you attend? What are the topics that you discuss at these meetings?

Overall Strategic Environment of the Company

5.   What are the factors of your business environment that affect the results of the work of your company the most? Which of these factors are changing most frequently? How do you personally face these factors in your daily work? How much are you able to have an impact on dealing with these factors?
6.   For which time horizon do you plan your decisions? Can you bring some examples, as presumably it is different for large-scale investments and your daily routine activities?
7.   Who are the primary competitors of your company? How do you monitor their activities?

Understanding Strategy

8.   How do you understand - what constitutes "strategic" in your company?

9.   What activities in your own practice are "strategic"? What activities have clear linkages or outcomes that are important for the strategic direction of your company?

Generic Issues of Strategy Process, incl. Hart (1992) and Burgelman (1983) Typology

10.   How do you discuss issues of importance in your company? How do you decide what is important and what is not? Can you name the current priorities of your company? What are your own personal / team priorities at the present? How are these to change during the next periods?

11.   Have you written down any of these priorities? Do you have a formal plan of activities? How do you follow it up or revise it? When you decide upon your daily tasks (or participate at meetings etc) - do you refer to these priorities? What happens if you are unable to meet your targets? Is there a sanction?

12.   Can you please describe the primary mode how do you plan the future activities in your company? How did you plan your future activities in [the previous period]? How do you foresee your future planning activity change in [the future][31]?

13.   Can you describe any structured / systematic tools or mechanisms that help you to plan the future activities or allocate resources? Can you describe what the positive and negative aspects of these mechanisms are?

14.   If there is a potential conflict between many priorities or individuals - who will mediate or decide upon the "middle road"? Is there somebody "ultimately responsible", who will single handedly decide upon the best choice of action in the case of stalemate? Can you bring some examples on when this has happened?

15.   Do you have some important strategic issues that tend to be recurring from year to another? Can you name some examples?

16.   How / where are ideas born in this company? What happens thereafter with these ideas? In what forms do you discuss these ideas? How do ideas turn into initiatives? Can you describe what the positive and negative aspects of managing those ideas are?

17.   Can you give different examples of either intentional planning activity or emergent strategic initiatives in your company?

18.   Can you bring some examples on how your company values had an impact on the way you prioritize your long-term goals or daily work?

Strategic Decision Making and Communication

19.   What is your scope of authority - what can you decide upon and for what decisions do you have to seek for approval from your bosses? Which decisions you consult your peers and colleagues?

20.   What types of factors do you usually take into account before taking decisions? What is more prevalent - making quick decisions and correcting the course during the implementation - or discussing long time before taking decisions and thereafter performing according to agreed plans?

---

[31] The previous and following period referred to particular years preceding or following the given interview.

21.   How do you ensure that people in your company understand what is important the same way? Do you have some regular meetings to discuss issues of importance?

22.   How do you coordinate your activities with the other departments / divisions?

Present, Past and Future Degree of Exploration and Exploitation

23.   What is the degree of attention in your company that is paid presently to bringing new products and services to the market, using new suppliers or entry to new markets compared to working with increasing efficiency of existing products / services, working with existing customers on existing market? How much has this changed during the past? How much will it likely change in the future?

24.   Can you describe some examples that show the degree of how much people in your company have been involved in experimenting, working with interesting ideas and selling the ideas to the higher ranks vs working on increasing efficiency, cutting costs and managing the bottom line? How much has this changed during the past? How much will it likely change in the future?

25.   Can you describe the degree by which the managerial authority has been either centralized or decentralized? How much has this changed during the past? How much will it likely change in the future?

26.   Have you implemented any initiatives that have been based on playfulness, discovery, innovation, blue ocean strategy, business idea garages, skunk works, partnerships with universities or R&D companies? Can you point out and describe some particular examples?

27.   Have you implemented any initiatives that have been based on quality management, ISO, cost cutting, lean management, six-sigma, process or supply chain optimization? Can you point out and describe some particular examples?

28.   What has been your personal involvement in any of the initiatives (either innovation or efficiency related) that we have asked questions in this section?

29.   Can you describe how did you cooperate your activities with other people in order to achieve these goals in this framework? How did you get their buy-in, how did you share information with them, what kind of coordination and collaboration were you looking for?

Exploratory or Exploitative Shift across Multiple Levels

30.   Can you describe some examples on how did the work on strategic / important issues look like during [the previous period]? Who and how decided what was important and what was done? Can you describe the strategy process during [the previous period]?

31.   Can you describe - what brought about the change in perception that [your company] needed a change? Can you remember an exact moment of what triggered the change for the company? What triggered change for you personally?

32.   With whom and how did you discuss the need for change? Did you describe it somehow? Did you use any colorful metaphors?

33.   How did you deal with change? Was it inevitable or was it something that you could do something about? Did you discuss the upcoming change between yourselves? Were there some

people who found it more difficult to cope with changes than you did? Did you support them somehow? Did you have some company-wide support tools that helped you to deal with change?

34. What started happening after the company changed its course? Can you please describe the chain of events? Can you describe your own role during the change process?

35. Were there some temporary systems, procedures or routines that were put in place during the changes?

36. Has the change been radical or is the situation for you still largely the same as it was? Can you bring some examples on what is different? Can you bring some examples on what has remained the same throughout the change process?

37. Can you describe the speed and duration of change - was it rapid or did it take time? What were the things that went smoothly? What issues were more difficult?

38. Was it the first time in your experience that your company went through this type of change or has something similar also happened before? Can you bring some examples from your earlier experience - what was similar, what was different this time?

39. Overall - are you sorry for these changes or did you embrace the change – in other words, were these "good old days" or "bygones are bygones"? Can you identify some examples on what was better during the [previous period] and what is better now?

40. As a result of this change - has your company introduced any new rules, procedures? Can you please describe them?

41. Because of this change - have you yourself started doing something much differently than you used to before? Can you explain - what and how?

42. In retrospective, have you changed your perception about what business your company is working in during the change? Have you changed any principles of how you work because of this change?

43. Can you recall - if there were any approaches, concepts or words that you used frequently before that you no longer use?

44. Can you describe if the situation that has now been achieved - is it a stable state or is it likely that it is going to change soon again? Can you please use some examples to justify your claim? How likely it is that after certain while the situation is going to revert to before [the shift]. Can you justify your claim?

Summary Question

45. Is there anything else that you would like to tell us about the issues that we asked you?

Thank you!

Annex 2 - Summary of Studies Measuring Exploration and Exploitation

Author	Content	Method	Exploration Measure	Exploitation Measure
March (1991, p. 77)	Balance of exploration and exploitation in organizational learning	Conceptual paper	Entrepreneurial learning-related activities including search, variation, risk taking, experimentation, play, flexibility, discovery and innovation	Expertise learning-related activities consisting of refinement, choice, production, efficiency, selection, implementation and execution
Floyd & Lane (2000, p. 159)	Strategic renewal consists of 3 sub-processes with different managerial roles: exploring (competence definition), exploiting (competence deployment) and shift between the two (competence modification).	Conceptual paper	The magnitude of competence definition - at which: • operational management is dealing with experimenting (learn, improve, initiate autonomous initiatives, experiment and take risks), • middle management with championing (nurture, advocate, champion, present alternatives) and • top management with ratifying (articulate strategic intent, monitor, endorse & support) roles?	The magnitude of competence deployment - at which: • operational management is dealing with conforming (follow the system), • middle management with implementing (adjust, monitor, inspire, coach) and • top management with directing (play, deploy resources, command)?
McGrath (2001, pp. 122, 131)	Extent of exploratory variation seeking and learning in new business development	Survey on learning behavior among managers	Newness of the product, technology, resources employed or markets sought. Are the following new to your organization: • People on the project • Product or service offered • Market or clients served • Client need to be met • Those funding the offering • Users of the offering • Competition faced • Systems used • Skills and know-how of the team • Technology used • Distribution channels	Exploitation not measured
Rosenkopf & Nerkar (2001, pp. 295-7)	Impact of type of exploration to R&D activities	Structural equation modeling of patent data for causal linkages	Exploration defined as either "external", "boundary spanning" or "radical" technological search that generates new patents that either cite patents of other firms or do not cite any existing patents at all.	Exploitation defined as "local technological search": building on similar technologies residing within the firm whereby new patents cite the existing patents within firm.
Katila & Ahuja (2002)	Conceptualizing search scope and search depth	Analysis of patent data	Search scope = high new patent citations ratio compared to overall patent citations	Search scope = low new patent citations ratio compared to overall patent citations
He & Wong (2004)	Ambidexterity is positively correlated with firm performance	Survey of innovation behavior among	Introduce new generation of products Extend product range	Improve existing product quality

Author	Content	Method	Exploration Measure	Exploitation Measure
		managers of Asian firms	Open up new markets Enter new technology fields	Improve production flexibility Reduce production cost Improve yield or reduce material consumption
Gibson & Birkinshaw (2004, pp. 216-7)	Ambidexterity mediates performance management, and social context with business performance	Multi-method: interviews with managers, survey and feedback sessions	The management systems in this organization encourage people to challenge outmoded traditions/ practices/ sacred cows The management systems in this organization are flexible enough to allow us to respond quickly to changes in our markets The management systems in this organization evolve rapidly in response to shifts in our business priorities	The management systems in this organization work coherently to support the overall objectives of this organization The extent of coherence of management systems to allow to quickly following up on standardized activities. The structure of the organization is formal and centralized enough to guarantee coordination among employees.
Auh & Menguc (2005)	Competitive intensity as a moderator between ambidexterity and performance	Survey of 20 managers of manuf. industries in Australia	Research and development expenditures for product development Research and development expenditures for process innovation Rate of product innovations Innovations in marketing techniques	Modernization and automation of production processes Efforts to achieve economies of scale Capacity utilization
Lubatkin et.al. (2006, p. 656)	Mapping antecedents of ambidexterity in SMEs	Survey data from managers of SMEs	Looks for novel technological ideas by thinking "outside the box" Bases its success on its ability to explore new technologies, Creates products or services that are innovative to the firm, Looks for creative ways to satisfy its customers' needs, Aggressively ventures into new market segments Actively targets new customer groups	Commits to improve quality and lower cost, Continuously improves the reliability of its products and services, Increases the levels of automation in its operations, Constantly surveys existing customers' satisfaction, Fine-tunes what it offers to keep its current customers satisfied, Penetrates more deeply into its existing customer base.
Jansen et.al. (2006, p. 1672)	Linkages of exploratory and exploitative innovation, coordination mechanisms, environmental aspects and performance.	Survey among managers of European firms	Our unit accepts demands that go beyond existing products and services. We invent new products and services. We experiment with new products and services in our local market. We commercialize products and services that are completely new to our unit.	We frequently refine the provision of existing products and services. We regularly implement small adaptations to existing products and services. We introduce improved, but existing products and services for our local market.

Author	Content	Method	Exploration Measure	Exploitation Measure
			We frequently utilize new opportunities in new markets. Our unit regularly uses new distribution channels.	We improve our provision's efficiency of products and services. We increase economies of scales in existing markets. Our unit expands services for existing clients.
Sidhu et.al. (2007, p. 35)	Exploration and exploitation manifest themselves in various forms of information acquisition. Local information search is associated with exploitation while distant information search is associated with exploration.	Survey among managers of Dutch firms	On the scale 1…7: do you agree with the following statements (1 - exploitation, 7 - exploration): **Supply-side search**: 1. We are well aware of technological and technical developments within our industry. 2. Our information-gathering efforts cover all industries that employ the sort of technology that we use. 3. A careful watch is kept on industries that are technologically related to ours (e.g., telecom and computer industries are technologically related). 4. We acquire little information on opportunities to employ our existing production facilities in new product domains. (reversed) 5. We closely monitor companies not active in our product area, but that have skills and expertise comparable to ours. 6. In our company, there is close surveillance of advancements in product and process technologies in supplier industries. **Demand side search**: 1. Marketing strategies of companies targeting our customers are closely followed by us. 2. We have a finger on the pulse as far as changes in the product preferences of our customers are concerned. 3. Little information is gathered on product preferences of customer groups that we do not currently serve. (reversed) 4. Developments in industries that fulfill the same customer need as we do, albeit with a completely different product, are well known to us (e.g., air and train transport both fulfill customer need for mobility). 5. We keep close track of activities of companies that offer complementary products (e.g., cameras and film rolls are complementary products because they are used together by customers). 6. We know the product and process innovation efforts of our customers well. **Geographical search** 1. We are knowledgeable about all important opportunities in the geographic regions in which we operate. 2. We hardly acquire any intelligence about potential opportunities in new geographic markets. (reversed) 3. We are well informed about the price and quality aspects of products in neighboring geographic regions. 4. We closely follow the activities of companies in our industrial sector but operating outside our geographic area.	
Uotila et.al. (2009, p. 231)	Analysis of company strategic orientation and its linkages to performance.	Content analysis of news articles and annual reports	Exploratory action: explor*, search*, variation*, risk*, experiment*, play*, flexib*, discover*, innovat*	Exploitative action: exploit*, refine*, choice*, production*, efficien*, select*, implement*, execut*

Author	Content	Method	Exploration Measure	Exploitation Measure
Mom (2006, pp. 96-107); Mom et.al. (2007, p. 919; 2009, p. 820)	Assessing manager's relative ambidexterity and its linkages with coordination mechanisms	Survey among managers in Europe	To what extent did you, engage in work related activities that can be characterized as follows: • Searching for new possibilities with respect to products/ services, processes, or markets • Evaluating diverse options with respect to products/ services, processes, or markets • Focusing on strong renewal of products/services or processes • Activities of which the associated yields or costs are currently unclear • Activities requiring quite some adaptability of you • Activities requiring you to learn new skills or knowledge • Activities that are not (yet) clearly existing company policy	To what extent did you, engage in work related activities that can be characterized as follows: • Activities of which a lot of experience has been accumulated by yourself • Activities which you carry out as if it were routine • Activities which serve existing (internal) customers with existing services/ products • Activities of which it is clear to you how to conduct them • Activities primarily focused on achieving short-term goals • Activities which you can properly conduct by using your present knowledge • Activities which clearly fit into existing company policy
(Lechner & Floyd, 2012, p. 495)	Linkages of degree of exploration of group's activities and performance of strategic initiatives	Survey of people involved in initiatives in three insurance firms	When the initiative was launched, how compatible was the initiative with regard to the following characteristics of the organization? (1 = low compatibility; 5 = high compatibility) ~ degree of exploration: 1. Management skills 2. Employee skills 3. Information technologies 4. Business process systems 5. Long-term strategic plan 6. Operational technologies 7. Investment guidelines 8. Financial control systems 9. Beliefs about what makes the organization successful 10. Assumptions in the organization about how things are done 11. Organizational values 12. Informal norms in the organization about how to do things	

CURRICULUM VITAE - MARKO RILLO

Personal Data

Date of Birth:	11 July 1976
Nationality:	Estonian

Education

01/2007-12/2015	**University of St. Gallen, Institute of Management**
	Pursuing doctorate degree of business administration on "Strategy"
09/2000-06/2003	**Tallinn University of Technology**
	Master of Science in Economics
09/1994-06/2000	**Estonian Business School**
	Bachelor of International Business Administration

Practical Experience

01/2007-present	**5MPC**
	Freelance Strategy Consultant
03/2011-01/2012	**Nicolaas Witsen Foundation**
	Key Expert - Management of the strategic management capacity-building project in the Ministry of Development, Ankara, Turkey.
03/2011-01/2012	**ECORYS International B.V.**
	Team Leader of the project for European Union Regional Economic Development initiative in Kosovo
09/2002-01/2011	**Tallinn School of Economics and Business Administration**
	Part time Lecturer of Management
07/2003-12/2006	**East West Consulting, SIPU International** and **Nomisma SpA**
	Team Leader of management consultants for Croatian Government
07/2001-07/2002	**AS Andmevara**
	CEO, Member of Board
12/1997-06/2001	**Phare Central Finance and Contracts Unit in Estonia**
	Director
05/1997-12/1997	**Price Waterhouse**
	Junior Consultant

Membership

Academy of Management (since 2005), European Group for Organization Studies (since 2005), Strategic Management Society (since 2006)

Achievements

2009, Academy of Management Outstanding Reviewer Award for Business Policy and Strategy Division; Swiss National Foundation scholarship 2008; SIAR Foundation and Carpe Foundation scholarship for PhD Studies in field of Strategy 2005, 2006, 2007 and 2008.

www.ingramcontent.com/pod-product-compliance
Lightning Source LLC
Chambersburg PA
CBHW070929210326
41520CB00021B/6864